PRAISE FOR

WHAT THE FACT?

★ "Journalist Yasmin (*If God Is a Virus*, for adults)
effectively explores contemporary media literacy's
barriers and how to overcome them in this eye-opening
work told via contagion and vaccine metaphor."
—*PUBLISHERS WEEKLY*, starred review

★ "A savvy, accessible, and critical guide to media literacy."
—*KIRKUS REVIEWS*, starred review

"It's a book every library and classroom should have."
—*SLJ*

these are the Facts you can trust.

WHAT

WHAT THE FACT?

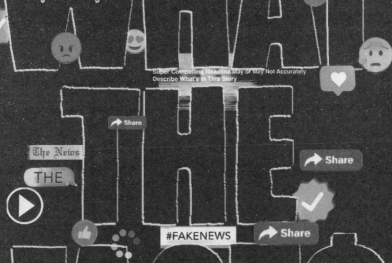

Super Compelling Headline May or May Not Accurately Describe What's in This Story

The News

THE

#FAKENEWS

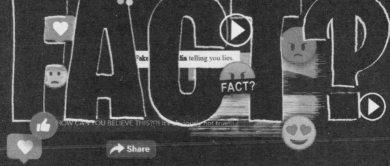

Fake media telling you lies.

FACT?

HOW CAN YOU BELIEVE THIS?!?! It's obviously not true!!!

DR. SEEMA YASMIN

SIMON & SCHUSTER BFYR

New York   London   Toronto   Sydney   New Delhi

An imprint of Simon & Schuster Children's Publishing Division

1230 Avenue of the Americas, New York, New York 10020

Text © 2022 by Seema Yasmin

Cover design by Laura Eckes © 2022 by Simon & Schuster, Inc.

For information about special discounts for bulk purchases, please contact Simon & Schuster Special Sales at 1-866-506-1949 or business@simonandschuster.com.

The Simon & Schuster Speakers Bureau can bring authors to your live event. For more information or to book an event, contact the Simon & Schuster Speakers Bureau at 1-866-248-3049 or visit our website at www.simonspeakers.com.

Also available in a SIMON & SCHUSTER BFYR hardcover edition

Interior design by Laura Eckes

The text for this book was set in Adobe Garamond Pro.

Manufactured in the United States of America

First SIMON & SCHUSTER BFYR paperback edition October 2023

2 4 6 8 10 9 7 5 3 1

Library of Congress Control Number 2022930951

ISBN 9781665900034 (hc)

ISBN 9781665900041 (pbk)

ISBN 9781665900058 (ebook)

FOR MUHAMMAD-AYMAN,
a journalist-in-training.
May your path shine bright
with the light of truth
and your pen illuminate
the world's darkness.

CONTENTS

INTRODUCTION: HI, FREETHINKER 1

CHAPTER 1: CONTAGIOUS INFORMATION 11

SIDEBAR: Fake News Is Old News 14

When Bad News Goes Viral 17

Social Networks of Contagion 19

Viral Vectors and Patient Zero 25

SIDEBAR: How to Spread a Lie—The Disinformation Playbook . . 30

Words Matter 33

SIDEBAR: Red Flags for False Information 44

Information Disorder . . . and Pasta 45

CHAPTER 2: BIAS, BELIEFS, AND WHY WE FALL FOR BS . . 61

Tell Me a Bedtime . . . *Fact?* 61

Your Brain on Stories 66

SIDEBAR: Changing Minds 74

Your Biased Brain 75

SIDEBAR: Spurious Science 84

The Backfire and Pushback Effects 87

Why Your Brain Is Weird (ǝldoǝd ɹǝɥʇO :ɹǝʍsu∀) 89

Can You Believe *Anything*? The Sunrise Problem 95

CHAPTER 3: NEWS, NOISE, AND NONSENSE...........103

Nineteenth-Century Clickbait...............................103

Not-So-Neutral News: A Partisan Press......................110

Breaking News . . . via Pigeon and Pony.....................113

"What Hath God Wrought?" Twentieth-Century News,

Twentieth-Century Problems..........................117

SIDEBAR: Breaking News....................................124

What Is Newsworthy? Who Decides What Is News?..........127

SIDEBAR: Blavity, the *Defender*, and Black America's News

Publishers...134

All the News That's Fit to Print . . . ? Local News, National

News, and the Flint Water Crisis.......................138

Ghost Papers and News Deserts: What Happens When Your

Town Loses Its Local Newspaper?......................144

SIDEBAR: Timeline of (Mostly American) Journalism.........150

How the News Is Made: Facts . . . or Framing?..............155

The Framing of Operation Iraqi Freedom...................157

SIDEBAR: Contagious News—The Vienna Subway Suicides.....162

Does News Influence Behavior?............................166

"Alternative Facts" and the Myth of Objectivity..............170

Like Eating Poop...192

SIDEBAR: Journalists under Attack.........................194

How to Consume News Like a Pro: Fact-Check the News

and Create Your Media Diet...........................198

CHAPTER 4: SOCIAL MEDIA............................207

Algorithmic Bananas.....................................207

Your Brain on Social Media...............................217

Into the Rabbit Hole 226

It Doesn't Have to Be This Way! 237

CHAPTER 5: HOW TO DEBUNK AND DISAGREE 241

Is There a Vaccine against BS? 241

SIDEBAR: Critical ~~Thinking~~ *Feeling?* 256

Prebunking versus Debunking 259

How to Disagree 261

The Ten Steps for Effective Disagreements 265

What Is Good Conflict? 283

SIDEBAR: The Socratic Method (and the Sad Fate of Socrates) 286

How to BS-Proof Your Brain 294

EPILOGUE: HI, CRITICAL THINKER! SO . . . WHAT NOW? . . .301

GRATITUDE 305

SOURCES 307

INDEX 345

INTRODUCTION

HI, FREETHINKER.

THIS BOOK IS *not* going to tell you what to think. Let's just get that out of the way. You can think what you like, believe what you want, see the world how you choose to see it . . .

Or can you? Are you really free to think your own thoughts and come to your own conclusions? Are you in control of the information that passes in front of your eyes, seeps into your ears, and swirls around you every minute of every single day?

HEADLINES, BULLETINS, TWEETS, MEMES, TEXTS, ALERTS! BREAKING! BREAKING! EVERYTHING! IS! BREAKING! PING! PING! PING!

It never stops. An endless stream of information zigzags its way through your eyeballs and into your ears where it collides with your brain, which processes up to one hundred terabytes of data through your one hundred billion neurons.

That's one quadrillion, ninety-nine trillion, five hundred eleven billion, six hundred twenty-seven million, seven hundred seventy-six thousand bytes of information processed and stored in your brain.

Some of these (approximately) 1,099,511,627,776,000 bytes are accurate nuggets of data. Congratulations! Some of them . . . well, I'm sorry to break this to you, but some of the data stored in your brain is not accurate. Some of it is like a snowball that started off as a pinch of frost (a fact) but was crusted over with thick chunks of myth, coated with one ounce of misremembered history, and finished off with three knobbly layers of bias.

How did you pick up and add to that snowball of information in the first place? Maybe one friend gave you a chunk of misremembered history, then a TV show offered a piece of questionable data that has stuck ever since, and at least four family members contributed to some of the bias that's in your head.

You're not blameless either. How many times have you shared "facts" that weren't that . . . factual? You may not have even realized what you were doing. It's like when you have a runny nose and you wipe your nose with your hand and then touch the door handle, and your friend touches the door handle and reaches for her not-yet-snotty nose, and then two days later she's sneezing and shoving tissues up her nostrils as well. That's because you left a virus on the door handle and the virus was contagious.

Guess what else is contagious?

Ideas.

Rumors.

Myths.

Lies.

Information spreads from one person to another, just like a virus, until myths and hoaxes and lies and facts and conspiracies have crept far and wide, taking on new shapes and mutations. Your snowball of information, layered with myth and misremembered history, was spread to you by others, and you spread it to someone else, who shared it with someone else, who keeps the chain of information contagion going and going and going.

This book is about that viral spread of information, how it courses its way across the internet, crackles through the airwaves, and lands in your hands through messages and news articles sent to your phone, computer, and TV. A piece of false information can travel faster and farther than accurate information, "infecting" millions along the way.

Knowing what information to believe can be tricky. But before we dive into the murky In-Between Territory that surrounds the islands of Fact and Fiction, don't forget: this is *not* a book that will tell you what to think.

You, after all, are a freethinker.

(Right?)

YOU make up your OWN mind.

This book won't try to change what you think. Nope. Not going to go there. Not going to try to convince you that swallowing apple seeds is safe, for example, when those tiny seeds contain deadly cyanide! If you want to take that risk, have at it.

This book is just here to show you how your beliefs, thoughts, ideas, actions, likes, dislikes, hobbies, favorite color, love of dogs, fear of bees, cravings for Indian food, number-one football team, interests, passions, and disgusts are influenced, molded, sculpted, bolstered, and strengthened by the hundreds of information sources that bombard you. Daily. By the second.

But you're a freethinker. So this book—this book that is *not* going to tell you what to think—is here to let you know a couple of things. First, your attention is one of the most precious commodities on the planet. Did you know that? Your attention is like a courtside seat at the NBA playoffs—everybody wants access. Everybody wants to make room for themselves in that coveted position, to fill that seat with their ideas. They are vying to have their side *and only their side* of the story heard. They want you to join their club, subscribe to their newsletter, buy their cookies and whatever else they are selling.

You might like to *think* you're a freethinker, a fair human, a real "show me all the sides and I'll make up my own mind" type of model citizen. After all, you are a truth-seeker, an information gatherer, a reader! And not just any reader; you're a *smart* reader. I mean, you did pick up this book. And you're even thinking about taking it home and reading some more. . . .

I hate to break this to you. I really do. It's not the way I like to start things off. But here's the second thing this book is here to tell you. You might like to think that you—independent, informed, balanced, freethinker you—make up your own mind, but the . . . Damn, I can't say "truth" because "truth" is a whole can of worms that we are just not ready to open yet, so let me call it something else . . .

Here's the something else: you make up your mind based on information from sources such as journalists, online friends, teachers, movie directors, presidents, rock stars, scientists, classmates, songwriters, cousins, your cousin's best friend's big sister . . .

. . . and they all get their information from a source, and those

4

sources get their information from sources who get their information from . . .

You get where this is going.

Every bite-sized byte of information spooned into your eyes and ears and cemented into your brain came from *somewhere*. Every chunk of data has its own origin story.

You might think you can smell crap a mile away, like that time someone said you should starve a fever but feed a cold (wait, you didn't fall for that, did you?), but it turns out that we are *all* vulnerable to influence, scams, and bamboozling. Thousands of us can be swindled in one fell swoop.

Picture this: In 1683, King Charles XI of Sweden ordered the German doctor and explorer Engelbert Kaempfer to investigate if lambs grew on trees. That's right. Wooly, bleating, two-hundred-pound lambs were believed by many of the world's top botanical experts to grow on trees in India and in parts of Asia known to Europeans as Tartary.

These Vegetable Lambs of Tartary were said to be finger-licking delicious, their blood as sweet as honey and their wool as soft as cotton and white as snow. The Vegetable Lambs couldn't go far because, well, their bellies were tethered to a thick stalk that sprouted out of the earth, but they were life-sized and real and their meat tasted like tender fish! So said the world's top scientists, as well as knights and priests. For more than a thousand years, respected scholars, explorers, and clergymen professed in books, wrote in religious texts, and stated at prestigious lectures that Vegetable Lambs grew on trees. They had seen them, drawn scientific pictures of them, even tasted their blood and flesh. *Really real*, they said.

Henry Lee, an English scientist (who drew the picture below in 1887), said the first mention of Vegetable Lambs was in the Jewish text *Talmud Ierosolimitanum* in 436 AD. For centuries afterward, Vegetable Lambs were mentioned by Europeans who said the poor creatures could lean forward on their stalks to chomp on the surrounding grass, but when all the grass was eaten, the "little beasts" would die. Poor Vegetable Lambs.

From the fifth century to the seventeenth century, some of the brightest minds in Europe believed that lambs grew on trees. Source: Henry Lee, *The Vegetable Lamb of Tartary*, 1887.

So then we arrive at 1683, and the explorer Engelbert Kaempfer is ready with his orders from the king. He travels the world and arrives in Tartary to investigate these trees with lambs that taste of fish.

And guess what?

Engelbert Kaempfer returns empty-handed. *Lambs do not grow on trees!* he tells the king. And that was that. A 1,250-year-old belief was debunked.

Super weird, right? Who would have believed that lambs grew on trees, anyway? Well, it turns out lots of people, including the brainiest of the brainy, believed exactly that. How on earth does a belief like that spread around the world and dupe millions of people for more than a millennium?

Now, you might be thinking: *Lambs growing on trees sounds ridiculous, and this all happened way back when. A myth that bizarre would never persist nowadays, not when we can fact-check using the internet. . . .*

I have some news for you.

In the summer of 2020, eight engineers were kidnapped and held hostage in the mountains of Peru while they were fixing a radio tower, the kind of tower used to relay signals that keep the internet and cellphones working. The reason for their capture? A belief that 5G cellphone signals were spreading the coronavirus and causing a global pandemic.

In fear for their lives, the engineers pleaded with their kidnappers: *5G stands for fifth-generation wireless technology! It's going to make your phone calls clearer and your downloads faster and more reliable! It's going to make your life better, and it is definitely not capable of spreading any infection!*

Conspiracy theories about cellphones and radiation are not

new. Back in 1903, twenty-four years after the invention of the electric light bulb, doctors were talking about "radiophobia," the fear that all kinds of radiation could damage the body. Radiation exists on a spectrum; some types of radiation can hurt the body, including the sun's ultraviolet rays (which can cause skin cancer) and X-rays (which are okay in small amounts, say if you're getting a chest X-ray, but damaging in large amounts).

But that type of radiation, the harmful kind, is on one end of the electromagnetic spectrum. It's known as ionizing radiation, which means the radiation holds enough energy to break your DNA and damage cells.

But 5G radiation, along with microwaves and radiation from older cellphones, sits on the other end of the spectrum, the safe end. These are *non*-ionizing types of radiation that do not harm our bodies.

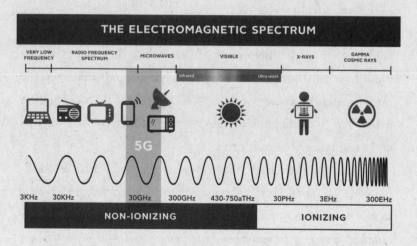

That information didn't stop the rumors from spreading. There were anti-microwave campaigns in the 1970s, fears of 2G cellphone towers in the 1990s, and then attacks against 5G cellphone towers in the twenty-first century. Hundreds of essential towers were burned by arsonists in 2020. On internet message boards and WhatsApp group chats (oh, the irony), some claimed that 5G radiation caused birds to fall out of the sky and trees to wither and die. People said 5G radiation would kill humans. None of it was true. And this was during the COVID-19 pandemic, when cellphone towers and communication were, you know, kind of important.

It can be confusing to separate fact from fiction, certainty from conspiracy, especially at times of crisis, when fear, anxiety, and panic are spreading alongside false information; when scammers are peddling falsehoods to sell their goods, to dupe us, to make us believe what they want us to believe without us even realizing it.

This book (that is very much *not* here to tell you what to think) is your map of the wild and gargantuan information ecosystem. This is your navigation guide for the treacherous terrains of Bias, the craggy mountains of Groupthink, and the slippery ravines of Disinformation. Along this journey, we'll be asking why false information travels faster and farther than the truth, what it is about your brain that leaves you vulnerable to "infection" with untruths, how you might unknowingly infect others with lies, and what you can do to tell apart fact from sophisticated fiction.

Dear freethinker, you've already fallen for one piece of false information. When I said swallowing apple seeds was unsafe because they contain cyanide, that was untrue—although my lie did incorporate a tiny bit of truth. (Apple seeds contain deadly cyanide, but you'd have to eat about four hundred crushed apple seeds to keel over dead.)

So you see how easy it can be for a lie about apple seeds or 5G cellphone signals or Vegetable Lambs or even a *person* to spread from one mind to another, one continent to four more, until millions of people believe a viral untruth that in some cases could cause real harm. Let's jump into one of these real-life stories. But brace yourself. Traveling through the universe of misinformation and disinformation is a wild and bumpy ride.

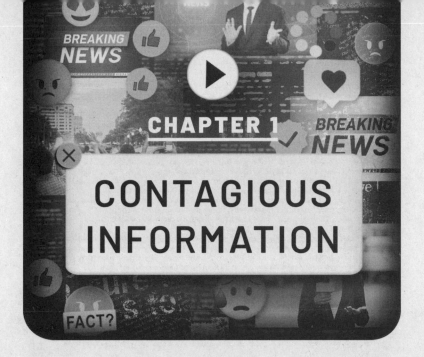

CONTAGIOUS INFORMATION

ON THE AFTERNOON of February 27, 2020, Peter Lee Goodchild, an 84-year-old retired art gallery owner from Buckinghamshire, England, posted a message on his Facebook page. "Last evening dining out with friends, one of their uncles, who's graduated with a master's degree and who worked in Shenzhen Hospital (Guangdong Province, China) sent him the following notes on Coronavirus for guidance . . . "

Peter's Facebook post offered a friendly list of warnings and tips about a new coronavirus that had sprung up in China around Christmas 2019. The infection was quickly making its way around the world. "If someone sneezes with it, it takes about 10 feet before it drops to the ground and is no longer airborne," wrote Peter, via his friend's uncle.

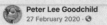

Peter Lee Goodchild
27 February 2020 · 🌐   •••

IMPORTANT ANNOUNCEMENT - CORONAVIRUS
1. If you have a runny nose and sputum, you MAY have a common cold/flu it isn't necessarily that you've caught the virus
2. .The term pneumonia describes the swelling of lung tissue. It's usually caused by a bacterial infection, and has been seen in Covid-19 patients. One of the most common symptoms of Covid-19 is a dry cough
3. Because the virus is relatively new, there's a lot not known about it, like the temperatures it can withstand.so early after the discovery of the virus. What we can do is look at related viruses. Coronavirus is a family of viruses including the common cold, SARS, and SARS-CoV-2
4.It's difficult to say exactly how far droplets spread when you sneeze, as it depends on a factors like humidity and temperature. Research in recent years has shown that droplets from sneezes have the potential to spread several metres from the sneezing person.
5The WHO says "Studies suggest that coronaviruses (including preliminary information on the COVID-19 virus) may persist on surfaces for a few hours or up to several days.
6. On fabric it may survive for some hours. normal laundry detergent will kill it.
7.you should avoid drinking liquids with ice..
8. Wash your hands frequently as the virus can live on your hands for 5-10 minutes, but - a lot can happen during that time - you can rub your eyes, pick your nose unwittingly and so on.
9. Gargling with salt water is recommended by the NHS for adults who have a sore throat, but only to relieve symptoms once you have caught it, not as a preventative measure.
10. Can't emphasise enough - drink plenty of water!
THE SYMPTOMS
1.It will first infect the throat, so you may have a sore throat lasting 3/4 days
2. The virus can blend into a nasal fluid that enters the trachea and then the lungs, causing pneumonia. This takes about 5/6 days further.
3. With the pneumonia comes high fever and difficulty in breathing.
4.In general, 1-3 are roughly an accurate description of the common symptoms of Covid-19, although some patients may experience other symptoms and the timing of those symptoms may differ.
The CDC (Centre for Disease Control) says that sore throat has been reported "in some patients". More commonly, symptoms include fever, a cough, muscle pain and shortness of breath, as the post claims. Not everyone who has Covid-19 will get pneumonia though. The NHS does not mention nasal congestion that 'feels like drowning' as a specific symptom for Covid-19.

It does advise that you use its 111 online coronavirus service, your doctor but don't visit

SPREAD THE WORD - PLEASE SHARE.AND ALSO SEE RECENT UPDATES FROM NHS AND ELSEWHERE AND

A post containing all sorts of nonsense about the novel coronavirus went viral on
Facebook in the early days of the COVID-19 pandemic. Source: Snopes.com.

Pictured is one version of the viral Facebook post that was shared in February 2020. The post "mutated" over time as it was updated, shared, and translated into dozens of languages.

Peter's post included advice about swishing the throat with liquid to prevent infection: "A simple solution of salt in warm water will suffice," he said. He included a timeline of the illness that said the virus "will first infect the throat, so you may have a sore throat lasting 3/4 days. The virus then blends into a nasal fluid that enters the trachea and then the lungs, causing pneumonia."

Peter also issued this warning: "The nasal congestion is not like the normal kind. It can feel like you're drowning." There were even details about exactly how many hours this new virus could survive on metal and fabric, alongside advice to avoid ice-cold drinks.

Peter's Facebook post was liked by his friends, who shared it with their friends, who shared it with their friends . . . until it was shared more than 400,000 times in a matter of days. And that was just on Facebook.

A few days after Peter hit "post," his Facebook message went from Buckinghamshire to Melbourne, from Hong Kong to Cape Town and beyond. Translated into Arabic, Spanish, French, Italian, Amharic—around a dozen languages in all—Peter's list of tips and warnings popped up on websites, on internet message boards, and in private group chats from Bali to Bologna.

Peter's virus post was read by millions of people all over the planet. Peter had gone viral.

The problem was this: Most of Peter's viral message about the new virus was nonsense. Throat gargles don't get rid of the coronavirus that causes COVID-19. Avoiding icy drinks won't obliterate the infection. And had you asked any honest scientist back in February 2020 about the exact timeline of infection and how long the virus lingered on metals and fabrics, they would have said, "Umm, can I get back to you on that? We're still trying to figure it out."

But it didn't matter that Peter's message was mostly nonsense. A new disease was spreading, fear was brewing, and people were desperate for information. And here, right when we were ravenous for facts and figures, was a helpful post from a man whose Facebook profile photo showed a smiling, grandfatherly face.

SIDEBAR: FAKE NEWS IS OLD NEWS

ON WEDNESDAY, OCTOBER 2, 2019, PRESIDENT DONALD Trump told reporters he invented the term "fake news." "I'm the one that came up with the term—I'm very proud of it, but I think I'm gonna switch it to corrupt news."

This was a lie. Unless Trump was the author of a 1925 *Harper's Magazine* article called "Fake News and the Public." (He wasn't. The author was one Edward McKernon.) Fake news was "a source of unprecedented danger," wrote McKernon. But his worry that humans might fall for false information dates back even further.

In 1620, the English philosopher Francis Bacon wrote that humans are prone to "seize eagerly on any fact, however slender, that supports his theory; but will question, or conveniently ignore, the far stronger facts that overthrow it." Yikes. We now have a name for this selective acceptance of information, **confirmation bias**, and there's more information about it in chapter two.

Bacon also pointed out that words can be used to obfuscate the truth, writing, "The ill and unfit choice of words wonderfully obstructs the understanding." In 1646, Sir Thomas Browne, an English doctor, published a book titled *Pseudodoxia Epidemica*, which translates to something like "An Epidemic of Fake News." Browne warned of charlatans, quacksalvers, and saltimbancos, a word he invented to describe a charlatan who sold fake medicines, usually by leaping onto a bench to hawk snake oil. It comes from the Italian *saltare in banco*, meaning "to jump on a bench."

Fake news used to be the stuff of *news*papers. In the late 1800s, some American newspaper publishers believed that sensationalist, fabricated "news" would spark interest and sell copies. Author Edwin Diamond wrote that William Randolph Hearst, publisher of one of the major newspapers at the time, is said to have wanted "readers to look at page one and say, 'Gee whiz,' to turn to page two and exclaim, 'Holy Moses,' and then at page three, shout, 'God Almighty!'"

There's even a term for this hyped-up news: **yellow journalism**, named after the rivalry between Hearst and his nemesis, Joseph Pulitzer, publisher of the *New York World*. Pulitzer's paper ran a cartoon strip featuring a character called the Yellow Kid. But in the 1890s, Hearst hired the cartoon's creator to his newspaper so he could publish the Yellow Kid cartoons as well. And since both newspapers ran embellished stories and used the "news" to stoke public support for the Spanish-American War, this sensationalist style of journalism was called "Yellow-Kid journalism" and later shortened to "yellow journalism."

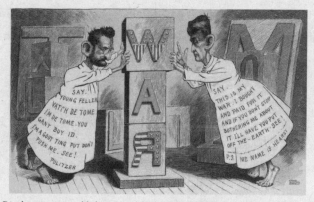

Rival newspaper publishers Joseph Pulitzer and William Randolph Hearst are dressed as the popular cartoon character the Yellow Kid in this 1898 cartoon. The term "Yellow-Kid journalism," later shortened to "yellow journalism," has since been used to describe sensationalist journalism because both publishers ran hyped-up stories in their newspapers. Source: Public domain.

There's no need to use the term "fake news" when the English language is replete with words for lies, the people that peddle falsehoods—and those who fall for them. A *gudgeon*, or *gudgin*, is a gullible person apt to believe in quacks and their fake remedies, according to texts from around the 1600s. *Factitious*, a word used since that same time, can actually refer to something that is *not* a fact.

But some of the best words describe those who spread false information. An *ultracrepidarian* is someone who goes on and on discussing things they don't know much about. A *taradiddle* is a lie, according to one dictionary from 1796, which defines a taradiddle as "a fib or falsity," and says that one who tells a taradiddle is a *taradiddler*.

The words are plenty and the history is long. So next time someone tells you that the term "fake news" is a twenty-first-century invention because "post-truth" was the *Oxford English Dictionary's* word of the year for 2016, you can tell them they are an ultracrepidarian and that "fake news" dates back centuries and is likely as old as humanity itself.

▭

WHEN BAD NEWS GOES VIRAL

ACROSS THE ATLANTIC Ocean, in Florida, Brian Lee Hitchens was picking up asthma medicine for his wife, Erin. It had been five weeks since Peter's post had gone viral, and both Brian, a taxi driver, and Erin, a pastor, had spent hours on Facebook reading up on the new coronavirus.

The couple had come across posts similar to Peter's that were written by people in different parts of the world, as well as social media posts that told them the new virus wasn't real, the pandemic was a hoax, and wearing a face mask and keeping a safe distance from people meant you were scared and weak. They believed much of what they read. But then Brian and Erin came across Facebook posts that made them change their beliefs. These messages said the virus *was* real but that it was spread by 5G cellphone signals. The virus wasn't anything to worry about, though, some of these Facebook posts said. It caused only a mild infection. Nothing serious.

So Brian went to pick up Erin's medicine without putting on a face mask. He drove his taxi around Palm Beach County as if the world wasn't in the grips of a historic pandemic. In early April, he began to feel breathless, as if he'd run ten miles, except he hadn't even been for a jog. All of Brian's energy was zapped. Erin felt sick. Her stomach churned. She couldn't keep her food down.

The couple hunkered down at home, feeling hotter, more tired, and less hopeful by the day. If this was that new virus they had been reading about on Facebook, then their illness wasn't anything serious, they thought. They would just wait it out at home. But they got sicker. Finally, on April 19, Brian mustered all his remaining energy to drive them to a local hospital. "You both have COVID-19," the doctors said, as they admitted the couple straight to the intensive care unit. Brian was stunned. The virus they had called a hoax was invading their bodies. The disease they had believed was mild had sent both him and his wife to the ICU.

Over the next month, as Brian slowly got better, Erin's lungs and heart became weaker. Doctors put her on a ventilator and told Brian that he was only allowed to stop by her room for minutes at a time to say a quick hello. Erin was unresponsive, but sometimes her eyes moved. Brian wondered if she knew he was there.

"Many people still think that the Coronavirus is a fake crisis," Brian wrote on his Facebook page on May 12. "I did too and not that I thought it wasn't a real virus going around but at one time I felt that it was blown out of proportion and it wasn't that serious. . . . Looking back I should have wore a mask in the beginning but I didn't and perhaps I'm paying the price for it now . . ."

Brian wondered if his wife would ever breathe for herself. Doctors eventually gave him some good news: He could go home. But he would have to go alone. Erin was too sick to leave the ICU. Then the worst news came: Erin suffered a heart attack and died on August 6.

Brian shared details of Erin's memorial service on Facebook. He also pleaded with his friends in a message that said, "Please use wisdom and don't be foolish like I was . . ." His Facebook post went viral.

Messages about this new infection zigzagged around the world, crossing oceans and jumping borders. But the virus wasn't the only thing spreading. News of its ferocity, whereabouts, and symptoms was a pandemic of its own.

SOCIAL NETWORKS OF CONTAGION

WE USE THE word *viral* to talk about silly cat GIFs and dance videos that spread like wildfire, jumping from one person's phone to another until millions have giggled at the same grumpy cat, or tens of millions have shimmied, twerked, and uploaded a trending dance to social media.

But that word, *viral*, reveals something critical about the nature of rumors and news. Disease is not the only thing that is transmitted between humans: we spread memes, ideas, and morsels of fact and myth. Peter's Facebook post about a virus was behaving like a virus itself. It spread from one Facebook user to that person's cousin, then to that person's coworker and that person's niece, until millions of susceptible people, from Italy to America, from Japan to Australia and beyond, were "infected" with false information that claimed the new coronavirus could be killed by gargling salt water or avoiding ice-cold drinks.

Humans have lived with epidemics for as long as we've been around. In recent years, we've figured out a way to predict where a disease might spread next and how many people it might infect. We call these prediction machines **mathematical models**, and there's nothing psychic or even that fancy about them. Mathematical models to predict the spread of disease work like this: You plug in data about a disease, like how quickly it spreads, how contagious people are when they're sick, and how long it takes for the average person to fall ill. Then you add information about the region that's affected, such as if people in the epidemic area live in crowded housing, or the place where the infection is spreading has only one hospital.

All these factors about the people, place, and pathogen impact an infection's speed and reach. You shove these numbers into the model and out pour the predictions. You get best-case scenarios, worst-case scenarios, and all the scenarios in between. The model might tell you this new disease will spread to nine cities by June, and this is how many people will be infected by July. The mathematical model could help you figure out how much it would help to build a second hospital or bring in lots more doctors and nurses to the worst-affected areas.

These mathematical models don't paint an exact picture of how the future will look. They're not time machines that let you jump forward a month to see what devastation a disease has caused. But by feeding the prediction models as many data points about contagiousness, sickness, housing, and hospitals as possible, you can get a decent idea of what the future might look like.

We can use the same prediction models to track the viral spread of *information*. Everything from tweets and memes to the spread of Facebook posts can be modeled.

Take a look at this messy picture. It's a diagram of a flu outbreak in a high school based on a mathematical model that looks at how much the flu virus could spread. Each dot is a person. They represent students, teachers, and other staff members who work in the school.

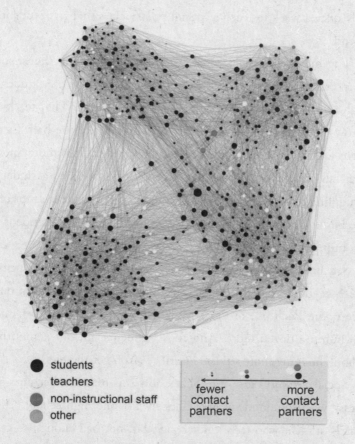

students
teachers
non-instructional staff
other

fewer contact partners — more contact partners

This diagram shows the connections between people infected with flu in a high school outbreak of the disease. Graph by Salathé lab, Penn State University, from Katrina Voss, "Flu Outbreaks Modeled by New Study of Classroom Schedules," Eberly College of Science, Penn State, February 11, 2013, https://science.psu.edu/news/flu-outbreaks-modeled-new-study-classroom-schedules.

The bigger the dot, the more people that student, teacher, or staff member is connected to. A big dot might be a super-popular student or a student who is connected to lots of people, say because they hand out sheet music and set up the stands at the beginning of band practice and touch the hands and equipment of many students. A small dot could be a teacher who comes into school only once a week to teach a special poetry class that five students attend.

The messy grey lines connecting the dots are the thousands of interactions between students, teachers, and staff. A student high-fives a teacher during gym class: that's a line. That teacher throws a football to another teacher, who catches the ball, then turns around to shake hands with a new teacher. Two more lines. The new teacher leaves the gym and offers a hand to a student struggling to balance a stack of textbooks. That student drops off the books to the head of history, who gives the helpful student a fist bump. Line. Line. Line.

See how connected we are? One student might swap pens, share keyboards, shake hands, and hug a dozen students in one afternoon. Each one of those students might hug, high-five, and fist-bump a dozen more. And those students fan out across the school, hugging more students until . . . You get the picture.

Social networks are vast. That's how this diagram becomes so messy with thousands of grey lines in just one high school. One sniffly student who feels kinda rough but not bad enough to call out sick might hug a dozen students in first period before being sent home because they became really sweaty with a high fever. If that student was in the early throes of flu that morning, a full-blown outbreak could sweep through the school the next week.

Now look at this picture. It looks similar, right? Dots of various sizes connected by lots and lots of lines. The dots are still people and the lines are still connections.

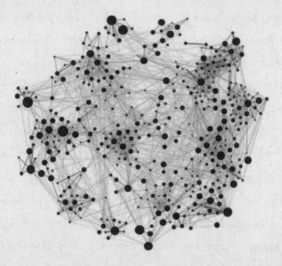

This diagram shows the connections between people spreading and receiving false information about COVID-19. Portion of figure, "Results from Numerical Simulations of a Rumour Spreading in Real-World Networks," in Jessica T. Davis et al., "Phase Transitions in Information Spreading on Structured Populations," *Nature Physics*, March 2, 2020, fig. 3, https://www.nature.com/articles/s41567-020-0810-3#citeas.

But it's not flu that's spreading this time: It's a rumor about COVID-19. In this diagram, the dots (people) don't have to be in the same school to be connected. They don't even have to be in the same town or country. They could be connected via Facebook groups or online chat rooms, or maybe they play video games together on the internet, separated by thousands of miles but connected through an online gaming platform.

Same networks. Different "infection."

And the parallels between viruses and viral rumors don't end there. In many outbreaks of disease, a small proportion of people spread the most amount of disease. We call these people superspreaders. (There's been lots of talk, rightly so, about the stigma attached to this idea of super-infectious people. For now, we'll stick with this word, bearing in mind we are not interested in pointing fingers or shaming people, which is cruel and doesn't help solve the problem of virus/rumor contagion.)

Say the average person in an epidemic infects two people, and those two people go on to infect two more people each. Well, a superspreader might infect eight people. What's different about the superspreader? It might be that they have a ton of friends, more than the average person. Or it might be that they have the kind of job that brings them into close proximity with lots of people (ice-cream seller, cheer captain, teacher). In any case, superspreaders can spark new and bigger outbreaks, which can make it difficult to break the chain of transmission and bring the epidemic under control.

Rumor superspreaders exist too. These are people who can make a rumor, tweet, meme, you name it, spread far and wide. They might be an Instagram influencer with a gazillion followers. They might be the president of a country with the power to hold televised press conferences at the drop of a hat or use social media to reach even more people. They might be a journalist with access to a respected news site where they can publish two stories a day. They also might just be a retired art gallery owner in Buckinghamshire, England, who has a face that appears trustworthy and a lot of Facebook friends. Superspreaders of information help rumors go viral, fast.

On the flip side, we have stiflers. Whether it's a disease that is spreading or rumors about a disease, stiflers are people who break the chain of transmission. They put an end to the spread of a rumor or the spread of a virus. Maybe they prefer alone time and only hang out with friends once or twice a month. Or maybe they work in a booth at a bank where a plastic partition separates them from other employees and the public, and they prefer to eat lunch alone while reading a book. Either way, stiflers are the opposite of superspreaders. When a rumor or disease gets to a stifler, it ends with them. They don't spread it to anybody else. In the case of disinformation, a stifler could be a person who spots the lies in a cleverly worded social media post or article, flags the content as false, and warns others to not believe it.

VIRAL VECTORS AND PATIENT ZERO

YOU CAN CALL anyone who spreads a rumor or a virus a **vector**. A vector is just a thing that spreads a thing. Mosquitoes are vectors for malaria because when a mosquito bites you, it can pass on the parasite that causes the disease.

In the case of disease and rumors, vectors can be human and nonhuman. For a virus, a nonhuman vector could be a doorknob or a keyboard, some temporary resting place for a pathogen so that when a sniffly person wipes their nose with their hand and touches the doorknob and you open the door after them . . . well, you know what happens next.

When it comes to rumor-spreading, vectors can be human, like you, or nonhuman, like bots. Bots, short for "robots," are software programs that run social media accounts that are designed to post specific messages, respond to particular hashtags, and follow certain kinds of accounts. (Bots are not to be confused with trolls. Trolls are real people who hide behind online personas to push our buttons and start fights. More on trolls in a moment.)

They might sound harmless and merely annoying, but bots—especially lots of them, fighting the same fight—can be powerful. Governments have even weaponized Twitter bots against enemy nations, programming huge numbers of social media accounts to look out for people tweeting in support of things like government-run vaccination programs, all in an attempt to stir up distrust in foreign governments.

Some of these bots have been programmed to look for tweets by real people who were saying things like **YAY! VACCINES SAVE LIVES! VACCINES ARE SO AMAZING!** The bots would react with messages of disagreement, some of them spreading outright lies: **NO! VACCINES SUCK. THEY'RE TOXIC! DON'T GET VACCINATED!**

Bots provoke arguments and instigate online attacks. There are a lot of them out there. As many as one in six Twitter accounts is a bot. Bear that in mind the next time "someone" argues with you online.

Looking back at those two messy diagrams of flu spreading in a high school and a rumor spreading around the world, you might notice a pattern. Sometimes it's clear that one blob—a person (or bot)—is a central figure. Hundreds, even thousands, of grey lines shoot out from that one circle. Sometimes this central figure turns out to be our patient zero.

You may have heard about patient zero during the COVID-19 pandemic. Patient zero is the first person to be infected in an outbreak, the first person to spread the virus to another human. There can be one patient zero for an entire pandemic and different patient zeros for separate, smaller epidemics. (Again, keep in mind the potential harm of lumping lots of blame onto patient zero, as if they are responsible for an outbreak. In reality, lots and lots of factors contribute to the spread of disease—and rumors—and it's pointless and inaccurate to point fingers and try to put the blame on one person.)

You probably won't be surprised by this: Rumor epidemics also have a patient zero. In our case, could Peter, the eighty-four-year-old English man who posted a viral Facebook message, be patient zero? He did share a mostly nonsensical Facebook post with advice about preventing and recognizing the symptoms of a new disease.

It turns out Peter is not our patient zero! There was no friend he had dinner with who had an uncle in China. "His" Facebook post that began, "Last evening dining out with friends . . ." wasn't about an actual dinner that Peter had attended the night before. Peter had seen that message elsewhere. He was exposed to this message and "infected" by someone else who inspired him to post his own false version of the message.

But who is that original person? It's hard to know because Peter won't share the details of what he saw and who it was posted by. When journalists asked Peter where he first spotted the message about a friend's uncle, Peter wouldn't give a name. He just said, "I believed him actually to be a relation of this scientific guy, a medical guy who'd given all those facts and figures."

That doesn't help us find our patient zero. But if we keep digging around online and following the connections between people, we see that three weeks before Peter posted his message, someone who belonged to a Facebook group called Happy People shared a similar message with the group's nearly two thousand members. The members of Happy People shared that Facebook post with their friends, who shared it with their friends, until the message popped up on the screen of a man called Glen.

Glen lives in India, and he posted his message about dinner with a friend who had an uncle in China to a bunch of Facebook groups, including one group that was for Catholics who worshipped at a local ashram.

Glen might be our patient zero—the first to type that mostly nonsense message and share it online. Or at least, because this is all so convoluted and tricky, Glen seems to be the first person we can trace the Facebook post back to. Three weeks later that message landed on Peter's screen, and Peter's Facebook post about "his" friend's uncle was shared more than 400,000 times and received nearly 40,000 "reactions," many more shares and reactions than Glen's message and other earlier versions of the post had received. That means that while Peter isn't patient zero, he played a critical role in amplifying Glen's Facebook post and helping it spread around the world. You could call him a superspreader.

The parallels between viruses and viral rumors continue, because after spreading like a virus, Peter's message did something else that viruses do: it mutated. A word was added to the post as another person shared it. Then one item on the list disappeared. Then another sentence was tweaked. Two more items were added. Another word deleted. The long list of advice from Peter's friend's uncle (but not really) in China evolved as it spread, just the way a virus evolves and mutates as it replicates inside a cell and spreads from one person to the next, making tiny changes here and there in its shape, size, and capabilities.

In America, a woman called April posted an edited version of Peter's post to a Facebook group called Coronavirus Updates. April's message didn't mention a friend's uncle. This time, the message had mutated to say the coronavirus information came from "a friend's nephew in the military," but the advice it listed was very similar to Peter's post. April told journalists she had copied the message from a friend. "Looks like most of it is false," she told the journalists. "I use Facebook all day long, everyday. I have found lots of helpful information . . . I don't watch the news."

Then the viral post mutated *again*. This time the attribution shifted from a friend's nephew in the military to an institution: Stanford University. Trustworthy, credible, known for producing excellent medical research (I'm biased; I work there), adding "Stanford" to the Facebook post helped it spread even farther. In fact, it spread so far that the university had to issue a warning that the information was false and definitely did not come from Stanford.

Tell that to the Ghanaian TV presenter who shared it anyway. Or the American actor who posted the message online. The post kept mutating. At one point it said "Taiwanese doctors" had shared the list of warnings and advice. Then it was attributed to "Japanese doctors." Then it was on Twitter, then it was on Instagram. Then it was everywhere.

Viruses. Rumors. Transmit. Infect. Amplify.

REPEAT. REPEAT. REPEAT.

SIDEBAR: HOW TO SPREAD A LIE— THE DISINFORMATION PLAYBOOK

INFORMATION WARFARE IS NOTHING NEW. THERE'S EVEN A playbook with tips and tricks for effectively spreading a lie. Created in the early 1900s by Soviet Union operatives and popularized in the 1950s by the nation's secret police, the KGB, the playbook has been adapted to keep up with the times.

The KGB used to work hard to recruit journalists to disseminate its lies far and wide. Now, disinformation spreaders need only a few desks and keyboards and a small army of trolls to unleash lies around the world. Here are six easy steps from the disinformation playbook that was invented years ago but is still followed by some today.

STUDY YOUR TARGET

What makes your target angry? What upsets them? What do they really care about? Is it jobs, the economy, education? What keeps them up at night with worry? How can you make your target more worried about these things, sow divisions, and make them question their fellow citizens?

PICK A LIE

Make it emotional so it triggers the divisions and worries that you identified in step one. Make the lie a little bit new and unique. Researchers have found that humans like to be the first to share new information, acquiring what they call "status points" for being the first in their social group to share something important and new. If your lie is framed as breaking news, that could make people want to share the lie as soon as they come across it.

ADD A KERNEL OF TRUTH

The government-run "news" operation *Russia Today*, which is an English-language outlet, produces somewhere around 80 percent factual journalism mixed with 20 percent Russian propaganda, according to researcher Claire Wardle. She told the *New York Times* "Eighty percent of their coverage is actually excellent coverage. And because 80 percent of the time they're doing quality journalism . . . it enables people to say, 'Well, no, look at this. We are journalists. We have policies. We know what we're doing.'" It's hard to separate a lie from the truth when the two are so tightly woven together. How can you tell which "news" story is factual and which is government advertising?

"IT WASN'T ME"

Pretend the lie is truthful information that came from elsewhere—not from you.

FIND USEFUL IGNORAMUSES[1]

Call on people who will spread your lie far and wide without knowing that it's a lie or that you're behind it. Influencers, celebrities,

---

1. The political terminology still repeats the original language, which used the phrase "useful idiots." But *idiot* is an ableist term once used to malign people who were born with learning difficulties.

other countries' presidents . . . Any of these can be your allies in the lie-spreading mission.[2]

"IT WASN'T ME!" (AGAIN.)

Deny. Deny. Deny.

2. Depressingly, people don't have to believe a lie is *true* in order to spread it; sometimes they spread the lie with full awareness that it is an untruth. In some cases, info that is a blatant lie serves as a signal to make the target think they are in on a secret. For example, President Donald Trump told an average of 21 lies each day during his presidency but remained popular among some groups. Why might that be? Trump was using a well-known strategy that's been exploited by leaders for hundreds of years. By saying things that were obvious lies, he was violating the norms of our society and signaling that he was willing to go against the status quo. So, to anyone listening who felt left out by mainstream society, Trump's lies signaled authenticity. *Ahh, this is a man who's not scared to go against the establishment and be different.* There's even a name for this weird duping: the **authenticity of the lying demagogue**.

WORDS MATTER

YOU MIGHT BE tempted to shout **"FAKE NEWS!"** at Peter's Facebook post. After all, it was a jumble of nonsense with some good advice thrown into the mix. (One version suggested regular hand-washing, never a bad thing!) But then there was that weird stuff about the new virus causing so much congestion in your nose that you would feel like you were drowning. False. There was some bogus information about avoiding ice-cold drinks, and there were very specific (but inaccurate) details about how long the virus could survive on metals and fabric.

So I get it if you want to shout **"FAKE NEWS!"** But if you say "FAKE NEWS!," you would be guilty of uttering nonsense too. Here's why. First, that term is unhelpfully vague. "Fake news" can refer to a whole jumble of things, from rumors and myths to carefully crafted government propaganda.

We need words that separate this mishmash of confusing falseness. It's like when you're trying to help someone. First, you have to figure out what is wrong if you're going to be of any use. Once you know what you're dealing with, that's when you can really help. "Fake news" is too broad and nonspecific for our purposes. We need precision when it comes to the words we use to describe this mess.

Here's another reason for avoiding this term. "Fake news" has been weaponized and lobbed like a word-grenade by people in power toward anyone saying anything they don't want to hear. "Oh, you're accusing me of embezzling funds from a children's charity?" a politician might say at a press conference. "THAT'S FAKE NEWS!"

The typical word-grenade throwers: presidents, politicians, CEOs. The victims: journalists, especially those asking probing questions, challenging people in power, and revealing their dirty secrets. "FAKE NEWS!" gets thrown about to undermine journalism and discredit reporters. It's used as a convenient tool for shutting down a conversation and silencing people who are speaking truth to power.

Here's yet another problem with the term, specifically the second word: news. Is it news if it's "fake"? Doesn't that word, "news," make you think of information that is based in fact and reality?

Luckily, we have alternative language. Specific, helpful words that precisely describe the problems we are dealing with. First up, there's **misinformation**. This is false information that's spread by people who don't realize it's false and who share it without any intention of causing harm. It's like your best friend saying that if you eat a ton of garlic, you won't get COVID-19. Is that true? Nope. But did your friend think they were correct? Yes. And was your friend trying to harm you? Hopefully not. (Unless they wanted you to have really bad breath. But that's the worst they thought would happen.) We can classify this type of unintentionally wrong information as misinformation because the person sharing it didn't realize it was false and they weren't trying to hurt you.

We could label Peter's viral Facebook post as misinformation. He wasn't trying to hurt anyone. In fact, he told BBC journalists that he wanted to help others and that he shared the list because he thought it might save some people from becoming infected. And his message, unlike many others out there, didn't share advice that encouraged people to do dangerous things like drink bleach. But it was inaccurate, it wasn't based on the best available science, and it could mislead people who might think drinking warm water or gargling with salt water is enough to keep the virus away. Because Peter didn't realize he was sharing false information, and because he says he didn't intend to cause harm, we can classify his Facebook post as misinformation.

Now, if Peter's Facebook post had been first sent to him by secret government operatives who wired him cash to spread information that was known to be false, in the hopes that lots of Brits would read it and become infected, that would make it **disinformation**. Disinformation is false information that is known to be false and is spread with the intention of causing harm. Peter didn't share disinformation, but we did see disinformation campaigns spread during the West African Ebola crisis of 2014–2016 and during the COVID-19 pandemic.

In 2014, news of an Ebola outbreak in Atlanta spread online with the hashtag #EbolaInAtlanta. It wasn't true. The messages were posted by a group of internet trolls linked to the Russian government. Their goal was to seed confusion and chaos in Atlanta when fears were already heightened about the Ebola epidemic in West Africa. That's disinformation.

Disinformation can turn into misinformation. Once it's been put online, information that is intentionally false might be repeated by someone who doesn't realize it's false. *Like a virus, evolving and morphing from one shape to another.*

Next in our new vocabulary of precise words is **malinformation**. Unlike misinformation and disinformation—which are false—malinformation is based on reality. It's accurate information that was never intended to be shared publicly, or it's accurate information that's shared out of context with the intention of hurting people.

One example of malinformation is this 2017 photo of a person who came to be known as the Muslim Woman on Westminster Bridge. In this photo the woman is seen looking at her phone while a person is lying on the ground and seven others are watching over and attending to that person.

The context: A fifty-two-year-old man had just attacked and killed five people near the Houses of Parliament in London on the afternoon of March 22.

Source: Jamie Lorriman.

The photo of this supposedly carefree woman in a hijab, walking past a victim of an attack while absorbed in her phone, went viral online with captions like "The main difference between Muslims and Christians."

But here's some more context: The woman had just finished talking to witnesses of the attack and was figuring out a way to help. She used her phone to call her family, who she knew would be worried about her when they heard the news of the attack and realized her proximity to the Houses of Parliament. After calling her family and trying to assist at the scene, the woman helped another woman get away from the chaos and onto public transport before making her own way back home to her family.

Carefree? No. Distraught? Yes. But if you saw only this photo frame plus the Islamophobic messages that spread alongside it, you might believe that the Muslim Woman on Westminster Bridge was unbothered by a deadly attack and that she represents all Muslims who apparently don't care about the victims of such tragedies.

You would be so wrong. But that's how malinformation works. It takes a snapshot of information, scrubs it of context, strips it of vital nuance and data, and pushes a narrative that can cause harm to many people. The Muslim Woman on Westminster Bridge received threats, and people misled by the image believed that many Muslims support terror attacks and don't care about the victims.

This photo, an example of how an image can be used to push a false idea, morphed from malinformation to something else entirely. Here's what happened. A Twitter user called @SouthLoneStar, whose bio read "Proud TEXAN and AMERICAN patriot," posted this tweet:

The Twitter user was delighted at the reach of their tweet. "Wow . . . I'm on the Daily Mail front page! Thank you British libs! You're making me famous," they said when their tweets appeared in prominent British newspapers. The next day they tweeted: "I'm on The Sun! Thank you again, British libs! Now I'm even more famous!"

Another tweet by @SouthLoneStar showed the Muslim Woman on Westminster Bridge next to a photo of a British Conservative politician, a White man, performing CPR on another victim of the attack.

Texas Lone Star @SouthLoneStar · 6h

The main difference between Muslims and Christians.
#PrayForLondon #Parliament #Westminster

These two images are based in reality. The Muslim Woman on Westminster Bridge really was looking at her phone and walking past a victim. A White male politician really was performing CPR on another victim. But without the context that the Muslim Woman on Westminster Bridge was helping in her own way and that she was visibly scared and distressed (as shown in other photos), and with captions that used her image to speak about all Muslims and the politician's image to speak about all Christians, you can see how hatred and falsehoods are spread.

So is it malinformation, or is it something different?

What if you found out that while @SouthLoneStar's Twitter bio said they are a Texan and a patriot, @SouthLoneStar wasn't a Texan? They weren't even in Texas. In fact, @SouthLoneStar was six thousand miles east of Texas in St. Petersburg, Russia. They were part of a Russian disinformation campaign, and their Twitter account was a "soldier" in a "troll army" of hundreds.

Remember the false #EbolaInAtlanta story that was spread

during the West African Ebola crisis? The same group that spread that disinformation created @SouthLoneStar's account in 2015. The group is called the Internet Research Agency and is also known as the Trolls from Olgino in Russian internet slang (Olgino is a neighborhood in St. Petersburg). The Internet Research Agency operates from an ordinary-looking building in the city. But rooms in that building house around two dozen people, each paid $400 to $1,400 a month for working twelve-hour shifts, or longer.

During these shifts the troll army sends out lots and lots of tweets. There are tweets about cake recipes and music videos, pretty regular stuff. But every now and again they throw in a tweet about the Ukrainian government, saying it is run by fascists. Then there'll be another cake tweet, maybe a tweet about the weather, a new music video, and then a tweet saying Russian troops were right to violently occupy Crimea.

It turns out the Internet Research Agency is linked to the Kremlin, and its likely financier is a billionaire who just happens to be friends with the Russian president, Vladimir Putin. What started off as a group with a mission to boost public support for Russia's actions in Ukraine morphed into an effort to meddle with other countries' democracies. Why would they do that?

Information warfare, which is what this is, was a big part of military operations throughout the 1900s. It was a method that didn't require bombs and fighter jets. Instead of missiles and air raids, you could use propaganda to weaken enemy states. Many thought this method of warfare dropped out of fashion after the Cold War, but it never went away, and now it's back with a vengeance. Why go to the bother of bombing a country (which would stir up all sorts of international problems and backlash) when you can just meddle with that country's elections by convincing its citizens to vote for the corrupt politician who happens to be your buddy? And you can do all this from the comfort of a discreet office building with only a laptop and a bag of snacks.

In December 2015, the Russian troll army in St. Petersburg began tweeting in favor of one particular American presidential candidate. "Donald Trump is my president!" wrote one troll. Then, on October 6, 2016, hours before embarrassing emails from presidential candidate Hillary Clinton's campaign chairman would be leaked (file that leak under "malinformation"—private information that was never supposed to be public), the trolls upped their game. Aggressively. More than eighteen thousand tweets went flying through cyberspace, at a pace of a dozen tweets a minute, the day before Hillary Clinton's emails were leaked. The *Washington Post* labeled it "the busiest day by far in a disinformation operation with an aftermath still roiling U.S. politics." More than fifty thousand Russian-linked accounts tweeted about the US election, and Twitter alerted at least 1.4 million users to let them know that tweets they had seen in the months leading up to the 2016 election were actually Russian propaganda. But those 1.4 million only included those who had retweeted, replied, or liked tweets that were disinformation. It's likely that many more people were exposed to Russian disinformation, but Twitter didn't notify users who had read Russian troll tweets in their feeds without interacting with them. A year later, Facebook revealed that in the run-up to the election, 126 million Facebook users were exposed to lies stemming from just one Russian disinformation factory, the Internet Research Agency.

Some of these accounts were later flagged as spreaders of dangerous disinformation, and some were even shut down. But by then it was too late. The damage was done, and potentially millions of Americans were duped into believing falsehoods about presidential candidate Hillary Clinton. Any existing worries about Clinton's future as president, any lingering, misogynistic biases about a woman president, were confirmed by the false information spread by outsiders looking to influence America's election result. Disinformation flooded social media, trickled into homes and communities and conversations, and influenced which boxes voters checked in the voting booth on election day. No need for air raids or bombs to weaken an enemy state; all the Russian troll army needed was a broadband connection and a keyboard.

It wasn't just the US election the troll army disrupted with its information warfare. There was the UK's vote on leaving the European Union, also known as Brexit. Half of the Internet Research Agency's troll accounts were created in the run-up to the 2016 Brexit vote. Amid the tweets about cake recipes and music videos were messages that spread anti-immigrant sentiment and seeded doubts about the UK's place in Europe. Exploiting the fears of those who already held racist or nationalist beliefs (see step one in the disinformation playbook), the Russian trolls drove those people deeper into their prejudiced rabbit holes.

The troll army has also unleashed disinformation campaigns against the Black Lives Matter movement. And it was this same troll army that descended on the Muslim Woman on Westminster Bridge, retweeting and liking @SouthLoneStar's tweets until they landed in the pages of British newspapers and strangers threatened the life of the woman who was caught up in a terrorist attack.

SIDEBAR: RED FLAGS FOR FALSE INFORMATION

NOW THAT YOU KNOW WHY AND HOW FALSE INFORMATION can go viral, what can you spot in Peter's original Facebook post that sets off alarm bells about information disorder?

Think especially about the timing of the post (in the context of the pandemic), the attribution it includes, and the language used.

In chapter four, we'll talk more about the psychological impact of likes and shares, but take note of them here and consider how they might influence a person's likelihood of believing a message and sharing it with others.

Peter Lee Goodchild
February 27 at 2:55 PM · 🌐

IMPORTANT ANNOUNCEMENT - CORONAVIRUS
Last evening dining out with friends, one of their uncles, who's graduated with a master's degree and who worked in Shenzhen Hospital (Guangdong Province, China) sent him the following notes on Coronavirus for guidance:
1. If you have a runny nose and sputum, you may have a common cold/flu
2. Coronavirus pneumonia is a dry cough with no runny nose to start off with..
3. This new virus is not heat-resistant and will be killed by a temperature of just 26/27 degrees..
4. If someone sneezes with it, it takes about 10 feet before it drops to the ground and is no longer airborne.
5. If it drops on a metal surface it will live for at least 12 hours - so if you come into contact with any metal surface - wash your hands as soon as you can with soap (an alcohol-based one is good)
6. On fabric it can survive for 6-12 hours, normal laundry detergent will kill it.
7. Try not to drink liquids with ice.
8. Wash your hands frequently as the virus can only live on your hands for 5-10 minutes, but - a lot can happen during that time - you can rub your eyes, pick your nose unwittingly and so on.
9. You can also gargle as an added prevention. A simple solution of salt in warm water will suffice.
10. Can't emphasise enough - drink plenty of water!
THE SYMPTOMS
1. It will first infect the throat, so you may have a sore throat lasting 3/4 days
2. The virus then blends into a nasal fluid that enters the trachea and then the lungs, causing pneumonia. This takes about 5/6 days further.
3. With the pneumonia comes high fever and difficulty in breathing.
4. The nasal congestion is not like the normal kind. It can feel like you're drowning. It's imperative you then seek immediate attention by telephoning 111 or your doctor - don't visit..
SPREAD THE WORD - PLEASE SHARE.AND ALSO SEE RECENT UPDATES FROM NHS AND ELSEWHERE

A post containing some false information about the novel coronavirus went viral on Facebook in the early days of the COVID-19 pandemic. Source: Facebook.

INFORMATION DISORDER . . . AND PASTA

YOU'VE PROBABLY HEARD the term "fake news" a million times, but now you know it's a useless term. It describes a massive mess of false information, some of it spread with bad intentions, and some of it spread by well-meaning friends and family who just don't know any better. Using precise language to describe *exactly* what kind of false information we're talking about can help us clear up the mess and get to the root of the problem. Specific terms are not only going to make us sound much smarter but they can help us better understand who created the false information, who is spreading it, and why.

Back to that word "disinformation." You might think this is a new problem and that this is a new word. But it's thought to come from the Russian word *dezinformatsiya*, which means "to spread falsehoods among your enemies to confuse and disorient," and it's a word that was invented by Joseph Stalin, who ruled the Soviet Union from the early 1920s until his death in 1953. *Dezinformatsiya* stems from the earliest years of the Cold War and was used as the name of the KGB's propaganda office. (The KGB was the Soviet Union's main security agency.)

While we think these problems are new, the fact that these words are old shows just how long-standing these problems of false information really are. It turns out the word "misinformation" isn't modern either. The English writer Samuel Johnson said the king of Prussia "declares himself with great ardour against the use of torture, and by some misinformation charges the English that they still retain it." That was in 1756.

Misinformation, disinformation, and malinformation can be grouped together under the umbrella of information disorder. Like a disease that is transmitted from one person to another and another, information disorder spreads, sowing doubt and hatred, meddling with people's opinions, influencing the way ordinary folks vote in elections, and interfering with democracies.

If you want to get really descriptive (and who doesn't?), we can break these categories down into a spectrum of seven types of misinformation and disinformation and rank them on a scale of falseness and intent. That last part is important: understanding who shared the information and what they were trying to gain from it is crucial in helping us spot patterns in the spread of falsehoods and protecting large numbers of people from falling for a lie.

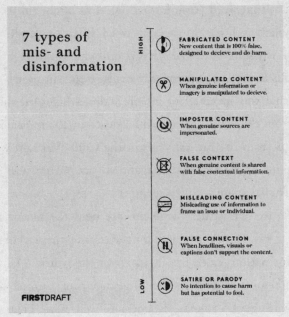

7 types of mis- and disinformation

HIGH

FABRICATED CONTENT
New content that is 100% false, designed to decieve and do harm.

MANIPULATED CONTENT
When genuine information or imagery is manipulated to decieve.

IMPOSTER CONTENT
When genuine sources are impersonated.

FALSE CONTEXT
When genuine content is shared with false contextual information.

MISLEADING CONTENT
Misleading use of information to frame an issue or individual.

FALSE CONNECTION
When headlines, visuals or captions don't support the content.

SATIRE OR PARODY
No intention to cause harm but has potential to fool.

LOW

FIRSTDRAFT

Source: Claire Wardle, "Information Disorder: 'The Techniques We Saw in 2016 Have Evolved,'" *First Draft News*, October 21, 2019, https://firstdraftnews.org/articles /information-disorder-the-techniques-we-saw-in-2016-have-evolved/.

At one end of the information spectrum is satire or parody, which a comedian might unleash to crack an audience up but could leave the audience thinking, *Well, hold on a second. Did a Texas politician really go on a sunny vacation while people in his state were freezing to death, or . . . is that a joke? It must be a joke!* Satire and parody are meant to be a little believable, which is exactly how they can cause confusion.

There's even a term for that head-scratching moment when you read a headline and say to yourself, *Hold on . . . is this real or . . . ?* Poe's Law states that satire and parody can be mistaken for the real thing, and that the opposite can also happen. If a real thing sounds extreme, you can be left turning the page and thinking, *Ah, well, that sounds ridiculous. It can't possibly be true.* On the other hand, if you read the parody of something extreme, it can ring true when it's not.

Poe's Law was in full effect when the *New York Times* printed an article that featured a picture of a doctored magazine cover. *Tiger Beat* was a teen magazine that was published from 1965 until 2019, and in 2007, the satirical news site the *Onion* printed a made-up cover of the teen magazine featuring a picture of then-presidential-hopeful Barack Obama to make a point about the senator's hunger to appeal to the "tween vote." It wasn't true, of course, but there was Obama on the fabricated front cover of the magazine, grinning next to Vanessa Hudgens and the Jonas Brothers. And there he was on that same cover printed inside the *New York Times*, which had to publish a correction: "A series of pictures last Sunday of covers of the magazine Tiger Beat, with an article about how the original teen-girl tabloid has remained virtually unchanged since its inception in 1965, erroneously included a parody cover, produced by the satiric newspaper The Onion, that featured a picture of President Obama."

Satirical news site the *Onion* created a parody front cover of the magazine *Tiger Beat* featuring a photo of Barack Obama. The *New York Times* published the cover as if it were real. Source: The *Onion*.

Oops.

But the *Times* is not alone. ESPN reporters and long-standing lawmakers are among those who have succumbed to Poe's Law. And in 2012, China's state newspaper *People's Daily Online* reported that North Korea's Kim Jong-un was the "Sexiest Man Alive" after the *Onion* printed a farcical story claiming that his "devastatingly handsome, round face, his boyish charm, and his strong, sturdy frame" meant the "Pyongyang-bred heartthrob" outranked the likes of Ryan Gosling and Will Smith. A South Korean news site, the *Korea Times,* also reported the *Onion*'s "Sexiest Man Alive" satirical story as fact.

Next up is a false connection, when a headline or photo caption says one thing but the story or photo says or shows something different. This photo of two young children hugging one another was published on social media sites with the caption "Two-year-old sister protected by four-year-old brother in Nepal." The image and caption went viral after a devastating earthquake in Nepal in 2015. Except the photo was taken eight years earlier . . . in Vietnam. It had nothing to do with the Nepal earthquake. The photographer, Na-Son Nguyen, said they took the photo while traveling through a remote village and posted it to their personal blog. They were shocked when the photo went viral years later, branded with a false connection to a 2015 natural disaster. There have been other cases where the same picture has been used but with a caption saying the children were victims of Syria's civil war or Burmese orphans.

Na-Son Nguyen
@nasonnguyen

This is my photo about two Vietnamese Hmong ethnic children taken in 2007 in Ha Giang province, it's not about Nepal

Then there's misleading content, like the caption that accompanies this next photo that was printed by the news

organization Reuters. The caption says an older man "clashes" with Ukrainian police officers. But who is clashing with whom? And do the power dynamics illustrated in the photo match what the caption says? This photo-caption combo can be classified as misleading content.

A supporter of the former Georgian president clashes with police officers in Kiev
REUTERS

Source: Reuters and Ethical Media for Active Citizenship.

Next on the list is false context, where something real is shared alongside context that is false. This could be the subcategory for the Muslim Woman on Westminster Bridge photo.

Imposter content is when false information is said to be affiliated with a brand or influential person. It's like the time during the COVID-19 pandemic when viral Instagram posts by the actress Megan Fox said that she didn't believe in wearing face masks to protect against the virus. She never said that. But the posts were made to look as if they came from her Instagram account. And because they showed her name and profile photo, people shared them thinking that the actress really believed those things. Sometimes it's not clear who creates content like this and why, but we can see that it can be a powerful way to influence opinions on things as important as mask-wearing, all while using a celebrity's status to push a particular way of thinking.

Higher up the spectrum is manipulated content, which is when real information (written or visual) is manipulated, like with this photo. Depending on how you crop the image, soldiers are either shooting or saving this man.

How we saw it   How it really happened   How other people saw it

Source: Ethical Media for Active Citizenship.

Top of the list is fabricated content, which is completely false but made to look legitimate. Take this front cover of the *Washington Post*, which was published in January 2019 but dated May 1, 2019. It's not real. The headline "Unpresidented" is plastered across the page above a slew of stories "reporting" that Donald Trump had resigned the presidency. It looked real. Thousands of copies of this fabricated newspaper were circulated on the streets of Washington, DC, and there was a digital version too. The *Washington Post* freaked out and said, "We will not tolerate others misrepresenting themselves as The Washington Post, and we are deeply concerned about the confusion it causes among readers."

In 2019, an activist group called the Yes Men created and distributed a fabricated version of the *Washington Post* newspaper that said President Donald Trump had resigned.
Source: Tasos Katopodis/Stringer/Getty Images.

The culprits behind the fabricated newspaper and digital site were the Yes Men, a self-described "trickster activist collective" who said the goal was to present "a sort of road map to the future." That road map cost the group $40,000 and caused a ton of confusion among people walking the streets of DC that day.

See why it's important to have specific language to explain the wild world of false information? Using one catchall term, like "fake news," to speak to *all* these different types of false or misleading information oversimplifies the problem we're dealing with and doesn't help us get to the root of the problem, such as why anyone would create this content in the first place and how millions of people can be duped into sharing and believing it.

As false information blooms, so does our vocabulary. There's even a specific word to describe Peter's viral Facebook post: copypasta. It has nothing to do with spaghetti and everything to do with material that is copied and pasted, meaning it's typed out instead of just being retweeted or reshared. Copypasta makes a post look unique, as if Peter really was the person who had dinner with a friend whose uncle worked in a Chinese hospital. . . .

Copypasta made Glen's Facebook post and April's Facebook post seem original too, like they really did have dinner with a friend whose uncle worked in a Chinese hospital . . . or whose nephew was in the military and came to know a thing or two about a new virus. Those posts were nonsense, but they were more *believable* nonsense because each of them, Peter, Glen, and April, had typed out the coronavirus list and shared it as if they were writing the original post. And this is what so much of information disorder contagion comes down to: Trust. Social networks.

While navigating the world of information disorder, it can be helpful to think about the motive behind the creation and sharing of false news so we can separate those who think they are sharing helpful information, which sadly turns out to be nonsense, from those desperate to dupe us with dangerous info. But it's even more helpful to understand *how* false information is created and spread. Digging into five key techniques used to make us believe lies helps us have those essential *Aha!* moments when we spot these techniques in action. It also leads us toward two key strategies for protecting ourselves from believing lies.

Before we get to the protection methods, let's look at the five key techniques for pushing lies. These are often used by science deniers, but they're also used throughout various regions of the world of information disorder. Abbreviated to FLICC, these strategies were described in 2007 by Mark and Chris Hoofnagle and fleshed out into a meatier taxonomy by John Cook, a researcher who studies climate change lies and ways to build resilience against bunk. (The *L* in FLICC used to be a *U* until John tweaked the acronym.)

The first element of FLICC stands for **fake experts**. These are people who say things like "The science that claims climate change is real is actually fake, and I'm the expert, so I can explain to you how it's all a hoax." The use of fake experts to mislead is also known as the appeal to false authority, which speaks to our desire to believe the words of someone who has "Dr." or "Prof." in front of their name. (Think about it. There's a reason my editor chose to put "Dr." before my name on the cover and in the pages of this book. That credential can add credibility.) While fake experts are usually not actually experts in the area they claim to know lots about, they might hold qualifications in adjacent fields, which can mislead those of us who are not in the know about that particular area of study.

There are some exceptions, though, such as the case of so-called **frackademics**, who are actually experts in the area in which they are spreading falsehoods. Frackademics are scientists who are paid by corporations that use hydraulic fracturing, also called fracking, to drill for oil and gas. There's lots of evidence to show that fracking is dangerous to the environment and bad news for human health. Frackademics are often experts in fields such as geology and physics—which is very relevant to fracking and makes them quite believable—but their expertise is bought and exploited by companies that encourage them to publish "science" in support of fracking. These companies want them to say that fracking is safe, that it doesn't harm the environment, and that it doesn't pose a danger to human health.

While the words "frackademic" and "frackademia" were first coined and popularized in the 2000s by Sharon Wilson and Steve Horn, who both write blogs about gas and oil companies, the idea of paying seemingly neutral academics to portray dangerous things in a positive light isn't new. In fact, this first FLICC technique has been around for decades. Anahad O'Connor, a journalist for the *New York Times*, discovered in 2016 that sugar companies in the 1960s put money in the pockets of Harvard scientists so that these seemingly neutral, highly respected experts would say that sugar did not cause heart disease and that fatty foods were the real dietary demons. Fake experts were used by tobacco companies (which are sometimes called "the pioneers of fake news") in the 1950s and in later decades. (Tobacco companies even paid scientists to publish studies in the 1990s saying the link between secondhand smoke and cancer was based on bad science and should not be believed. We know how that turned out.)

Some of the worst—although some might say the best, since they're so effective at duping us—techniques for pushing lies and making false information look believable can be traced back to tobacco companies. In their book *Merchants of Doubt,* authors Naomi Oreskes and Erik M. Conway show how the "Tobacco Strategy" of seeding doubt and pushing back against credible science became the playbook in later years for Big Sugar, Big Oil, Big Gas, and others, including climate change deniers.

Sometimes a technique called the **magnified minority** is used to amplify the voices of lonely fake experts. You might have noticed this during the COVID-19 pandemic, when one or two highly unreasonable voices were given lots of airtime on TV and seemed to hog the mic as they shouted against the consensus. This magnified minority technique makes it seem as if scientists are fighting with each other about a topic when in fact most are in agreement. It amplifies the appearance of a debate when in reality there is scientific consensus.

While fake experts are sometimes deployed alone, other times they are unleashed en masse to make them look even more convincing. Shoving a dozen or more fake experts at the public can overwhelm the target audience with reams of data and make the fake experts look credible, as if they are backed up by their peers.

Next up is the technique of **logical fallacies**. This is where the conclusion made in an argument doesn't follow the basis of the argument. For example, say you're in the middle of a discussion about gun control and your interlocutor says, "Well, if you want to ban guns because they're dangerous, why not ban butter knives and forks as well?! Might as well ban cars while we're at it since they can run people over!" That kind of reasoning is called a **straw man argument**. It's where your intelligent thoughts about gun control are twisted to make them easier for the other person to rebut. Or say your interlocutor moves away from the topic at hand and starts attacking you as a person. They might say, "Why should we even listen to your arguments on gun control when we know you do karate and could hurt someone?" That kind of attack on a person's character, aimed at taking the focus off the topic, is yet another kind of logical fallacy called an **ad hominem attack**. In a way, every letter in FLICC represents some type of logical fallacy, but giving this technique its own letter in FLICC and its own spot on John Cook's taxonomy is a helpful way of remembering how often it's used to spread false information and how many types of logical fallacies exist.

Next up is **impossible expectations**, which is when a person demands so much proof that it would be impossible to provide enough data to convince them. Impossible expectations might be wielded to say more evidence is needed, or even absolute proof, which isn't always possible in the real world. The worst part of impossible expectations is that once you do hand over tons of evidence, the stakes are elevated and even more evidence is demanded! And then more evidence, and more evidence . . .

The first *C* in FLICC stands for **cherry picking**. This is where a falsehood-spreader selectively focuses on some small points of data to back their claim instead of looking at the bigger picture and all the rest of the data that contradicts what they are saying. John likens cherry picking to a person standing on the bow of a sinking ship saying that because the bow is rising, the ship can't be sinking.

John Cook
@johnfocook   ...

Replying to @WxCat62 and @tan123

The #CrankyUncle game will include cartoons using the same fallacy as this tweet...

I've actually been moving upwards since we started "sinking."

Conspiracy theories are the final technique to keep in mind. They are a convenient way of backing up a claim by pointing the finger at secretive, impossible-to-prove, evil plans, the kinds that are usually said to be run by giant corporations or governments working against the rest of humanity. Conspiracy theories are a bit like a safety blanket that offers comfort during nerve-wracking times. They provide a quick way to fill a knowledge void, especially because the real world is so murky and grey and rarely simple and not all our questions can be answered as soon as we would like.

Conspiracy theories can be difficult to counter, even when they sound wild and absurd, because governments and corporations have actually done and continue to do terrible, hard-to-believe things, such as unethical medical experiments on disabled people. This only gives untrue conspiracy theories more fuel.

Now that we can name and identify these five FLICC techniques for pushing misleading information, we can look at two key ways of protecting ourselves from them: the topic-based approach and the logic-based approach. The topic-based approach would go something like this: *See this Facebook post you shared that says climate change is a hoax? It's a lie because the data it shares comes from a study that was funded by a gas company that makes big profits from its customers burning fossil fuels instead of switching to renewable energy.* The topic-based approach digs into the nuts and bolts of the issue being lied about.

The logic-based approach to pushing back against lies would go something like this: *See this Facebook post you shared that says climate change is a hoax? It's using a so-called scientist who is a fake expert to convince you that fossil fuels don't damage the environment, and this fake expert is cherry-picking data to make it seem as if climate change isn't real.* Next, in the logic-based approach to fighting lies, you can move away from the topic of climate change to talk about how these two strategies, fake experts and cherry picking, have been used to spread very different lies, such as the lie that cigarettes don't cause lung cancer and that sugary drinks aren't bad for your heart.

The logic-based approach relies on correcting people who believe lies by teaching them about the deceptive FLICC *methods* rather than focusing on the facts about the topic being lied about. In research studies, this logic-based approach has often proved more effective at leading people toward evidence-based truths than the topic-based approach. In reality, you might use a combination of both, but bear in mind, teaching a friend or family member to spot the *techniques* used to spread lies can give them an umbrella of protection against lies about a bunch of topics.

Knowing that these techniques exist and are often used against us can make them easier to spot, but it doesn't answer the question of *why* we fall for lies and even help them to go viral, boosting falsehoods with millions of likes and shares while the truth sits quiet and alone in the corner. To answer that question, to *really* understand why we believe the sometimes strange things that we believe and why we might reject the truth and even dig in our heels when someone points out that we believe something false, we have to visit a very confuddling place: your brain.

CHAPTER 2

BIAS, BELIEFS, AND WHY WE FALL FOR BS

TELL ME A BEDTIME . . . FACT?

Strands of hair stuck to Sara's damp cheeks and forehead. Sweat dripped into her brows. She squeezed her pale blue teddy bear tightly against her chest as the doctor, a tall Black woman with red-rimmed spectacles and a singsong accent, peered into Sara's brown eyes with a special magnifying lens. She stepped back and looked apprehensively at Sara's mother, Laylah, with a stare that could only mean bad news.

Three months earlier, as school ended and the long summer began, Sara had giggled and squealed as she chased Mimi through the tall grass surrounding their home on the reservation. Mimi looked like a Chihuahua, but Sara couldn't be sure. The puppy's ears were a little too floppy and her body a little too chubby to be a Chihuahua, but Sara was certain of one thing: Mimi was 100 percent the cutest, most adorable puppy she had ever seen in her seven years on planet Earth. The abandoned pup with eyes as big and brown as Sara's became her new best friend.

Sara tied small white flowers into a loop, hung the necklace over Mimi's neck, and sniffed the petals when they cuddled. She scooped Mimi into the basket of her glittery purple bicycle and trundled along the dirt path in search of adventure. Sara and Mimi ate together, napped together, played together. Then Mimi fell sick.

As summer came to an end, Sara's best friend panted harder when they frolicked in the fields. She whimpered during their long cuddles. Mimi left kibble in her bowl and even turned away from the jerky that Sara made especially for her. Mimi lost weight. Sara held the shivering dog against her beating heart and begged her mom to take them to a vet. But Laylah said the closest vet was a four-hour drive off the reservation and that paying for gas and medical bills would mean no money for food.

That night, Sara emptied her piggy bank and cried into the small pile of coins. Mimi snuggled into Sara's pink-and-yellow bedcovers and fell into the deepest sleep. The next morning, Mimi didn't wake up. Sara buried her best friend in the same field where they had met.

Grief followed Sara into the clinic that grey morning. The corridors smelled of bleach and sadness. "She's not been eating, and she keeps saying her head and tummy hurt," Laylah whispered to the doctor. "I think she misses her dog." But the doctor said Sara was very sick. She said Mimi likely had suffered a serious infection and Sara had caught the same bug. A bacterium was spreading across American Indian reservations in the southwestern United States. The bug lived inside ticks that bit children and puppies, causing a disease called Rocky Mountain spotted fever. Lots of pups and children were dying.

Sara wiped her sticky forehead as the doctor gave her mom some good news. "I'm so glad you brought Sara to me immediately, because I can treat this. Children die from RMSF if they don't get the right medicine straight away, and unfortunately, not a lot of doctors know about this disease because it's new to the area."

The doctor handed Sara a piece of paper and gave her and her teddy bear a hug. Sara wrapped her arms around the doctor's neck and said thank you. "This is for an antibiotic called doxycycline that will make you feel better in just a few days," the doctor said. "But make sure you keep taking it for three days after your fever ends. And Sara, I'm so sorry about your dog. Mimi sounds like she was an amazing puppy. But if you see other strays around your home, please keep in mind that they might have this infection." Sara said she would be very careful and that she would tell her friends to be careful too.

This is a true story.

All facts.[3]

Now, say we want to raise awareness about this disease. We could give people the following information:

An infection previously contained to the north and southeastern United States is now spreading in epidemic proportions across American Indian reservations in the Southwest.

The infection is caused by a bacterium that causes a disease called Rocky Mountain spotted fever.

The bacterium is spread to humans via ticks that bite dogs and humans.

Symptoms of Rocky Mountain spotted fever in dogs include loss of appetite, depression, myalgia, and weight loss.

Symptoms of Rocky Mountain spotted fever in humans include high fever, abdominal pain, myalgia, headaches, fatigue, and nausea.

Children are especially susceptible to the infection and at high risk for death if not treated within one week of symptom onset.

Poverty and poor access to health care are barriers to reducing morbidity and mortality from Rocky Mountain spotted fever on American Indian reservations.

Attrition of the workforce and locum shifts in local hospitals can contribute to delayed diagnosis or misdiagnosis and incorrect treatment.

These are all facts too.

Which do you think you'll remember? The bullet point that

---

3. (Only names have been changed to protect privacy.)

says, "Symptoms of Rocky Mountain spotted fever in humans include high fever, abdominal pain, myalgia, headaches, fatigue, and nausea," or the part where strands of Sara's hair were stuck to her cheeks and forehead because she was so feverish?

Will you remember the line that says, "Attrition of the workforce and locum shifts in local hospitals can contribute to delayed diagnosis or misdiagnosis and incorrect treatment"? Or will you remember Sara hugging the kind doctor as she told her that a lot of health care workers didn't know much about this infection because they didn't have local experience?

Will you remember the bullet point about poverty making this epidemic worse, or will you remember Sara clutching Mimi to her chest, begging her mom to take her to the vet, and crying as she emptied her piggy bank?

In a few months you might vaguely recall something about a little girl who fell in love with a stray dog, and how their summer friendship ended in tragedy. You might not remember all the details, but . . .

Cute pup!

Aww, they became besties

Something bad
happened to the pup

Then the girl got sick

*So glad they found a doctor
who could help her*

Rocky Mountain . . .
spotted . . . something???

. . . these fragments of facts might stick in your brain. But guess what? These are more than facts. These are **FEELINGS**.

LOVE!

ADORATION!

All the heart feels about the little girl and her new pup made you think for a second about *your* BFF and *your* favorite dog when you were growing up. (Now we're talking about feelings *and* memories!) And then . . . fear. Like a pile of rocks in your stomach. The dog is losing weight. Dread. Panic. Sadness. *Sniff. Sniff.* And ohhh, relief. Relief! The girl is going to be all right!

FEELINGS. LOTS OF FEELINGS.

YOUR BRAIN ON STORIES

SARA AND MIMI'S story did more than give you information. It took you on an emotional ride. While you were reading about the seven-year-old girl and the dog that was possibly a Chihuahua frolicking in the tall grass, making flowery necklaces, and taking bike rides together, your brain was very, very busy. Not only was your brain absorbing facts, but it was also processing memories and feelings.

Love. Empathy. Panic. Trepidation. Fear. Sadness. Relief.

Here's what was happening inside your brain as you read Sara and Mimi's story.

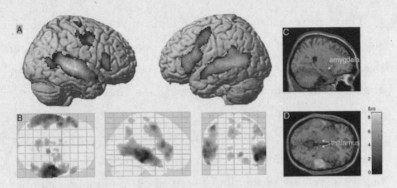

Different parts of the brain are activated and light up when we read, watch, or listen to a compelling story. Reprinted from Mikkel Wallentin et al., "Amygdala and Heart Rate Variability Responses from Listening to Emotionally Intense Parts of a Story," *NeuroImage* 58, no. 3 (October 1, 2011): fig. 4, https://doi.org/10.1016/j.neuroimage.2011.06.077.

Lots of areas lit up, such as the visual cortex and either the parts of the brain that process written text (if you were reading Sara and Mimi's story) or the auditory cortex (if someone was reading the story to you). Wernicke's area, the brain region that processes words, was active too. And in some cases, the olfactory cortex could light up, say when you read about Sara smelling the flowers she had strung around Mimi's neck.

But hold on a second. *You* weren't running in the field with Mimi and Sara . . . and yet, your brain was helping to transport you there. Nerve cells called mirror neurons started firing. Mirror neurons activate when you see or think about someone doing something, like cuddling a dog, for example. But mirror neurons also fire when *you* do the same thing. So when you read that Sara was cuddling Mimi and sniffing her necklace, mirror neurons fired as if *you* were cuddling a puppy and *you* were smelling flower petals. (This is called narrative transportation, and it's how a good story can make you feel like you're on the other side of the world . . . or on a different planet.)

Those areas that lit up in the middle of your brain, on both sides, are a part of the brain called the hippocampus. These are places where your memories are stored . . . because didn't thinking about Sara and Mimi make you think about your bestie and summertime friendships too?

Scientists have found that when you hear moving stories, the parts of the brain involved with emotion light up. Not only that, but when you are sucked into a story about a mountain climber whose fingertips are digging into hot and sandy rock as she desperately clings to a cliff face and tries not to tumble deep into a crevice, the parts of your brain responsible for helping you move *your* limbs become activated, almost as if *your* fingers need to grip onto a cliff edge for dear life.

There's even scientific evidence that when you hear a story unfold, your brain waves start to synchronize with the brain waves of the storyteller, and when you're at that point when the storyteller has totally pulled you in and got you holding your breath and wondering what's happening next, that's when your brain waves really match up with the brain waves of the storyteller.

Now let's think about your brain as you read the bullet point list of facts. The part of your brain that processes sound or text was active because you were reading the list or listening to someone read it. Wernicke's region was active because you were processing words.

But that's about it.

Two sets of information: One story. One bullet point list.

One packed with tension, drama, conflict, and **FEEEEEEL-INGS**, even the kinds of feelings that bring back tender memories, all of which led to a surge of chemicals deep inside your brain and tons of brain activity.

The other was . . . just the facts. Blah.

We use a lot more of our brains when reading, watching, or listening to a story. Our brains are *biologically susceptible* to stories. Give a human a list of facts and . . . **YAAAAAWN**. But your brain while listening to stories? ON. FIRE.

Neurotransmitters! Hormones! Signals! Cortisol! Dopamine! Oxytocin!

Let's talk about some of the chemicals that went surging through your body as you read about Sara and Mimi and consider the subtle ways those hormones influenced your thinking.

"*She squeezed her pale blue teddy bear tightly*" and "*sweat dripped into her brows.*" When you read those lines, your body released cortisol, a stress hormone that makes your heart beat faster, your blood vessels tighten, and your blood pressure rise. You were like, *Wait, what's going on with this girl? Something isn't right.* It was cortisol that helped you stay focused on the story. It was cortisol that helped you pay attention to what could be wrong with Sara. Cortisol went from your adrenal glands, which sit above your kidneys, to the parts of your brain involved with attention and awareness. When cortisol surged, you sat up and focused. You stuck with the story.

When you read that the clinic smelled of bleach and sadness (whatever smell sadness conjures up for you), the parts of your brain that process smell, the olfactory sensory areas, were active. As Sara trundled over a dirt path on her glittery purple bicycle with Mimi in her basket, your motor cortex was firing up.

As the story became emotionally charged—with friendship, illness, poverty, death—your brain released dopamine, a chemical involved with arousal and reward. Dopamine is released when you expect or experience a reward. When you read a good story, one that's full of tension, drama, and suspense, dopamine surges, and you feel good for paying attention and following along. Dopamine also helps to lay down memories.

The narrative transportation that zipped you into the fields with Sara and Mimi occurred because of those nifty mirror neurons. All of this is how a story lets you walk a mile in another person's snowshoes while your own feet are tucked beneath a blanket. It's how a story can transport you into the world of a nine-year-old boy who lives ten thousand miles away, speaks a different language, and loves the things you hate. This brain chemistry fires even when the person you are reading about is fictional. These chemical and electrical brain mechanics are how reading opens our minds, deepens our understanding of the world and other people, and broadens our perspectives.

Stories do even more than that. Stories hold the power to shift our beliefs and influence our behaviors. As you read about Sara and Mimi falling into a beautiful summertime friendship, as they stared into each other's big brown eyes and Mimi snuggled into Sara's blankets, your brain released oxytocin.

Oxytocin is a chemical known as the love hormone. It's released when a parent looks at their baby (and, coincidentally, it surges through your veins and through your brain when you stare into the eyes of a cute dog). It's also released when a person breastfeeds, and it speeds through your brain when you feel love and affection toward others. Oxytocin makes your pupils dilate, your blood vessels soften, and your heart relax. Here's why it is important to us as we explore the connection between stories, our brain, and our behavior: Oxytocin promotes friendship and social connection. It makes us empathic and caring toward other humans. Oxytocin helps us be human.

As you read Sara and Mimi's story, especially in those moments when you could relate to Sara's happiness, fear, sadness, and hope, it was the oxytocin coursing through your brain that was helping you identify with Sara's life. As the little dog whimpered and shivered in Sara's arms, as she grew sicker and weaker, oxytocin worked in the empathy regions of your brain, lighting them up. Oxytocin helped you to connect and care.

Even beyond helping you relate to other people's feelings, oxytocin can change your behavior and make you kinder and more giving. Here's how scientists figured this out. First, they set up an experiment where people watched a compelling story, the kind that tugs at your heartstrings and makes you feel lots of feelings. Next, the same people had to watch a boring story. The second story was bare bones and missing drama and tension.

While people were watching the stories, scientists took blood samples to measure levels of oxytocin. After watching the first story, the moving version full of detail and drama, people were more likely to feel empathy toward the characters. Those who said they felt lots of empathy had 47 percent more oxytocin in their blood than those who watched an emotionally neutral video. People watching a boring story weren't as moved, and their oxytocin levels weren't as high.

The scientists took things a step further. To understand how oxytocin impacts behavior, they gave the story watchers money and told them to spend it however they wanted. The people with the highest levels of oxytocin in their blood gave more of their money away to charitable causes. They wanted to *do* something to help others after watching the emotional story.

The lead scientist of the experiment said stories can "change behavior by changing our brain chemistry." He also said that oxytocin release makes you more likely to trust a storyteller, more likely to trust a situation, and more likely to take a particular action.

That's the power of a good story. Stories can change us.

So . . . awkward question. What if it's an evil story? A story filled with lies and misleading stereotypes about certain people? What if it's a story that demonizes one group of people, telling us, for example, that immigrants are dangerous, when that's not the truth?

That *bad* story is . . . *bad* news. As we have just witnessed—and *felt*—stories hold the power to shift beliefs and influence behaviors. The inner workings of our brain chemistry can be exploited for good and evil. Those chemicals and electrical signals can be manipulated to evoke feelings and sway beliefs, to make us think we came to a particular belief—that immigrants are dangerous—ourselves, and not through strategic storytelling designed to tweak our brain chemistry and make us feel hatred toward certain people.

The same cortisol, dopamine, and oxytocin that coursed through our veins as we read about Sara and Mimi, those same mirror neurons that made us feel as if *we* were the ones cradling a small, whimpering dog, can be fired up to make us feel bad feelings toward some groups of people and to build our allegiance, our sense of belonging, with others.

We can walk away with our lovely dopamine and oxytocin surges after falling deep into a story even when there is no evidence to support what the story is saying. How could this happen? Even if our brains are biologically susceptible to stories, how could we believe a story that's not based on evidence?

Those same hormones and neurotransmitters that flow when we get lost in a good story can lead us into a trap. Our brains seek more dopamine, more oxytocin, more information that backs up what we've come to believe, while conveniently ignoring evidence that contradicts our beliefs. Basically, we love stories, we come to love the beliefs we learn through stories, and we live life looking for more stories to back up what we already think about the world.

This pattern can make you feel warm and fuzzy inside . . . all that dopamine and oxytocin. Yum. It can be comforting to hold fixed beliefs about a world that is constantly changing and full to the brim with unanswered questions and uncertainty.

But it's a trap. A big trap. Imagine that you are constantly surrounded by these stories that shape your beliefs. Oh wait, you don't have to imagine. This *is* your life. The 24/7 news cycle, the constant allure of social media posts . . . all these stories bombard your brain, which leaks chemicals into your bloodstream and takes you on an emotional journey of surprise, intrigue, glee, horror. Ensnaring us in this trap are cognitive biases. (Cognitive just means anything to do with reasoning, thinking, perceiving, or knowing.)

SIDEBAR: CHANGING MINDS

THINK OF A TIME YOU CHANGED YOUR MIND ON A TOPIC.
What did it feel like to have an existing belief challenged? What eventually led you to change your mind?

Think of a time when you tried to change someone else's mind. What was the outcome? What worked or didn't work in that process? What would you do differently now?

YOUR BIASED BRAIN

I KNOW WHAT you're thinking: **WELL, I'M NOT BIASED. NOT ME. I'M LOGICAL, REASONABLE, THOUGHTFUL, PERCEPTIVE, KNOWLEDGEABLE.**

Unless you are a robot reading this book, you *are* biased. (And even robots, because they are programmed by humans, can be biased!) You might not be aware of your biases because some of them are so deeply ingrained. In fact, these automatic biases that you don't even think about, sometimes called implicit or unconscious biases, are some of the most dangerous biases, precisely because you are unaware that you have them. But whether you want to admit it or not, whether the biases are unconscious or conscious, we are all biased to some degree. Understanding and acknowledging our biases can protect us from falling into traps of simplistic thinking.

Here's one example. Have you been scared of riding a bike ever since you saw a movie where a kid comes flying off their bike, hurts their back, and never walks again? When you get invited to go biking, do you picture bike crashes and quickly drum up an excuse? Do memories of all the times you've safely ridden a bike stay buried while you imagine every pebble that could flip you over your handlebars or every way a brake cable could come loose and snap? That's a cognitive bias.

Biases are not accidental, and they're not all entirely terrible. They can be helpful, in their own way. Think of them as stemming from mental shortcuts that we use to speed up our assessments of the world and our decision-making. These shortcuts are often based on prior experience and are known as **heuristics** or **heuristic techniques**. Heuristic techniques (aka mental shortcuts) are highly imperfect, but they can make problem-solving more efficient and picking a solution easier. Here are some examples of heuristics that you probably use all the time: making an educated guess, using the rule of thumb, using trial and error to figure something out. These heuristic techniques come in handy.

Here are three important heuristics you should know about.

The horror of hopping onto a bike and suddenly having every image of a bike crash flash through your mind is an example of the **availability heuristic**. This mental shortcut is all about how easy it is for certain memories to come to mind while other memories stay buried when you are trying to make a decision. Say you're not even on a bike yet; you're at home wondering how to reply to the friend texting you about going on a Saturday afternoon bike ride. The availability heuristic might quickly bring to mind horrific stories of bike crashes—which might be pretty rare in real life, at least when it comes to really serious ones, but they are front and center in your memory, so you text back, "Sorry, but I must wash my hair and do laundry on Saturday" and quickly slam down your phone and vow to walk everywhere instead. Next time this thought pattern creeps through your mind, shout "Availability heuristic!" and call that shortcut out! Now you know it's a mental time-saver that brings to mind some memories more easily than others but doesn't necessarily lead to decisions based on *accurate* information. Just because some memories are easier to retrieve does not mean they are based on fact or that you should pay more attention to them.

Next heuristic. Imagine you're in the library and you see an older woman, maybe in her eighties, reading a book. You think, *Ahh, she must be a kind person; let me go say hello.* You assume this older woman is sweet and kind and possibly apt to feed you special candies from the bottom of her purse, because she reminds you of your grandmother and that's what your grandmother likes to do. But when you approach the woman, you see she is reading a book titled *How to Scam Foolish People in Libraries* and you take a step back. You were almost ensnared by the **representative heuristic**. This mental shortcut can get you in all kinds of trouble. The representative heuristic allows you to quickly compare a new situation with the most representative prototype in your mind. This could come in handy . . . but it can also land you in trouble. Because of the representative heuristic, you see an older woman and you think of your granny and all that she represents. This shortcut plays a role in assumptions such as women are nurturing and maternal, people born in India love spicy food, bicyclists believe in climate change, religious people are judgmental, etc.

A third heuristic is the **affect heuristic**. It's all about how our feelings affect our beliefs and choices. Imagine that you walk out of class and find that someone has secured their bike to yours instead of locking their bike to the stand. You can't release your bike until they return . . . and now you're going to be late for soccer practice. But say you just found out your poem won a national award and your best friend brought you a cake to celebrate and it's sunny outside and you're feeling fantastic. Well, the locked bike and being late to soccer practice might not feel like such a big deal. You sit next to your bike, eat your cake, smile about your award-winning poem, and wait for the other bike owner to return.

But if you were having a crappy day, and your English teacher had laughed and rolled his eyes at your poem, your friend had brought you a cake that set off your peanut allergies and caused you to break out in hives so that you had to be stabbed in the thigh with an adrenaline injection, and now you're slumped next to your bike, which you can't unlock, all the while getting later and later for soccer practice . . . well, now the locked bike might feel like a message from the universe that your life is doomed and that you always, *always* attract bad luck. The affect heuristic leads you to make decisions and form beliefs that are heavily influenced by your current emotions. Is your life doomed? Probably not. Are you having a bad moment with hives, a locked bike, and an underappreciated poem? Sure. The affect heuristic can have you thinking that everything related to bikes is annoying and attracts bad luck, and before you know it, you're posting an ad for your bike and vowing to skateboard everywhere.

Commercials exploit the affect heuristic. First, they make you feel good with images of people dancing, having fun, and looking happy. Then you see the same people drinking alcohol, and suddenly, a product with some harmful side effects can seem very enticing.

Heuristics, and the biases they lead to, can help us out with the many decisions we have to make day to day by allowing us to sidestep the overload of information that threatens to drown us. It's easy to think, *Older woman . . . She must be like my granny*, when in reality, that older woman is a person with her own life, who may have chosen not to have kids because she would rather not be anyone's grandmother. But when you saw her, you thought of your own grandmother and connected traits of kindness, trust-worthiness, and candy-giving to a stranger.

You can think of heuristics as mental shortcuts, or rule-of-thumb strategies, and biases as the mistaken and oversimplified ways we sometimes see the world. While they might be useful at times, biases can cost us our ability to be reasonable, rational, and logical. Imagine you go for a walk in the park and see a poodle jumping all over its owner and apparently mauling her. You come to believe that dogs are vicious beasts. After that, the odd story here or there about a badly behaved dog becomes more noticeable and memorable to you, more so than the gazillions of stories about dogs who are cuddly, cute, and have even saved their owners' lives. Those happy stories go right over your head. Because of this bias, you might end up leaving a park every time you see a dog playing. Sure, some dogs attack people, but it's a rare occurrence relative to the number of dogs who nuzzle, lick, and love on their humans.

This type of bias is called *confirmation bias*. Confirmation bias is the tendency to seek out information that backs up your existing views and to dismiss anything that disagrees with them. Confir-mation bias leads to you interpret new evidence (a dog jumping all over its owner) as confirmation of your existing beliefs (dogs are killers!). Here's another example of confirmation bias. Say you've come to believe that everyone who dances ballet is a great singer. Maybe you believe this because you once met a few people who were good at both. But what happens next is that every time you meet someone who happens to be a great ballerina *and* a great singer, your brain places greater weight on this evidence that supports your existing belief. All the great ballet dancers you meet who sing like they're gargling rocks . . . they don't stick in your memory. You dismiss those points of evidence and keep strengthening your belief by remembering the evidence that supports your point of view.

This is how biases can work. You have a belief. You seek out more evidence to back up that belief. You put greater weight on anything that affirms your belief. You dismiss anything that contradicts your belief. And on and on. Biases can trap you in a vicious loop of fixed thinking and false beliefs.

There's a particular kind of confirmation bias called **assimilation bias** that we need to pay careful attention to. Imagine that you believe that people who play violent video games are more likely to be violent in real life but your friend thinks the opposite. Your friend says that playing these games doesn't make you more likely to fight a real person. You and your friend are presented with data from experiments that measured people's aggression after playing violent video games. A ton of studies found a strong link between playing the games and being more violent. And then a ton of studies showed that people who play violent video games are not more aggressive.

You look at your friend and say, "Look, I *told* you violent video games make people want to fight in real life. There's so much data!" And your friend says, "Look at all the experiments that found players of violent video games are *not* more aggressive in real life. What are you talking about?!"

Assimilation bias is dripping all over this scenario. Because of assimilation bias, you looked at the data that agreed with your viewpoint in a more favorable way. You put more weight on the evidence that backed up what you already believed. Meanwhile, your friend who believes the opposite put more weight on the studies that back up her belief. Because of assimilation bias, both of you paid attention to the evidence that reaffirmed your existing beliefs, and both of you became more convinced that you were right and the other person was wrong. Instead of saying, "Well, hmm, this is a mixed bag of results, isn't it? Maybe this is more complicated than we thought," you both clung to your opposing views.

Does this sound familiar? This story about video games and violence is based on a real study about assimilation bias, but you can switch out video games with so many other things, such as climate change, gun control, genetically modified food, vaccines, religion, and political parties, and you can see how our biases can keep us firmly entrenched in our beliefs while obscuring evidence that might lead us to change our mind.

The world is a trillion shades of grey, not black and white, and our biases can help filter out some of the uncertainty that could otherwise feel overwhelming. But as we've seen, they can land us in trouble as well. There are a ton of different biases that get in the way of our assessing information and situations fairly. There's the **Dunning-Kruger effect**, a cognitive bias that makes people mistakenly think they know more about an issue than they do. (Sound familiar? Politicians exhibit this bias frequently.)

In a 2014 survey, Americans were asked what they thought their government should do about Russia invading Crimea, an area that some say is an autonomous part of Ukraine. First, respondents were asked to point to Ukraine on a map. Next, they were asked if the American government should send its troops to that region.

Some of the people who took the survey were wildly off target. They pointed to countries thousands of miles away from Ukraine, believing those areas were Ukraine. And it turned out that the people who were the least likely to know where Ukraine was on a map were the most likely to favor American military intervention in the region.

Justin Kruger and David Dunning, the psychologists who investigated this bias in the 1990s, said the most ignorant people were often the most overconfident in their understanding of a particular topic. The two researchers famously demonstrated that people who scored the lowest in tests were most likely to predict they would ace the tests! In reality, the more you know, the more you realize you have yet to learn. In fact, learning about the complexities and uncertainties of the world can feel discombobulating, which is where our biases like to step in and take us by the hand back into our comfort zone of fixed thinking.

Many biases sound obvious and recognizable once they're pointed out, but on a day-to-day basis these same biases are deep-seated and barely noticeable. While we're in the middle of quickly deciding if someone is trustworthy or if climate change is real, these implicit or unconscious biases are ones we need to keep in mind.

Now, if you *knew* you were biased in some ways, you might try to lessen your biases and think differently. This is what scientists do (or should do). Aware that experiments are imperfect and that they bring all their biases into their labs with them, scientists like to think ahead about which biases might end up influencing their studies and how to lessen the effects of these biases. This even includes the biases that volunteers who participate in studies carry with them. Designing an experiment to learn about the effects of vitamin D on babies' lungs? Better make sure the babies come from all different kinds of families, not just the families who live in the area near the lab. Planning a study about food poisoning that requires people to remember what they ate for breakfast ten days ago? Better keep in mind that people might remember only the tastiest or strangest foods they ate that long ago.

But you can't work to lessen the effects of biases unless you acknowledge their existence in the first place. Many people would rather not admit to being biased because admitting to having biases can make them feel less than perfect, and who doesn't want to feel great about themselves?

Sure, acknowledging your biases can make you feel a little guilty or bad, but holding a bias . . . or ten . . . doesn't automatically make you a bad person. Leaving biases unexplored and unchecked, however, can contribute to all sorts of assumptions and problematic behaviors. You can wind up treating people differently because of how they look, or the kind of family they come from, or the way they talk, or the religion they practice. These biases might come from stories you've read or seen in the press, reporting on immigrants, for example, or a lack of reporting on the lives of disabled people. These exposures can reinforce biases you may already have. If you continue to live your life without challenging these thoughts and without critically evaluating what you read and watch and hear, you can get very comfortable in your cozy biases and worldview. But becoming more aware of your biases can help lessen their effects on the way you make decisions, piece together information, form beliefs, and treat other people.

SIDEBAR: SPURIOUS SCIENCE

TWENTY YEARS AFTER SCIENTISTS DECLARED PRECISELY which atoms the sun was made of, they changed their minds. Some said they were no longer certain. Sure, the sun was a bubbling ball of hydrogen atoms fusing two by two with helium and expending tons of energy in the process, but in 2018, astrophysicists announced they weren't sure exactly what *else* was in the sun. And the *what else* has serious ramifications for how long we have until the sun explodes. Even relatively small amounts of metals can alter the life span of a star.

Even more discombobulating: If we don't know exactly which metals and how much of them are in the sun, then we don't know how much oxygen is in the universe. (The sun acts as a kind of yardstick for the composition of everything else.) Based on newer data about the sun, there could be 40 percent less oxygen in the universe than we previously thought. *Gulp.*

Scientists have been wrong in the past. Ask a good scientist about the limitations of their results, and they might reel off so many flaws and possible biases that you're left wondering if you should believe their results at all.

Some philosophers of science say this should make us more uncertain. They call this quandary **pessimistic meta-induction**. It's the idea that past errors can point to present and future mistakes. After all, scientists have been REALLY wrong. Miasma, a kind of bad air, was thought to be the cause of tuberculosis and other infectious diseases for decades. Then we discovered bacteria and viruses. Oops. Scholars said for centuries that the sun revolved around the earth. Double oops.

Not only have scientists been wrong, but they've also been racist. Karl Pearson (originator of statistical tools such as the Pearson coefficient, the chi-squared test, p-value, linear regression, and histograms) and his buddy Francis Galton (Charles Darwin's cousin) were fanatical about measuring the differences between Black and White people to prove that White people, like them, were superior. In fact, Galton is credited with inventing the word **eugenics**, the "science" of improving the human species by selectively mating so-called superior people to produce "ideal humans." In Galton's terms, that meant White humans.

Some historians say the entire field of statistics grew out of the pair's need to measure the differences that they believed existed among various, artificially created races. Still love statistical tests? Still wanna shout "Believe science!" from the rooftops?

Science has been wielded as a weapon by people in power seeking to oppress other humans. Science was used to justify the creation of racial categories, which were in turn used to justify slavery. Science is not neutral, and scientists are not unbiased robots conducting experiments in a vacuum away from the cruel realities of the world. Acknowledging scientists' human biases helps us interpret their results with deeper understanding. And it helps us grapple with the problem of pessimistic meta-induction, the idea that because science has messed up in the past, it will mess up again. And not only science. Pessimistic meta-induction applies to economics, law, medicine, and politics. All these fields have murky pasts (and presents) replete with biases and mistakes.

Diligent scientists think carefully about this. They swim around in uncertainty, semi-comfortable that the experiments they run and the data they produce inch us closer to some version of the truth—a truth that can be disproved at any time.

The disturbing, dehumanizing origins of statistics don't mean we have to throw out the entire discipline. Statistics has given us useful tools, some of which even help us fight back against racist stereotypes. And the problem of pessimistic meta-induction doesn't have to be so . . . pessimistic. In fact, uncovering and acknowledging past mistakes is a great way to shine a light on all that can go wrong so that we can try to stay out of the dark and prevent the repetition of similar errors in the future.

The same goes for acknowledging the uncertainties of the world. Uncertainty doesn't have to mean we believe or don't believe something, since life isn't that simple. Whether it's the questionable life span of the sun (yikes) or the sunrise problem (more on this in a bit), accepting that uncertainty exists in *everything*, and assigning different strength levels to our beliefs, can help us navigate life's uncountable unknowns.

THE BACKFIRE AND PUSHBACK EFFECTS

THERE'S A SMALL problem, though. You might think that explaining to someone that they're biased, that a belief they hold is a little bit skewed or maybe outright wrong, would help correct them. You might hope they'd say, "I appreciate your correcting me. I didn't know that information, and based on my assessment of the new evidence, I am going to change my mind!"

It doesn't always work this way. When you challenge a person's thinking, there's a small possibility that they will dig their heels in deeper and hold on more tightly to their belief. Let's say their existing belief, the one you're challenging, takes the form of a furry little creature. You're saying, "But that furry creature is not a kitten! You're cuddling a *possum*! Put it down!" Your truth-telling can backfire, and the person you are shouting at might clutch the kitten-that's-really-a-possum even more tightly in their arms, all the while telling you to back away and stop lying. Being challenged puts them into protection mode. They feel they have to safeguard their existing belief, even though the "kitten" is a hissing possum with razor-sharp teeth.

This so-called **backfire effect** has been described by political scientists who ran experiments where they asked volunteers to read a story. The story said that weapons of mass destruction were found in Iraq. Next, they gave the volunteers a second story. This story was in fact the correct story. It said the first report was wrong and that weapons of mass destruction had *not* been found in Iraq.

But some people in the study would not believe the correction.

Many of them stuck with the belief they formed after reading the *first* report, and they outright dismissed the second story that said the first was wrong. Not only that, but the more they were told the first story was wrong, the more they rejected the correction and created counterarguments against the truth. Trying to correct their belief led to a deeper belief in the incorrect information! The scientists running the experiment said it can be easier to fool a person than to convince a person that they have been fooled.

Here are two important things to know about the way humans form ideas: "truth" is about community, and belief is connected to belonging. This means that our beliefs are not as individual as we might think. They are tied to the communities we are a part of and have a lot to do with our sense of belonging. In fact, consensus can act as a natural heuristic. When people around you whom you trust are saying one thing, a safe mental shortcut might be to agree with the crowd.

Say the person you're shouting at is cradling a possum (which they think is a kitten) and then a second person comes along and says, "Awww, that is one cute kitty." And then a third person and a fourth person also compliment the kitten with its tiny ears and pointed teeth. Now that makes four people who hold the same belief. It's not factual, but there's safety in numbers and these four people are now connected through a shared belief, which can feel really good. They have formed a community. Meanwhile, you're saying, "Umm, hello? How is that possum a kitten?," so you are the odd one out. You look isolated and lonely in your belief. What you need is to find other possum-seers in order to have a sense of community and belonging, because you definitely do not fit into this other group that is busily petting a possum but calling it a cute kitten. *Miaow.*

It's funny that we like to think of ourselves as fiercely independent freethinkers when oodles of evidence shows that we have a strong need to connect with others and experience a sense of belonging—and that we do this through shared, collective beliefs.

Our beliefs are bolstered by affirmations from other people who say they believe the same things. In fact, studies show that the four people stroking the kitten-that's-really-a-possum not only quadrupled their affirmation that the possum is a kitten but also *exponentially* increased their assurance in this belief. That's how much buy-in from other people makes a difference in what we believe and the strength of our beliefs.

WHY YOUR BRAIN IS WEIRD
(ANSWER: OTHER PEOPLE)

SOME COGNITIVE SCIENTISTS say we came to be this way because cooperation and collaboration were once absolutely critical to our very existence. Dan Sperber and Hugo Mercier argue that our ability to work nicely with others was humanity's biggest advantage over other species. It's what gave humans the edge to fight off attacks and persist as we evolved over millennia, threatened by natural disasters and beasts that feasted on human flesh.

Our thinking evolved in a similar way: Not to help us sift through large data sets and analyze social media posts, but to quickly solve the problems of collaboration—collaboration that we needed to survive. The scientists describe humans as "hyper-social" animals who had to depend on other humans to endure the cruel, unfriendly world.

Things that we do and ways that we behave that might seem super strange from what these scientists call an "intellectualist" perspective actually make sense when you think of them from an "interactionist" point of view.

Try this experiment. Ask five people if they know how a toilet works, and likely all of them will say, "Duh, yes." Then ask them to explain, step by step, exactly how the fill valves, rim jets, and siphon jet function to flush away waste and return water to the bowl. You might start hearing some "umms." (In fact, this exact question was asked to graduate students at Yale University and many of them couldn't explain the inner workings of toilets, so don't feel too bad.)

Let's face it: all of us think we understand some things better than we really do. Cars, sewing machines, the internet. This phenomenon is called the **illusion of explanatory depth**. It's when you don't fully understand something but you *think* you understand it really well.

Say you believe that fluoride in tap water is bad for your health. A friend asks, "What even is fluoride and why would drinking it be bad?" You start to explain your perspective about how fluoride causes . . . wait . . . What *does* it cause? As you're trying to answer your friend's questions, you realize you don't have answers about where fluoride comes from, how much is in tap water, and precisely what it does inside the human body.

Oops. Again, we've all been there. A healthy response to this humbling experience would be something like: "You know what—I'm less confident about my thoughts on fluoride now because I realize I still have some unanswered questions. Let me go do some research and then I'll get back to you."

Becoming *less* confident in your previous belief that fluoride is bad can make you *more* receptive to information that goes against this belief. This is a good thing.

Your lower confidence level opens you up to new perspectives and more evidence. (Hopefully, your next round of research leads you to better evidence than your previous searches, since fluoride in tap water is perfectly fine for your body and has prevented millions of people from losing their teeth to decay.)

The illusion of explanatory depth is a BIG problem in the age of the internet. Humans have 24/7 access to information. Tons of it. Does that mean we all deeply understand the inner mechanics of flush toilets, trends in global migration patterns, and the latest science on the ozone layer? Nope. Does it mean we have a higher level of *confidence* that we know a lot about a lot of things? Possibly. We may lap up information frequently, but that doesn't mean our understanding runs deep. Awareness about the illusion of explanatory depth can keep you on your toes and remind you that humans are susceptible to thinking they know more than they do.

Besides humbling us, why is this important when it comes to bias? Having to explain something—including things like exactly how a toilet or the internet works—forces you to confront the world in all its beautiful and annoying complexity, and to realize you don't know it all. This revelation, that we don't know everything about everything, that our beliefs are sometimes based on incomplete information, is a crucial first step in coming face-to-face with our own biases and asking them to pipe down.

Grappling with the illusion of explanatory depth can help us lessen political polarization, which is the problem of extremely held beliefs. In one study, volunteers were asked to do four things: Rate your understanding of political issues, including taxes, health care, and a policy to limit carbon emissions. Next, explain how taxation, health care, and a policy to limit carbon emissions work. Third, re-rate your understanding of these issues. Finally, rate the extremity of your beliefs on taxes, health care, and pollution.

The results were wild. People who started off as know-it-alls and described themselves as holding extreme beliefs (meaning they strongly agreed or disagreed with particular policies and issues) changed their minds after they were asked to explain how things actually worked. That's when things got a little uncomfortable because they realized they couldn't exactly explain this stuff. When that happened, they realized they didn't fully understand all the inner workings of taxation, health care, and carbon emissions, and so they decided they no longer extremely supported or opposed a particular policy. Their confidence—or lack of confidence—in their knowledge brought them right back to reality, and they became less willing to donate money to groups that advocated strongly for particular positions on taxes, health care, and carbon emissions. That's why researchers say awareness of the illusion of explanatory depth can be an effective tool in helping to shift people away from strongly held, ill-informed beliefs. When you realize you're not an actual expert, it can be humbling and make you more open to listening to different points of view.

The illusion of explanatory depth reveals something about why we hold on to our beliefs, even the belief that we know exactly how a toilet works or the belief that we deeply understand health care policy or carbon emissions and taxation. The reason for our wonky thinking is . . . *other people.* In the case of the flush toilet, humans invented a mechanism that works very well and is used the world over. We know it works, and so we trust the judgement and design of other, more flush-savvy humans. In fact, we exploit other people's talents so well that it's hard to know where our personal understanding of a topic ends and another person's begins.

Does all this mean you shouldn't challenge or try to correct someone? Not exactly. Take the backfire effect, for a start. While many scientists say it's a concern, others remind us that the backfire effect doesn't occur every time you challenge a person about their beliefs. Social psychologists who study the way humans shift beliefs say it's more likely you'll see a pushback effect rather than an outright backfire effect where a person becomes even more resistant to the truth. A person demonstrating the **pushback effect** might engage with you and push back on your correction but take away some of what you are saying. This relies on the understanding that while humans might be fact-*resistant,* we're not all the way fact-*immune.* For the most part.

The existence of the pushback and backfire effects should not put you off countering falsehoods or challenging people's firmly held beliefs. But they should make you aware of this: presenting only the facts is not enough to shift a person's perspective on the world. Why would it? If "truth" is tribal and beliefs are connected to our sense of belonging, if facts are tied up with feelings and we walk around brimming with biases that we're mostly unaware of, why would something as simple and boring as facts convince a person they need to consider a different perspective? Keep in mind, they've probably already heard the facts about vaccines, climate change, gun safety, immigration, etc., previously, and *rejected* them. As impressive a communicator, texter, or tweeter as you might be, do you really think repeating facts that a person has probably already heard and dismissed over and over will make any difference? Especially when challenging their beliefs—which we now know have a lot to do with their sense of belonging—most likely feels like an attack against their sense of identity and community.

Here's where our knowledge of storytelling and biases comes in handy. Do you remember many of the bullet points from the list of facts about the disease at the beginning of this chapter? Or do you remember more of the details from the story about Mimi and Sara?

We know that the brain is biologically susceptible to stories and that stories are what might have led people to believe false things about the world in the first place. We know that people think they know more than they actually do and that this can embolden them to hold on to beliefs because they think those beliefs are well-informed.

We can use this knowledge about the weird and wonky human brain to avoid simply deluging people with more information in the hopes that facts alone will change their minds. What might change minds is more complex than that. It includes understanding that we arrived at our personal "truths" not from individualistic thinking but by thinking about what others who we trust believe. We're not as freethinking as we like to imagine.

But don't lose hope. There are ways to challenge our own assumptions and beliefs *and* to help those around us consider new ways of looking at things. (Spoiler alert: use stories.) We'll get into much more detail about this later, but first, a question. Is all this making you question your ability to assess evidence fairly and make calculated decisions based on data rather than just past experiences and present feelings? All those heuristic techniques you employ every day . . . all those biases you whip out to efficiently make decisions and solve problems without even realizing it . . . all that subconscious consideration of what other people think . . . How can you trust that your beliefs were formed fairly and in truly evidence-based ways?

CAN YOU BELIEVE ANYTHING?
THE SUNRISE PROBLEM

IF BIASES RUN through our brains, if we unwittingly push back when confronted with the truth and become less confident about our beliefs the more we learn . . . what on earth *can* we believe? Anything? Nothing?

It's more realistic to talk about *levels* of belief instead of simply considering beliefs as yes/no things. Let's face it: you're probably more certain of some beliefs than others. For this reason, we can talk about credence—a measure of belief strength—instead of just *yes, I believe* or *no, I don't.*

Here's a question for you. Is there anything you are 100 percent sure of? Anything that makes you say, "Yep, I am definitely certain that this thing is true." What about the sun rising? The sun rose today and it rose yesterday . . . so will it rise tomorrow?

If you answer yes, can you be *100 percent* sure that the sun will rise tomorrow simply because it rose today and every day before that? The sun, after all, is an expanding ball of gas, held together by its own gravity. It will keep expanding until it runs out of hydrogen, and then it will begin to collapse into a red giant before morphing into a white dwarf until . . . poof. No more sun. And no more humanity. Probably.

So are you still sure that the sun will rise tomorrow? If you were 100 percent sure that the sun will rise before reading about its expansion and eventual collapse, are you now a little *less* sure? Maybe the strength of your belief has dropped a bit, down from 100 percent to 98.5 percent.

The sunrise problem has been a source of investigation for centuries, since mathematicians, statisticians, and scholars tried to calculate not only if the sun would rise every day but how *sure* they could be in this belief. Tackling the sunrise problem brings us to the **problem of induction**, which helps us understand how our beliefs can end up less than rational.

There are two main kinds of thinking that we use to make sense of the world: inductive and deductive reasoning. Inductive thinking goes like this: I've only ever seen white sheep in my life; therefore, all sheep are white.

We can write the claims and eventual conclusions of inductive thinking like this:

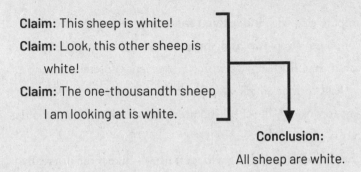

Claim: This sheep is white!

Claim: Look, this other sheep is white!

Claim: The one-thousandth sheep I am looking at is white.

Conclusion:

All sheep are white.

A different kind of reasoning is deductive. It goes like this:

Claim: Nneke is a vegan.

Claim: Vegans don't eat meat.

Conclusion:

Nneke doesn't eat meat.

We can also write deductive reasoning like this:

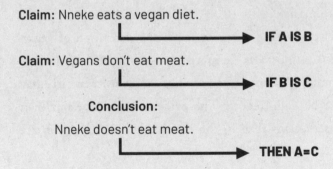

Claim: Nneke eats a vegan diet.

IF A IS B

Claim: Vegans don't eat meat.

IF B IS C

Conclusion:

Nneke doesn't eat meat.

THEN A=C

The conclusion, that Nneke doesn't eat meat, is backed up by the claims, and the claims are true (Nneke is vegan; vegans don't eat meat). Deductive reasoning leads to a logical conclusion that Nneke also doesn't eat meat.

Compare this with **inductive reasoning**, where the claims of sheep one and sheep two and sheep one thousand support your conclusion that all sheep are white . . . except those claims don't *logically* lead to that conclusion. Because of inductive reasoning, you may go through life thinking all sheep are white. You would be wrong.

It's hard to know anything with certainty—like if the sun really will rise tomorrow and the day after that just because it's risen every morning before this—because of the problem of induction. Unlike deductive reasoning, which holds that if the claims are true then the conclusion absolutely must be true, inductive thinking leaves us with this: if the claims are true, the conclusion is probably . . . *maybe* . . . true.

It's not that inductive reasoning leads to conclusions that are always wrong. It's just that inductive reasoning can lead to a conclusion that *could* be wrong. The conclusions of inductive reasoning are less certain than the conclusions we reach through deductive thinking.

Deductive thinking relies on facts: the definition of vegan includes not eating meat. Inductive reasoning—which we use every day, multiple times a day—relies on *evidence*, which may or may not be high quality. The evidence might be our own limited observations that all the sheep our eyes have seen are white.

It's humanly impossible to look at every single sheep on the planet. Hard as you might try, you'll miss some, and the sheep you miss might include the Dutch Spotted Sheep of the Netherlands, the gingery-yellow Bluefaced Leicester, or the chocolate-brown

Corriedale. See, all sheep are *not* white! But inductive thinking, which we use all the time, can lead us down a path that arrives at this faulty conclusion.

See, not all sheep are white. Source: iStock.com.

You might want to throw inductive thinking out of the window now—but hold on a second. We use it for good reason: it's impossible to get the data we need to reach every belief through deductive thinking. For example, I told you the sun is an expanding ball of gas that will eventually run out of hydrogen and begin to collapse. But have you checked the sun to make sure it's made of gas? Have you tested it for yourself to see if it's actually made up of hydrogen and helium atoms? Unless you are a helioseismologist, it's unlikely you have seen the evidence that the sun is made of hydrogen and helium, or that you could fully understand this evidence if it was given to you (in the form of three-dimensional, time-dependent hydrodynamical models that account for departures from local thermodynamic equilibria). I don't understand that either, and I certainly have not tried to take gas samples from the sun. I'm just going with what the helioseismologists say. I hope they're an honest bunch.

Here's where credence, the measure of belief *strength*, is a game-changer (and a sanity saver). We don't need to be 100 percent sure of everything to make smart decisions. We just need to be sure *enough* to survive and be successful. So instead of saying we believe all sheep are white, we can say we believe all sheep are white to a *certain degree*, and we can base that degree on the evidence. If the evidence is made up of only our own observations, based on however many years we've lived on the planet, the countries we've traveled, and the sheep we've seen, we might say this evidence is a little thin and our level of belief that all sheep are white is low. So now we might still choose to believe all sheep are white but to a lesser extent, which keeps us open to being challenged by new evidence so that if someone comes along and shoves a chocolate-brown Corriedale in our face, we'll say, "Okay, I was wrong. Not all sheep are white." Because we've set our credence at "low," a friend shoving said sheep in our direction leads us to change our belief.

Back to the sunrise problem. By now we realize we can't be 100 percent sure (unfortunately) that the sun will rise tomorrow, because arriving at that conclusion requires inductive reasoning. And we know how flawed that is. But we can say, "Based on the evidence that the sun has risen every day for all of recorded human history, I'm certain enough that the sun will rise tomorrow." And this certainty—being certain *enough*—is all you need to plan your schedule for the next day and the next week. Absolute certainty turns out to be unnecessary. You can still plan next week's picnic and assume there will be daylight at noon on a Sunday.

So the answer to "Can you believe anything?" is YES, you can believe things. You don't have to live your life super skeptical to the point of rejecting every single claim, and you can do away with the idea of binary yes/no beliefs about everything. But you do have to be thoughtful about the varying *strengths* of your beliefs. You do have to be aware of how you arrived at these conclusions, and you do have to be sensitive to the limitations of inductive thinking.

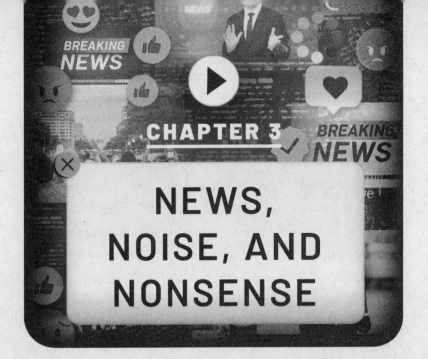

CHAPTER 3

NEWS, NOISE, AND NONSENSE

NINETEENTH-CENTURY CLICKBAIT

WHEN IT COMES to bias, you might think journalists don't have any, or that maybe they have a few biases but they must dump these, along with their feelings and opinions about the world, in the *Drop Your Biases Here* bin that sits at the entrance to every newsroom. Surely, no matter what a reporter believes about climate change, gun control, or animal rights, the journalism they produce on these topics must always be neutral and objective, right? Some news sites even brand themselves as "unbiased," boasting that their reporters tell only the facts and leave their feelings and biases at the door.

That's a Big. Fat. Lie. We expect our news sources to be accurate, on time, and reliable, but the history of the news in the West reminds us that journalism has always had its share of intentional lying and propaganda. It's not all bad, though. There's tons of journalism that digs into the facts, explains complex topics, and changes the world for the better by lifting the veil on corrupt presidents and scandalous CEOs. Even today, the news that appears before our eyeballs or seeps into our ears, even when we're not seeking it out, is a mishmash of fact-checked, credible reporting created by journalists who do their very best to uncover the truth, and stories that push false narratives and disinformation that can hurt people and even start wars and destabilize societies.

Presidents using journalism as a means of propaganda is not a new concept, as we'll see in a moment. Misinformation in the news is not a new problem either. In 1807, when a teenaged editor, John Norvell, wrote a letter to President Thomas Jefferson seeking advice on how best to run a newspaper, the president sent a pretty depressing letter back: "Nothing can now be believed which is seen in a newspaper. Truth itself becomes suspicious by being put into that polluted vehicle. . . . I will add, that the man who never looks into a newspaper is better informed than he who reads them."

President Thomas Jefferson's letter to teenaged newspaper editor John Norvell, written on June 11, 1807, mentions the misinformation printed in the newspapers of the time. Source: Library of Congress.

Jefferson sounds pretty cranky, but he wasn't wrong. Beginning centuries before his presidency, news-tellers in Europe had printed falsehoods to manipulate public opinion and even stoke riots. During the reign of King George II, printers in Great Britain published lies about the King's health in the hopes of destabilizing the monarchy. The attorney general complained that it was too tricky to figure out how often a newspaper needed to *repeat* a lie before it became a crime, but in 1693, a man named William Anderton was found guilty of high treason for printing lies about the king. He was hanged.

One of the wildest, most questionable newspapers of the time was the *New York Sun*. In August 1835, it ran a six-part series called *Great Astronomical Discoveries Lately Made by Sir John Herschel*. The series shared the "discoveries" of the British astronomer Sir John Herschel, who had traveled to the Cape of Good Hope in South Africa to study the night sky.

According to the *New York Sun*'s reporting, Herschel had invented a seven-ton telescope, lugged it from Britain to South Africa, and used it to discover never-before-seen planets and to peer at the moon's surface. Herschel, the *New York Sun* said, was able to project spectacular images from space onto the walls of the South African observatory using the new technology of "hydro-oxygen" microscopes.

Because Herschel's telescope was six times bigger than any existing equipment—according to the newspaper—the astronomer was able to gaze onto the moon's surface and see white sand beaches, great lakes, pyramids, and huge amethyst and ruby formations. The paper also said he spotted blue-grey goats, two-legged beavers, horned bears, unicorns, and . . . wait for it . . . humanlike creatures with wings.

Great Astronomical Discoveries Lately Made by Sir John Herschel captivated the public and sent the *New York Sun*'s readership soaring. More than seventeen thousand Americans are said to have bought the paper at the time; that's more than ten times the readership of the *Sun*'s competitors. Other newspapers and magazines republished parts of the series, and Sir John Herschel's apparent discoveries were translated into many languages. Possibly thousands of readers around the world fell for what later came to be known as the "Great Moon Hoax."

ALTRE SCOVERTE FATTE NELLA LUNA DAL SIG. HERSCHEL

In 1835, the *New York Sun* claimed that unicorns and humanlike creatures with wings had been spotted on the moon. Source: Smithsonian Institution Libraries.

The *New York Sun*'s moon series of 1835 was republished in various languages. This Italian lithograph from 1836, titled *"Altre scoverte fatte nella luna dal Sigr. Herschel"* ("Other lunar discoveries from Signor Herschel"), shows the moon landscapes and creatures the newspaper claimed had been discovered by astronomer Sir John Herschel using a seven-ton telescope.

The "Great Moon Hoax" stories were written by a Cambridge University–educated reporter who kept his name out of the newspaper when the series went to print. But eventually, when *New York Sun* editor Richard Adams Locke finally admitted to authoring the tales (it took him four years to confess), he said that the moon series of 1835 was meant to be read as satire, a kind of storytelling that pokes fun at people and societies to reveal the flaws in their beliefs. Basically, he used the "I was only joking" defense.

The front page of the *New York Sun* on August 25, 1835, when the paper launched a series of "satirical stories" about life on the moon that many believed were based on actual science. Reprinted from John Loeffler, "The Great Moon Hoax of 1835: The Birth of Fake News?" *Interesting Engineering*, June 11, 2021, https://interestingengineering.com/great-moon-hoax-birth-fake-news.

The *New York Sun* was far from the only newspaper spinning sensational stories. A new kind of newspaper was launched in the US in the 1830s. Known as the Penny Press, these cheaply printed papers sold for only one cent—six times less than the cost of the more serious newspapers of the time—and because they were so cheap, tens of thousands of copies could be printed to reach a massive audience. The Penny Press newspapers made money by selling advertisements for products such as morphine-laced cough syrup, face cream, and cigarettes. They used an entertaining style of storytelling, more like a novel, to peddle gossip and tell tall tales about politics and crime.

In the typical style of the Penny Press, the *New York Herald*, one of the most popular of the Penny Press newspapers, used its third page (which was considered the front page back then) to panic readers. On November 9, 1874, the *Herald* reported on "terrible scenes of mutilation," "savage brutes at large," and "a shocking Sabbath carnival of death" in a story about animals escaping from their cages at the Central Park Zoo after a zookeeper poked and prodded a rhinoceros through the bars.

Forty-nine New Yorkers were killed by the beasts and two hundred injured while police and the National Guard threw punches at lions and tigers in the Manhattan streets. Only readers who were able to stomach the gory details and read to the end of the *Herald*'s front-page story would have discovered this small print: "The entire story given above is a pure fabrication."

The front page of the *New York Herald* on November 9, 1874, told a tall tale about animals escaping Central Park Zoo and mauling New Yorkers to death. Reprinted from Mario Patti, "The Central Park Zoo," *My Destiny: Premium Car and Limo Service* (blog), https://mydestinylimo.com /blog/places-to-visit/the-central-park-zoo/.

Thomas Connery, the *Herald* editor who authored the ten-thousand-word story, later explained that his "reporting" was inspired by a real visit to the zoo. Connery had seen a leopard *almost* escape its cage when staff transferred the animal from one enclosure to another. The front-page story, Connery said, was meant to serve as a dramatic and public warning of what could go wrong if the zoo didn't implement serious safety changes. It was meant to be "a harmless little hoax, with just enough semblance of reality to give a salutary warning," he said.

If the point of newspapers is to tell the *news*, why were some publishers willing to print made-up stories and lose trusting customers? The publishers of the time, especially those printing Penny Press newspapers, were desperate to grab attention and sell copies. That's because they made money from selling newspaper space to companies printing advertisements, so the bigger the newspaper's readership, the more the publishers could charge advertisers for getting their ads in front of a greater number of eyeballs. Simply put, the Penny Press put profits ahead of accuracy. It's not unlike twenty-first-century clickbait, which lures you in with catchy headlines until you find yourself scrolling through superficial stories about "The Biggest Stars' Worst Fashion Mistakes!" Worse still, it's hard not to accidentally click on the dozens of autoplaying commercials and pop-up advertisements in those annoying, clickbaity stories.

Researchers who study the way Western journalism has changed over the centuries say the history and evolution of the press can tell us a lot about the problems we face with the news today, problems like the closure of more than a quarter of America's newspapers between 2004 and 2020, the loss of half of all local journalism jobs during that same time, information contagion, and dwindling trust in the press.

Some of these modern news problems, these researchers say, go way back to the days of the Penny Press, when profits ruled, reporters were loose with the facts, and readers were treated as eyeballs connected to wallets. But it could be that our modern news problems started even earlier. To really understand today's problems with the media, we need to look beyond the Penny Press to the earlier roots of the news.

America's first newspapers—even the more serious ones—were fiercely partisan, meaning they were openly biased and shared only the opinions of people who held the same ideals and beliefs about the world. These first news outlets, printed in what was a British colony on its way to becoming a republic, tussled with issues of government censorship, propaganda, and blatant bias.

NOT-SO-NEUTRAL NEWS:
A PARTISAN PRESS

THE FIRST NEWSPAPER published in the American colonies was a monthly edition printed in Boston in the late seventeenth century. *Publick Occurrences both Forreign and Domestick* covered the major news of Britain's newest outpost but left one of its four pages blank for readers to write in their own news and pass it along to another reader. It was published by Benjamin Harris, who fled England in 1686 because he was a wanted man. Police were on Harris's tail for printing pamphlets that criticized the Catholic church and the British government. Blimey.

It won't come as much of a surprise that not long after *Publick Occurrences both Forreign and Domestick* was launched in

September 1690, it was shut down by the governor. The same laws that Harris had fled in England were to be his demise three thousand miles away in Boston. British law prohibited any news to be printed without the government's permission. The people in power had created a law to suppress the news. They were desperate to protect their authority.

Reprinted from "September 25, 1690: First Newspaper Published in the Colonies," *Mass Moments* (almanac), https://www.massmoments.org/moment-details/first-newspaper -published-in-the-colonies.html.

All copies of *Publick Occurrences both Forreign and Domestick* were destroyed by government order, and only one surviving newspaper remains in the British Library in London. Fourteen years after that newspaper was shut down, a second newspaper, the *Boston Newsletter*, was published—this time *with* the governor's permission. It stayed in print until the 1770s.

When the British colony became a republic, one of its earliest papers, the *Gazette of the United States*, was not only permitted by the government but also used as its mouthpiece! The *Gazette*, first printed in 1789, was a part of George Washington's Federalist Party. That's right; the origins of the American media are political and biased. So much for neutral news.

By the time the *Gazette* was in print, the Continental Navy and Army had defeated the British military, won independence, established thirteen colonies, and put into operation the Constitution of the United States of America. The First Amendment to that Constitution prevented the government from restricting the press, even when the press criticized the government. The First Amendment said, "Congress shall make no law . . . abridging the freedom of speech, or of the press," a stark contrast to English colonial law.

America's first presidents were fans of the press (but, umm, maybe that's because newspapers were biased in their favor?). The newspapers, pamphlets, and bulletins of the time were unashamedly one-sided and often railed against the tyranny of the British government. In return, the British government tried to suppress the news. Some of the first American presidents helped to create newspapers because, to them, sharing information was an important way of staying in power. How else could they get people to vote for them if the public didn't know who they were or what they stood for? Newspapers were a handy way to spread political advertising.

Those earliest presidents also spent money establishing the United States Postal Service, not so much because they cared about people sending packages, but because the USPS would function as a news distribution service. Back in the early 1800s, 95 percent of the USPS's cargo was newspapers; only 5 percent was mail and personal packages.

So *this* is the origin story of the American press. And that brazenly political press evolved to become the profit-driven, clickbaity Penny Press. Newspapers went from being politicians' mouthpieces to printing elaborate stories about beavers on the moon and bogus, bloody zoo escapes. Instead of selling political ideas to voters like the early newspapers, the Penny Press of the mid to late 1800s sold products to customers. And who was in the driver's seat quietly controlling which "news" got covered and which was left out of the press? Advertisers. Advertisers were paying for American journalism and gently influencing what got written about. (Spoiler: it was whatever "news" would sell the most newspaper copies.)

As news shifted from power hungry to profit hungry, readers of the news were looked at differently. Before, they were seen as citizen-voters who needed to be sold political advertising about who was running for president and which candidate believed what. But now they were seen as customers who needed to be entertained with sensational, trivial stories so that they would keep their eyes on the page, drink in the advertising, and buy lots of products.

Sound familiar? Sure, this was back in the 1800s, but time hasn't made things much better. Pressure to entertain audiences can still mean that important stories are buried deep within news sites or broadcasts because editors believe they won't be of interest to many people. Instead, they might choose to lead with a sensational story that they hope will hook the audience's attention. If you watch the news, you might have noticed that journalists and editors often mix the two—the entertaining stuff and the "hard news"—to keep audiences interested. More on this and how it influences what news we see and what news stays hidden later.

BREAKING NEWS . . .
VIA PIGEON AND PONY

BACK IN THE 1800s, not only was the news often biased, made up, and profit-driven, but it was also *s l o w*. In fact, it traveled at a speed of around ten miles an hour, to be exact. In 1860, the Pony Express was launched as a new means of news distribution. Before then, if you were alive in the 1600s and 1700s when *Publick Occurrences* and the *Gazette* were in circulation, you would have received your news via a local printer that was maybe a few miles from your home. But by the 1860s, there was an appetite for delivering information from the East Coast to far-flung parts of the new republic.

The Pony Express used a network of 75 horses and 120 riders, many of them teenaged boys as young as fourteen. Weighing no more than 165 pounds, Pony Express riders delivered letters and newspapers across the newly carved-up nation, plodding along a nearly 2,000-mile-long track between St. Joseph, Missouri, and Sacramento, California, transmitting the news at the speed of a four-legged creature.

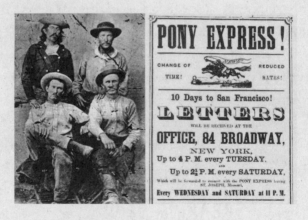

"Billy" Richardson, Johnny Fry, Charles Cliff, and Gus Cliff are thought to be some of the first riders of the Pony Express, a 2,000-mile-long network of horses and riders who transported newspapers and mail from Missouri to California in the record time of ten days. Reprinted from *Academic Dictionaries and Encyclopedias*, s.v. "Pony Express," https://en-academic.com/dic.nsf/enwiki/27594.

The newspapers they carried in leather pouches were designed to be small and light because riders and horses galloped one hundred miles up to four times a week. "Fresh in From the Pony Express . . . !" was often emblazoned across their front pages, and snippets of breaking news—not that different from our tweets, Facebook posts, and phone alerts—were printed and dispatched on horse in the hopes of sharing new information with people thousands of miles away.

It took ten days to send letters and news from Missouri to California. Riders switched horses across 157 stations, spaced ten to fifteen miles apart. Ten days might sound like a long time, but it was a huge improvement from the weeks or months it would typically take to send mail from New York to California via ship (or even longer if it was sent via stagecoach).

The Pony Express wasn't the first time horses had been used to distribute news in America. Fifteen years earlier, during the Mexican-American War (which began when the US annexed Texas in 1845), Moses Yale Beach, publisher of the *New York Sun* (yep, the same one that printed the Great Moon Hoax), wondered how he could get news of the war to his readers faster than sending dispatches via the USPS.

Beach asked four other New York publishers to band together and organize a group of horse riders to bring the news from the war zone to Montgomery, Alabama. From there, a stagecoach took the dispatches to Richmond, Virginia, and on to New York. This five-newspaper service is the origin of the Associated Press, or AP, a news service that still exists today.

Back then, the AP was likely the first news service that became known not only for the speed of its news delivery but for its balanced approach to telling the news. In fact, ten years after it launched, the AP's first Washington bureau chief, Lawrence

Gobright, boasted, "My dispatches are merely dry matters of fact and detail." A far cry from the fake moon tales of Beach's *New York Sun* and the made-up stories of the Penny Press.

Four years after the AP was launched, Daniel H. Craig, a journalist and pigeon trainer from New Hampshire, set up the news agency's first foreign bureau in Nova Scotia, Canada. It was the perfect spot to meet ships from Europe as they came ashore on their way to the US. As they moored in Nova Scotia, Craig would board one of the ships with baskets of pigeons and take the two-day trip south to Massachusetts. He would read as many European newspapers as he could get his hands on, write the headlines in tiny letters on tissue paper, and attach the tissue paper to the pigeons, which he had trained to fly to Boston as soon as the city came into view. While Craig was still getting off the ship, the pigeons would fly to his wife, Helen, who would unwrap the tissue paper headlines from the birds and sell the news to journalists in Boston and New York City.

Daniel, Helen, and others like them working at the AP saw the news as a business, a commodity, plain and simple; news was something Daniel and Helen could sell to buy food, pay the rent, and fix their clothes. As in any business, their product had to be good enough to fight off the competition. They decided that meant their version of the news had to be seen as accurate, reliable, and appealing to people who held a variety of political beliefs. The AP stripped the news of opinion and political bias because its bosses believed that was a good business decision. Beating the competition was one reason the AP chose to be nonpartisan.

To this day, people who study the news debate this question:

Is the news a public good, or is it a commodity? Public goods are things like streetlights and safe roads that benefit lots of people and are usually paid for through taxes. Commodities are things like chocolate, clothes, and cellphones, which can be sold, bought, and exchanged. So what do you think? Should access to credible news be looked at as a public good or a commodity? Should everyone have access to the news free of charge? And if that's the case, who should pay for it?

"WHAT HATH GOD WROUGHT?"
TWENTIETH-CENTURY NEWS,
TWENTIETH-CENTURY PROBLEMS

A NEW TECHNOLOGY was about to revolutionize the news. Only eighteen months after it was launched, the Pony Express was scrapped because electricity, cables, and Morse code were set to replace teenaged boys on horses. On October 24, 1861, the transcontinental telegraph connecting New York City to San Francisco was launched. This revolutionary invention made the sharing of information even speedier. Not only did the telegraph change the way the news was shared, it changed the way the news was written.

Samuel Morse dispatched the first telegraph message on May 24, 1844, sending "What Hath God Wrought?"—a super-duper upbeat line from the Bible—from Washington, DC, to Baltimore. But it wasn't until 1861 that telegraph cables were laid from coast to coast, transforming journalism. Those transcontinental cables allowed America's Civil War correspondents to deliver news from the battlefield back to their editors at a speed they had never before experienced.

Sending electric impulses along miles and miles of wires, the telegraph used electricity to convert a written message into a series of dots and dashes, which appeared as a printout of words and sentences at the other end of the line. These strings of paper with snippets of breaking news were taken by boys on bicycles to newsrooms. The use of electricity and boys on bikes—rather than teenaged boys on ponies, or stagecoaches and the Postal Service—meant the news could travel from San Francisco to New York, and eventually to London and beyond, within minutes instead of days or weeks. But getting the news to rural parts of the US could still take a while longer, so large news organizations bought their own telegraph machines to get breaking news to their readers as quickly as possible.

The telegraph was fast, but it was far from perfect. Telegraph lines weren't always reliable. Sometimes a bison would pick a fight with a telegraph pole, causing the pole to fall, or wind and snow would damage the wires and cause the system to stop working halfway through a transmission. Imagine sending an important message across the wires to your boss, only to be cut off: "BREAK-ING NEWS: PRESIDENT MAKES HISTORIC DECISION, DECLARES IMMEDIATE WAR WITH—" Talk about a cliff-hanger.

The telegraph was also expensive, costing a penny for every letter sent, so journalists shied away from the long-winded, flowery language that was in fashion at the time and turned toward a tighter, more succinct way of writing.

Tricky telegraph lines also led to a different way of organizing a story. Reporters switched from the chronological style of reporting—a method that told a story in order of what happened first, then second, then third—and instead put the most crucial details in the first lines of their stories, just in case the rest of the message was lost because a bison was in a bad mood in some field in the middle of America. This new way of ordering a story came to be known as the inverted pyramid structure, a style that is still used today.

The inverted pyramid begins with the summary news lede,[4] also known as the lede, which contains the most important information in the story, including the five *W*s: who, what, where, when, and why (you can also add in "how"). Have you ever heard the phrase "Don't bury the lede"? It refers to that annoying moment when you discover the juiciest details of a story submerged way down in its depths, hidden among less interesting facts.

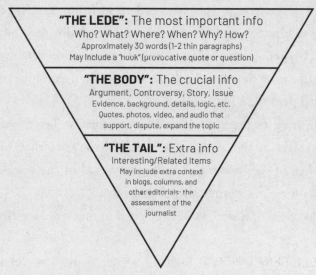

"THE LEDE": The most important info
Who? What? Where? When? Why? How?
Approximately 30 words (1-2 thin paragraphs)
May include a "hook" (provocative quote or question)

"THE BODY": The crucial info
Argument, Controversy, Story, Issue
Evidence, background, details, logic, etc.
Quotes, photos, video, and audio that
support, dispute, expand the topic

"THE TAIL": Extra info
Interesting/Related Items
May include extra context
in blogs, columns, and
other editorials: the
assessment of the
journalist

The inverted pyramid structure for storytelling puts the most important details (according to a reporter and editor's news judgement) first and less important information later in the story.

---

4. "Lede" is probably a misspelling of "lead" so that if the writer accidentally leaves the subheading "lede" in the story, the editor will realize the writer doesn't mean "lead" and know that the word is not supposed to remain in the published version of the story.

After the summary news lede comes the body of the story, which shares important but less critical information. The body offers details such as background, context, and conflicting perspectives. Finally, the tail of the story offers even less critical information. The inverted pyramid structure helps editors when they need to cut a story's length, because deleting paragraphs from the bottom means removing the least important information.

Some scholars say it wasn't bison, snow, and other problems with telegraph lines that led to the rise of the inverted pyramid structure. They point to a singular event: the assassination of President Abraham Lincoln in 1865.

When the president was attacked, news of the event was dispatched from the government to the *New York Herald*, which printed the statement word for word on its front page. Whether this gave rise to the inverted pyramid structure may be disputed, but reporting of Lincoln's death in the *New York Herald* on April 15, 1865, is certainly one of the earliest examples of the inverted pyramid style of reporting.

The story of President Lincoln's assassination begins with a lede that lays out the crucial facts, including the who, what, where, and when of the shooting. The body and tail of the story offer information of lesser and lesser importance.

Take a look at how the story appeared in the *New York Herald*:

PRESIDENT LINCOLN Shot by an Assassin.; The Deed Done at Ford's Theatre Last Night. THE ACT OF A DESPERATE REBEL The President Still Alive at Last Accounts. No Hopes Entertained of His Recovery. Attempted Assassi-

nation of SECRETARY SEWARD. DETAILS OF THE DREAD-
FUL TRAGEDY.

WAR DEPARTMENT, WASHINGTON, April 15—1:30 A.M.

Maj.-Gen. Dix:

This evening at about 9:30 P.M., at Ford's Theatre, the President, while sitting in his private box with Mrs. LINCOLN, Mrs. HARRIS, and Major RATHBURN, was shot by as [sic] assassin, who suddenly entered the box and approached behind the President.

The assassin then leaped upon the stage, brandishing a large dagger or knife, and made his escape in the rear of the theatre.

The pistoi [sic] ball entered the back of the President's head and penetrated nearly through the head. The wound is mortal. The President has been insensible ever since it was inflicted, and is now dying.

About the same hour an assassin, whether the same or not, entered Mr. SEWARD's apartments, and under the pretence of having a prescription, was shown to the Secretary's sick chamber. The assassin immediately rushed to the bed, and inflicted two or three stabs on the throat and two on the face. It is hoped the wounds may not be mortal. My apprehension is that they will prove fatal.

The nurse alarmed Mr. FREDERICK SEWARD, who was in an adjoining room, and hastened to the door of his father's room, when he met the assasin, who inflicted upon him one or more dangerous wounds. The recovery of FREDERICK SEWARD is doubtful.

It is not probable that the President will live throughout the night.

Gen. GRANT and wife were advertised to be at the theatre this evening, but he started to Burlington at 6 o'clock this evening.

At a Cabinet meeting at which Gen. GRANT was present, the subject of the state of the country and the prospect of a speedy peace was discussed. The President was very cheerful and hopeful, and spoke very kindly of Gen. LEE and others of the Confederacy, and of the establishment of government in Virginia.

All the members of the Cabinet except Mr. SEWARD, are now in attendance upon the President.

I have seen Mr. SEWARD, but he and FREDERICK were both unconscious.

EDWIN M. STANTON,

Secretary of War.

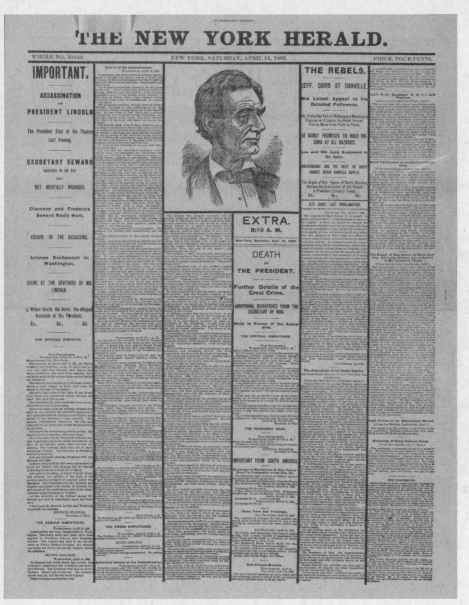

The *New York Herald*'s front-page story about the assassination of President Abraham Lincoln in 1865 was a word-for-word reprinting of a government statement that was structured in the inverted pyramid style. Source: Library of Congress.

SIDEBAR: BREAKING NEWS

ON APRIL 4, 1841, PRESIDENT WILLIAM HENRY HARRISON died of pneumonia, one month into his presidency, making him the shortest-serving president. It's popularly believed that Harrison became sick while giving a very long inaugural address in the cold outdoors (but many historians dispute this). Here's how long it took news of his death to reach newspaper reporters and editors, and their audiences.

April 6, 1841: News of Harrison's death is printed in the *Richmond Enquirer*, a newspaper in Virginia.

April 10, 1841: The *New York Tribune* reports news of the president's death.

April 12, 1841: The *Madisonian* in Washington, DC, prints the news.

April 13, 1841: Vermont's the *Caledonian* reprints a report from the *New York Express*.

April 14, 1841: News of the president's death is reported in the *North-Carolina Standard*.

April 17, 1841: *Boon's Lick Times*, the newspaper of Fayette, Missouri, reports news of the president's death almost two weeks after he died.

Is it still "breaking news" if it happened thirteen days earlier? Within how many hours—or minutes—of a president's death would you expect to learn this news?

ACTIVITY: In the first week of March 2020, as a new coronavirus spread across the globe, Italian authorities weighed an idea that hadn't been used since the Second World War: create a shelter-in-place order that would shut down travel and work for sixteen million Italians living in the north of the country. The central government shared information about the possible quarantine with local officials to get their opinions, but the same information about a possible massive quarantine was leaked to the press.

News editors had to make a quick decision: inform sixteen million people that their lives could drastically change, or wait and not reveal the news until *after* the government had reached a final decision and announced the news to the public.

You are the editor of a major newspaper. A local official who has received a document about a potential quarantine shares the information with you. You must decide if you should publish this breaking news or wait till the government makes a formal announcement. What do you do: print news of the possible quarantine, or wait to see if the quarantine is put in place before informing your readers? What are the potential consequences of your decision?

Don't read any further until you have made a decision . . .

WHAT HAPPENED: Editors decided to publish the leaked news about a potential quarantine ahead of the government's announcement (which came the next day). Thousands of Italians tried to flee the area that would be put under quarantine. As they flocked to train stations and onto buses, Italy experienced its highest day-on-day rise in deaths from COVID-19 up until that point. Some attributed this to the leaking of the news via the press.

🔋

WHAT IS NEWSWORTHY?
WHO DECIDES WHAT IS NEWS?

NOWADAYS, IT'S UNLIKELY that a news agency would print a government statement word for word in its pages or on its website without context, additional reporting, and fact-checking. Editors might decide to print parts of a press release from the government or some other institution, but they'd likely quote it within a longer story, and that story hopefully would include the perspectives of different people, including experts in the field and ordinary people affected by that news topic. These sources might disagree with each other and dispute what is being put forward by officials in the press release so that the news story doesn't only give the government's version of events—unlike the *Herald*'s front-page news about President Lincoln's shooting, which offers just one perspective.

But before we get into how stories are put together for the internet, newspapers, television, and radio, we have to look at the very important step that happens *before* a reporter is sent out to cover some news: a decision is made about which stories, issues, and people will be *excluded* from the news. This decision about what will be included in the news and what will be cut is known as **agenda setting**. It's similar to **gatekeeping**, the idea that there's a lot going on and not all of it can end up in one outlet on one day. Agenda setting and gatekeeping rely on a process known as **news judgement**, which factors in things like where the news outlet is based, how frequently it publishes news (hourly versus daily, weekly, or monthly), who the audience is, and how much money and person power the organization has to cover the news.

Let's say a new cosmetics store is opening in your neighborhood. Is this news important enough to include in your local newspaper? What if the opening is going to be attended by a YouTube influencer launching their first-ever makeup collection, and lines of hundreds of fans are anticipated to wrap around the block and mess up traffic for the town that day? What if we're talking about a news outlet with an audience that spans beyond your town? Maybe the audience covers the entire state: Would this store opening be considered news? What if the town's largest school is being shut down the same day because of some huge scandal? Would that change the newsworthiness of other events happening that day? Which is the bigger, more important news story? Who gets to decide?

Sitting around the table when these questions are being asked and these decisions are being made are the organization's editors and managers. Let's be clear here about who holds most of the power when it comes to these important decisions. In the US and much of Europe, many bosses at news organizations are White men (mostly older, cisgender, nondisabled, heterosexual men), which means decisions about what is and isn't newsworthy are made by people who don't fully represent the communities their news organizations are supposed to serve. We all experience the world a certain way, are treated in different ways, and have varied backgrounds and life experiences, and if many different lived experiences were represented in the rooms where news decisions are made, journalism would better reflect the lives of the people who consume it.

The mismatch between who decides what is news and who

consumes and is affected by the news is huge. Racial and ethnic minorities made up close to 40 percent of the US population in 2021 but only around 18 percent of newsroom bosses. Even in cities where minoritized people make up the majority of the population—places like New York City, Washington, DC, and Los Angeles—newsrooms are still predominantly White or have a history of overrepresenting White journalists. (In recent years, the *LA Times* has focused on diversifying its newsroom to better match the population of the region.)

Close to three-quarters of Angelenos are minoritized people, but only 38 percent of newsroom bosses at the *LA Times* were people of color in 2019. The newsrooms of the *Wall Street Journal* and the *New York Times* have been majority White while less than a third of New Yorkers identified as White in 2021. In fact, while 32 percent of New Yorkers are White, 63 percent of staff at the *New York Times* was White in 2020.

The *Washington Post* sits in a district where nearly half the population is Black, but only 9 percent of its news staff is Black while close to 70 percent are White. (Black and Brown staff at the *Post* have been making efforts to diversify the newsroom since 1972; some say the organization's mostly White leadership hasn't done enough to make sure its staff represents the communities it reports on. It's a similar story at news organizations across the country.)

But what difference does any of this make? How might these disparities between who sets the news agenda and who reads and watches the news influence which stories are told and how they are covered?

The *Disparity Times*. Source: Visual and data journalist Mona Chalabi.

Reporters in positions of lesser power, such as staff who are not senior editors or newsroom bosses, are often left in the tricky and uncomfortable position of pushing for sidelined stories to be included in the news. Here's a true story: A young Mexican reporter working in a newsroom in one of the US's Southern states had to convince her boss, an older White woman, that the launch of a celebrity makeup line—the celeb was a Latina legend—at a local high-end shopping mall was big news. The editor didn't think the event was worthy of including in the newspaper but eventually agreed to let the reporter visit the store, interview shoppers, and cover the launch. The editor was stunned when hundreds of fans, mostly Mexican women and girls, flooded the mall to buy the makeup. The story—which almost wasn't a story at all—was eventually understood to be so important that it ran on the front page of the newspaper's Sunday lifestyle section (which is a big deal because it's considered prime real estate in a newspaper).

This might sound like a trivial example since it's about celebrity and makeup, but think of all the stories that are left on the cutting-room floor because someone decided nobody would be interested in certain groups of people or particular issues, or that three other stories from the same day were more important and should be prioritized. Representation matters.

Here's another true story: Following a mass shooting in downtown Dallas in 2016 in which five police officers were killed, a young Black man who was in the area at the time was profiled as the possible shooter by the local police department. A photo of the man smiling and openly wearing his gun across his chest (which is legal in the state according to its open carry laws) was posted on the police department's social media account. But the man was not the shooter and there was no evidence that he had committed any crime. He was a law-abiding citizen whose gun was registered and who was exercising his right to openly carry a firearm. But when vigilantes saw his photo posted to the police department's social media account, they tracked down his home address and threatened his family until his wife and kids were forced to leave their home and hide in a hotel.

The local newspaper ran extensive coverage of the mass shooting but only a one-inch "brief"—a very short summary of a news event—about police posting his photo to social media and wrongly accusing an innocent person of being a mass shooter. The one-inch brief was not reported by journalists at the newspaper; instead, the editors used a technology called **news aggregation**, which pulls snippets of news from other news websites and wire services.

When a reporter at the local newspaper, a person of color, read the brief, she considered this incident to be of significance to the newspaper's audience. The attacks against the man raised important questions about whether the state's open carry laws applied equally to Black and White people, and what consequences people in positions of power should face when they post photos of innocent people to social media accounts and label them as potential perpetrators of serious crimes. The reporter's boss, who was White, said the story didn't seem newsworthy enough and the reporter should focus her time covering other aspects of the mass shooting.

But then, national TV and print news outlets covered the story and interviewed the man repeatedly, sparking outrage about how he was treated by police. So the editor changed their mind. The reporter was sent to interview the man and his family at a secret location, and when the story was published on the newspaper's website, it received thousands of hits from interested readers.

This is news judgement—and bias—at play. News judgement is said to be objective (lots more on this idea of objectivity in a moment), meaning decisions about what is news and what isn't should be based on fact rather than a person's opinions or feelings about a topic. But there isn't really a *Drop Your Biases Here* bin at the entrance to any newsroom, and how humans receive and perceive facts is based on personal experiences of living in a world that treats people differently. In these examples of disagreements about news judgement, White newsroom bosses had opposing ideas about what was newsworthy compared to journalists of color, whose lived experiences were very, very different.

But how are news organizations supposed to cover absolutely everything that matters to everyone? Newsrooms have limited numbers of reporters, editors, and photographers to cover the news, not to mention limited budgets to send staff to distant places. Decisions about what can and can't be included in the news, and whether the news organization will spend its own money to cover an event or pay a fee to pull information from other outlets or wire services, are made by taking all these factors into account.

But surely the internet offers unlimited space for a news outlet to publish tons of stories on its website? It might seem that way, but there are still significant decisions to be made about which stories will run on the home page, how prominently they will be displayed, and which stories (and people and issues) will be buried deep inside the website.

Keep this in mind toward the end of the chapter when you curate your media diet. How might the makeup of a news organization—its proportion of Black, Brown, queer, disabled, and otherwise minoritized reporters, editors, photographers, and bosses, relative to the audience it serves—impact its ability to accurately and appropriately report the news? How will you access this data given that many major news organizations in the US, including ABC, *Bloomberg*, CBS, Vice, *Vogue* magazine, *USA Today*, and others, refuse to share information about newsroom diversity? How does this data—or lack of data—affect your trust in the news?

SIDEBAR: BLAVITY, THE *DEFENDER*, AND BLACK AMERICA'S NEWS PUBLISHERS

WHEN MICHAEL BROWN, AN UNARMED BLACK TEENAGER, was shot dead by a police officer in Ferguson, Missouri, in 2014, Morgan DeBaun, a young Black woman who grew up not far from where the teenager was killed, read the news coverage with deep concern. Where were the voices of local Black residents? The stories and grievances of people in her community, especially young people, were being silenced, said DeBaun, and the coverage in media outlets such as CNN, the *New York Times*, and the *Washington Post* excluded the concerns of the people most deeply hurt by the teenager's death. "There was a huge gap of information between what I saw happening on the ground in St. Louis and what I saw in the mainstream media," she said.

DeBaun decided to do something about it. Along with her college friends Jeff Nelson, Jonathan Jackson, and Aaron Samuels, DeBaun—who was twenty-four at the time—started her own news organization, Blavity (a portmanteau, or combination word, made up of "Black" and "gravity"), with the goal of uplifting the voices of young Black people.

There was clearly a need for a news website like Blavity; within just a few years, the site grew into a digital media organization with a reach of more than one hundred million readers each month.

Blavity's leadership looks a lot different from the leadership at most US news organizations, where only around 7 percent of full-time newsroom employees are Black and only one-fifth of those

Black employees—that's around 1 percent total—hold leadership positions. DeBaun, Nelson, Samuels, and Jackson (who now advises the company) say their experiences of being Black, young, female, and Jewish—among other identities that they share—factor into how Blavity approaches the stories it covers, the people it hires, and the voices it amplifies. The news judgement of editors at Blavity, who consider the outlet's audience, the voices excluded from other news sites, and their own lived experiences, leads to news coverage that sets Blavity apart from most of America's news organizations, where more than 78 percent of newsroom bosses are White.[5]

Blavity Inc./AfroTech founders Jeff Nelson, Morgan DeBaun, and Aaron Samuels. Source: Randy Shropshire/Getty Images for Blavity Inc./AfroTech.

Blavity isn't the first news organization to cater to the information needs of Black Americans. Black America has a rich history of storytelling and newspaper publishing, dating back to at least 1827, when Samuel Cornish and John Russwurm launched America's first Black-owned and Black-operated newspaper, *Freedom's Journal*, in New York. The four-page weekly paper was created the same year that slavery was abolished in the state.

---

5. Data from a 2018 survey by the American Society of News Editors: https://members.newsleaders .org/diversity-survey-2018-tables.

More than forty Black newspapers were in operation by the 1860s, and by the 1920s, Black publishers were generating millions of dollars from printing the news. One of America's first Black millionaires was publisher Robert S. Abbott, who launched the *Chicago Defender* in 1905 with less than fourteen dollars to his name. The *Defender* grew to a readership of nearly a quarter of a million by 1929 and reached a readership of 500,000 people each week at the peak of its success. The *Defender's* reporting is said to have influenced millions of Black Americans to leave the terror of the Ku Klux Klan in the South and seek work in the North, sparking the Great Migration.

Young Salesmen. *Left to right*, Julius Vance, Laville Williams, and Allen Ware, stand and smile while selling newspapers on the streets of Chicago, 1982. These young salesmen are selling copies of the *Chicago Defender*, the leading African American newspaper. (Photo by The Abbott Sengstacke Family Papers/Robert Abbott Sengstacke/Getty Images.)

Black newspapers may have saved the lives of Black people. During the 1918 flu pandemic, White-run newspapers printed false news about the health of Black people, going so far as to claim that Black people were immune to pandemic flu. Black newspapers fought back, correcting the misinformation and disinformation. White newspapers in the early 1900s also declared that Black people were more likely to suffer diseases such as syphilis and tuberculosis, assumptions the White press tried to justify with nonsense claims about Black people being more promiscuous and less hygienic. Again, the Black press corrected the lies.

Among them was the *Pittsburgh Courier*, an influential Black newspaper founded in 1907 that published a weekly edition to an audience of 300,000 readers. While the *Courier* shut down in 1966, some older Black-run newspapers, such as the *Defender*, still exist as printed or online news sites, telling stories excluded from, or misrepresented in, White-run news organizations. Like Blavity, and many other news websites, podcasts, video documentaries, blogs, and more, these Black-owned and Black-run news organizations center the voices of Black Americans and continue the centuries-long tradition of Black journalism and publishing.

Boys at Courier Window. James Hamlett, Harry Kenny, Eugene Geller, and Leonard Wright wearing sleeve patch reading "Pittsburgh Public Schools Playground Leader," standing in front of the *Pittsburgh Courier* newspaper offices, Pittsburgh, Pennsylvania, 1941. (Photo by Charles "Teenie" Harris/Carnegie Museum of Art/Getty Images.)

ALL THE NEWS THAT'S FIT TO PRINT . . . ?
LOCAL NEWS, NATIONAL NEWS, AND THE FLINT WATER CRISIS

IN THE SPRING of 2014, Tammy Loren noticed that the water pouring out of her sink was green and brown. It smelled bad, tasted like sucking on a metal coin, and her children itched and rubbed at the rashes that covered their bodies after they bathed. Doctors said the boys had a fungal infection. Or maybe it was scabies. It could be ringworm. Maybe it was fleas? They prescribed ointments and pills. Tammy hired an exterminator in case their rental home in Flint, Michigan, was infested with bugs. Nothing worked. The boys scratched. Sludgy water poured out of the sink. Their stomachs churned. Tammy used what little money she had to buy bottled water, but sometimes she didn't have enough leftover cash and they were forced to drink the green-brown liquid that gushed out of the taps.

Managers at the General Motors factory in Flint noticed something was wrong with the water too. It wasn't skin rashes they were spotting—expensive engine parts were rusting and corroding when washed. The managers couldn't afford to lose valuable inventory, so they stopped using Flint's water and switched to a different supply.

One hundred thousand people lived in Flint in 2014. More than half were Black, and 40 percent were poor. All of them were exposed to toxic water when city officials made a big switch. On

April 25, 2014, the city's managers changed the source of Flint's water. Instead of paying for more costly water from Lake Huron, they bought cheaper water that came out of the Flint River—a river known for being scattered with rusting cars and decaying bodies. The city budget was in bad shape and the officials wanted to save money. But at the same time, they hiked the price of water in the city until Flint residents were paying the highest home water bills in the nation.

Flint residents noticed the change in their water immediately. They complained of diarrhea, clumps of hair falling out, blistering skin, vomiting. But government officials insisted the water was safe. There was even an outbreak of the bacterium *Shigella*, which spreads from feces, because Flint residents were unable to safely wash their hands. When the bacterium *E. coli*, which causes diarrhea and vomiting, was found in the water supply, residents were told to boil tap water to kill the bug. At the same time, a different bacterium, *Legionella*, was spreading through Flint's water, causing the third-biggest Legionnaires' disease epidemic in American history.

How did officials respond to the health problems and complaints? They dumped more chlorine into the water to try to quash the bugs, but that caused a new problem: the chlorine made the water even more toxic by increasing amounts of chemicals called total trihalomethanes, or TTHMs. Drinking TTHMs may increase the risk of cancers in the bladder and gut.

There was an even bigger problem lurking in the water, a problem that unlike the green-brown color and metallic stink was undetectable to the nose and eye.

One evening, a local pediatrician, Dr. Mona Hanna-Attisha,

was hanging out with old friends from high school, eating barbecue and having a good time, when one of her friends made a shocking revelation. The friend worked for the Environmental Protection Agency, the government body tasked with keeping America's air and water safe, and they were extremely worried that Flint's drinking water was now dangerous because it was coming from the Flint River. Not only that, but the water in the Flint River was very corrosive, they said, and it was running through the city's timeworn pipes—which were made of lead. Because the water was corrosive, it was leaching lead out of the old pipes and into the drinking water that Flint residents were sipping.

Lead is poison. No amount of lead is safe to the human body. Lead mimics calcium, a metal that is essential for brain health. Once inside the body, lead seeps from the blood into the brain and bones. It causes learning difficulties, speech problems, hearing loss, and seizures in children. It can make kids more likely to wind up in jail when they become teenagers and adults. Lead settles into the teeth, heart, kidneys, and liver and can hunker down in those organs for decades. In pregnant people, lead causes miscarriage and stillbirth. There were two outbreaks of miscarriages in Washington, DC, in the early 2000s because the district's tap water was poisoned with lead.

Shigella. E. coli. Legionella. TTHMs. Lead. The toxic facts raced through Dr. Hanna-Attisha's mind. Then, her friend shared a leaked EPA memo with even more information about Flint's poisonous water. Dr. Hanna-Attisha realized that her patients' brains—the brains of mostly Black and Brown babies and children—were being irreversibly damaged, and the children and their families had little idea of the harm being done to them. She began testing the children's blood for lead poisoning. The results were terrifying.

But not everyone was interested in Flint's historic, toxic crisis. As one of America's biggest tragedies of environmental racism was unraveling, national news outlets were nowhere to be seen. Hello, agenda setting! Hello, gatekeeping! See how this works? Who was affected by the tragedy in Flint, and who was making decisions about whether this was "newsworthy"?

Local news, on the other hand, was diligently covering the mass poisoning. Soon after Flint's water became poisonous, local news outlets such as the *Flint Journal* and *MLive* began telling the stories of Flint residents complaining of infections and rashes, as well as stories about the government officials insisting the toxic water was still safe to bathe in and drink. Michigan Radio, local NBC television station WEYI, and the *Detroit Free Press* told stories about the foamy, murky water flowing out of the taps, and reporters at those news outlets put the voices and concerns of Flint residents in their pages and on their websites and airwaves.

An investigative reporter at the American Civil Liberties Union of Michigan, Curt Guyette, went door-to-door handing out hundreds of lead-testing kits so residents could check their water. The ACLU is a nonprofit organization that uses donations from the public to fight court cases for people who they believe are in danger of having their civil liberties—things like the freedom to express their faith, or the freedom to petition against the government—threatened.

Guyette helped to make a documentary about Flint's water crisis, and he filed a request using the Freedom of Information

Act (FOIA), a law that forces government officials to share previously hidden information with journalists and citizens. His FOIA request unearthed the same EPA memo that Dr. Hanna-Attisha had been given by her friend. Through his reporting, Guyette discovered that the way state officials were testing Flint's water produced inaccurate results that made the water seem like it was safe when it was actually dangerous.

So, when *did* national news outlets begin to think the Flint crisis was news? Almost a year after disaster had struck. That's when national news outlets sent reporters to cover the mass poisoning. But even then, coverage was patchy and inconsistent. Agenda setting, gatekeeping, and bias struck again. By the time national news outlets were paying any attention to Flint, Dr. Hanna-Attisha had plenty of data to back up her concerns. But government officials were still denying the evidence. In September 2015, the doctor held up a baby's bottle filled with brown water at a press conference and warned the people of Flint not to drink what was coming out of their taps. "Lead is one of the most damning things you can do to a child in their entire life-course trajectory," she said.

At this point, the *New York Times*, a newspaper known as the "paper of record" partly because of its authority and international audience, sent some of its reporters to Flint. At the town hall, the reporters took notes as Dr. Hanna-Attisha shared the results of her investigation: The children of Flint had been poisoned with lead. The amount of the toxic metal in their blood was off the charts. Comparing the results to the time when Flint residents drank water that came from Lake Huron, she found that the percentage of children with high amounts of lead in their blood had now doubled, and in some areas, tripled. "It's our professional obligation to care for the children of Flint if we know something," the doctor said. "Lead poisoning is irreversible. This is not what our community needs."

By now, both local and national news outlets were reporting on the Flint crisis and the reaction to Dr. Hanna-Attisha's disturbing findings about lead poisoning in children. But there were big differences in the ways different outlets were covering the Flint tragedy, including which people reporters chose to interview, whose voices they included in their stories, and who they considered an authority or expert on the situation. Scientists? Sure, they were quoted as experts in many news stories. How about politicians defending their decisions or claiming the toxic water was still safe to drink? Plenty of them were quoted by journalists. What about Flint residents—the poor, mostly Black and Brown people whose lives had been upturned by the money-saving decision of the people in power? What about the children and teens of Flint who were most likely to suffer life-long health problems because of the cost-saving decisions of politicians who continued to lie and say the dangerous water was safe? Well, they weren't featured in national news stories as much, at least not to begin with.

National media outlets such as the *New York Times* were accused of helicoptering into the situation and only taking it seriously after President Barack Obama declared a state of emergency. One expert, Derrick Z. Jackson, who analyzed the way journalists covered Flint said national media did not take seriously the thousands of Flint residents who protested, organized water-bottle drives, and banded together to bring attention to the tragedy. It was only when people with authority spoke out—people such as officials, scientists, and doctors—that national outlets took the situation seriously. The people of Flint, especially the children of Flint, were ignored for months while the crisis deepened.

The Flint water poisoning was a public health crisis, an act of environmental racism, and an example of national media ignoring a tragedy afflicting poor, Black people. It's a crisis that can repeat, because most of the 134 million Americans who live near toxic sites are Black, Latinx, and poor. Of the nearly six million American children who live within a mile of a toxic site, nearly four million are children of color. Who tells their stories?

GHOST PAPERS AND NEWS DESERTS:
WHAT HAPPENS WHEN YOUR TOWN LOSES ITS LOCAL NEWSPAPER?

AFTER THE NINETEENTH-CENTURY newspaper boom— where thousands of publications flourished and even smaller, local papers had reporters stationed in bureaus in Moscow and Tokyo—twentieth-century readers began to turn to other forms of news. First, radio broadcasts were big competition to newspapers in the 1920s and 1930s, then TV news lured news-lovers away in the 1950s. But even then, reading the news over breakfast or on the train to work remained a popular way of keeping up with world events.

It was the 1990s when newspaper readership began to dip dramatically and the industry started heading for deep trouble. Readers began to find their news on blogs, online news sites, TV, and the radio more than in newspapers. Because the dip coincided with the creation of the internet and the launch of low-cost advertising websites such as Craigslist.org, some blamed the web for the downfall of print news.

But wait. Craigslist isn't a news site, right? Well, that's true, but Craigslist meant that if you wanted to sell a keyboard or a coffeepot or were in search of a roommate, you could post an online ad at a very low cost—or even for free. How could newspapers compete? In comparison, it would have cost around eight dollars to print each line of an ad in the *Washington Post* in 1996. Classified websites saved the public money and promised bigger audiences. One study found that Craigslist saved customers five billion dollars in advertising fees from 2000 to 2007. (That's another way of saying that newspapers *lost* a potential five billion dollars in advertising revenue.)

Total circulation of U.S. daily newspapers

The number of printed newspapers in circulation has decreased steadily since the 1990s, according to analysis by the Pew Research Center. Source: Paul Bedard, "RIP: Newspaper Circulation Lowest Ever Recorded," *Washington Examiner*, July 25, 2019, https://www .washingtonexaminer.com/washington-secrets/rip-newspaper-circulation-lowest-ever-recorded.

Newspapers also relied on the health of some of their biggest advertisers: department stores. But as department stores struggled, so did newspapers. It was a vicious cycle: The public was spending less money on placing newspaper ads and fewer people were reading print news, so big advertisers—such as car companies and travel businesses—spent less money on advertising in newspapers . . . and department stores were struggling at the same time, which meant less ad revenue for local newspapers, so fewer newspapers stayed in business . . . which meant fewer people spent money on newspaper ads, which meant big companies wanted to spend even less on newspaper advertising, which meant . . . You get the picture.

It's easy to blame just the internet or just the failing of big department stores for the demise of newspapers, but we already know the industry was primed for problems. Remember the days of the Penny Press and the not-so-neutral partisan press before that? The press had long modeled itself as a mostly for-profit business that relied heavily on income from advertisements to fund important journalism such as on-the-ground coverage of war zones or cultural events such as the Olympics. Because advertising subsidized journalism, advertisers held a level of influence over the stories the public consumed. Even if car company executives or food manufacturers weren't physically inside the newsroom, poking reporters and editors in the chest and saying, "Hey! Trash that story about the reduction in school funding and write about that new celebrity scandal! More people will read it!," they still had a ton of influence. They didn't have to be in the newsroom to make an impact.

News organization bosses saw the writing on the wall: if stories about celebrity love lives attracted more readers than stories about important (but possibly less high-profile) concerns such as the local councilman who gambled away money meant for middle school computers, then advertisers would pay more to print their ads in issues focused on celebrity gossip because more people were buying those copies. Newspapers could be motivated to dedicate more space to the stories that sold a lot of ads and less space to the stories that impacted local kids.

Plenty of fingers have been pointed at the internet as the cause of nearly all that's wrong with journalism. But don't feel *too* sorry for print news. Some say these big newspaper chains helped destroy their own businesses because they spent millions buying websites such as Apartments.com, Cars.com, and CareerBuilder.com to try to get in on the internet craze in the 1990s and early 2000s. It was a little hypocritical, too. In the 1980s, the CEO of the *Washington Post* had tried to stop AT&T from launching an electronic version of the popular yellow pages, which listed ads, because she was worried it would take away from the money the newspaper made through advertising.

But should you even worry about the state of local news? Well, just think about what happens to a town and its citizens when they lose their local newspaper. A solid local newspaper employs journalists who turn up to city hall meetings and listen for hours on end to make sure officials are doing their jobs. Local reporters sit through school board meetings to understand how students are being accommodated so that parents know exactly how their tax dollars are being spent. And local journalists painstakingly rake through thousands of pages of police department records in search of missing funds or other signs of corruption. So when a town loses its local newspaper, banks and businesses that lend towns money to build things start looking at the town as a riskier investment because it doesn't have a local newspaper keeping an eye on all that's going on. They might still lend the town money to build roads, libraries, and hospitals, but they'll charge the town more for this privilege. It becomes much more expensive for the town or city to make the improvements and advancements its residents need.

Losing your local newspaper isn't just bad for schools, hospitals, government, and other services; it's bad for democracy. If you live in an area known as a news desert—a region that lacks accurate local journalism that holds people in power to account—then you're more likely to live in a place where there's worse political polarization, where local residents disagree more on important topics such as education, the future of climate change, and access to health care. Living in a news desert means it's harder to learn about your local officials. Fewer people vote in news deserts, and there are fewer local candidates competing for votes and proposing ways to improve your life.

Local journalism, such as a great local newspaper, radio station, or TV station, can make a town a safer, healthier place to live. That's why some call local news the immune system of a democracy. Credible reporting by diligent journalists keeps those in power in check and means that residents are much more informed about what's going on in their backyards.

People seeking to exploit the vulnerable know exactly where to look. Like a virus that hunts down its victims' weak spots, preying on those with damaged immune systems, these disinformation spreaders zoom in on news deserts and spread dangerous lies about political candidates or important issues, knowing full well that the people who live in those areas don't have credible sources of information—like a local newspaper—to debunk the false information.

Even though a large percentage of Americans say they trust local journalism over national news sources, nowadays thousands more people live in a news desert compared to twenty years ago. Around two thousand newspapers shut down between 2004 and 2018, leaving nearly a thousand communities across the US without access to accurate news about how their taxes were being spent, what their elected officials were up to, and what was going on in city hall, the police department, the school district, and elsewhere. Those worst hit by the loss of local print news were mostly Americans of color living in low-income or rural neighborhoods.

Don't be fooled by the presence of just *any* local newspaper. Some long-standing newspapers have become ghostly versions of their past selves; in fact, they're called ghost papers. They've lost the substance of good journalism, and the flimsy pages are instead filled with tons of advertisements, even though the ghost paper has kept the title of its former self. Ghost papers and news deserts are on the rise, and while journalism has loads of room for improvement, its loss wreaks havoc on local communities and leaves the door wide open for false information to spread.

SIDEBAR: TIMELINE OF (MOSTLY AMERICAN) JOURNALISM

59 BC: Julius Caesar orders the printing of Rome's first newspaper, the *Acta Diurna* (or *Daily Acts*). The paper is sent to Rome's provincial governors, connecting distant government with the center of the empire.

Eleventh century AD: Chinese inventors develop movable type, a way of printing that uses individual blocks with letters carved into them. Although wooden and ceramic blocks had been around for a while, this newer method allowed for individual letters to be rearranged so that printing could happen more quickly and on a larger scale. It also made the words easier to read and more durable on paper.

1450: Europeans catch on and German inventor and blacksmith Johannes Gutenberg invents his version of the mechanical moveable type printing press.

1600s: Weekly and even daily newspapers are printed across parts of Europe.

1644: In response to the English Parliament banning newspapers for six years and declaring that every printed word must be approved, the English poet John Milton publishes *Areopagitica: A speech of Mr. John Milton for the Liberty of Unlicensed Printing, to the Parliament of England.*

1690: Benjamin Harris's *Publick Occurrences both Forreign and Domestick* is published in the British American Colonies.

The newspaper is immediately shut down for not having a license.

1695: English courts reverse the rule that every printed word must be approved by the government.

1735: Peter Zenger, publisher of the *New York Weekly Journal*, is arrested and put on trial for allegedly printing libelous things about the British government. His acquittal sets the foundation for freedom of the press.

1789: The *Gazette of the United States* is published. The publication is believed to have marked the beginning of the party press era (1780s–1830s) and the beginning of newspapers endorsing political parties. It is not just approved by the country's first president; it is the actual mouthpiece for George Washington's Federalist Party. The first president is known to use government funds to wine and dine journalists who promise to write in his favor.

1789: The US Constitution, written in 1787, goes into operation in 1789. It includes a First Amendment that describes a free and unhindered press.

1798: President John Adams signs the Alien and Sedition Acts. The Sedition Act states that any person writing or publishing literature that goes against the government, the Congress, or the president shall be in breach of the law. Adams uses the law to imprison newspaper publishers who write in favor of his opponent, Vice President Thomas Jefferson.

1800s: There are several hundred newspapers in print in the US by 1800. The number grows dramatically over the century.

1807: President Thomas Jefferson writes a letter to newspaper-man John Norvell complaining about the misinformation present in the newspapers of the day.

1833: Benjamin Day launches the *New York Sun* and creates the Penny Press, a new type of mass-printed, salacious newspaper focused on gossip and tall tales and profiting off advertisements.

1835: The fabricated and widely read "Great Moon Hoax" series appears in the *New York Sun*.

1844: America's first telegraph line is launched. It stretches from Washington, DC, to Baltimore.

1846: The Associated Press, or AP, is founded when Moses Yale Beach, publisher of the *New York Sun*, asks the publishers of the *New York Herald*, the *New York Courier and Enquirer*, the *Journal of Commerce*, and the *New York Evening Express* to join forces. The news publishers use pigeons and ponies, as well as stagecoaches, to transmit news of the Mexican-American War to readers as quickly as possible.

1851: George Jones and Henry Raymond make a point of featuring quality reporting and writing in their newspaper, the *New York Daily Times*, which later becomes the *New York Times*.

1860: The Pony Express, a network of boys on horseback who distribute newspapers between Missouri and California, is launched. The Pony Express lasts eighteen months before it is disbanded because . . .

1861: The transcontinental telegraph gets off the ground, allowing breaking news to be sent from San Francisco to New York City in minutes. This technology—and its unreliability—

leads to a more succinct style of reporting and, arguably, the inverted pyramid style of structuring a news story.

1861–1865: The American Civil War is one of the first major events of which news is transmitted quickly via telegraph. The war is also extensively photographed. General William T. Sherman regards war reporters as spies, so Secretary of War Edwin Stanton makes two major changes to journalism: he invents the press pass (which reporters must apply for in order to have access to people fighting the war) and the press release (written documents released to reporters that state the government's version of events). Stanton also imposes a news blackout . . . which he can do since he controls the telegraph lines.

Also during the Civil War, President Abraham Lincoln's White House shuts down several newspapers for printing what the president considered treasonous statements. Lincoln was known for leaking stories to the media, manipulating coverage, bribing editors, and ordering his personal aides to anonymously write favorable stories about him. Around the same time, General Joseph Hooker insists that reporters include their name in their stories and no longer publish anonymously. The byline—the line in the paper where a reporter's name appears—is born.

1897: Newspaper publishers and rivals Joseph Pulitzer and William Randolph Hearst go head-to-head using a sensational style of reporting known as yellow journalism to push their personal agendas and sell copies. Yellow journalism was named after the cartoon character the Yellow Kid, which first appeared in Pulitzer's *New York World* newspaper. (The cartoon artist was poached by Hearst, who printed the cartoon in his newspaper the *New York Journal*.)

1920: The first radio news broadcast in the US is transmitted by radio station 8MK in Detroit, Michigan. The station still exists as WWJ and is owned by CBS.

1934: Congress passes the Communications Act and launches the Federal Communications Commission (FCC) to oversee and regulate telephone, telegraph, and radio communications.

1963: Millions of television viewers watch President John F. Kennedy get shot in Dallas via a live CBS News broadcast.

1972: Two cub reporters at the *Washington Post* trace a string of crimes back to President Richard Nixon and his administration, leading to the Watergate scandal and Nixon's resignation in 1974.

1996: The *New York Times* begins publishing daily on the internet.

2004: Social networking site The Facebook is launched. It becomes Facebook in 2005, and in 2019, Facebook News appears, a part of the site dedicated to journalism.

2006: Twitter is founded.

2014/2015: The phrase "pivot to video," referring to a trend where news organizations poured considerable resources into short-form video content—and took resources away from written content—becomes synonymous with journalist-writers losing their jobs and the media bowing to pressure from advertisers, who favored video over written content.

HOW THE NEWS IS MADE:
FACTS . . . OR FRAMING?

LET'S DIG DEEPER into how newsroom bosses make decisions about what news we'll see versus what news is considered not so relevant. In an early-morning meeting, bosses, editors, and some reporters will gather around a table to talk about what's going on in the world or the town where they are based. Some news organizations focus on local news, while others cover global events, or both. Editorial meetings, like these morning meetings, are where staff gather to discuss what's going on and what (they think) will be of interest to their audience. Decisions are made about what will be covered, who will cover it, from which angle that news will be covered, and—of course—which stories will *not* be featured in the pages or on the airwaves, maybe because they're considered not interesting enough for the news outlet's audience or the newsroom just doesn't have enough people and money to cover that news.

A **news budget**—a list of stories that will be covered—is created and distributed to the newsroom. Reporters, editors, and photographers are assigned stories, and the work of reporting begins.

A reporter will usually talk to their editor about the story they've been assigned, or the idea they want to pursue, to hash out some early details. What is this story about? Whose voices will it include? Where can the reporter gather the information needed to tell this story? This early stage is a critical part of the reporting process. You might think that fact-checking, a step that happens later on (but also throughout the reporting process), is crucial to the accuracy of a story, and it is, but these initial decisions about which angle the story will be told from and whose voices it will feature—also known as the **framing** of the story—can change the entire story and the audience's perception of the issues the story explores.

If deciding what is news is known as agenda setting, and it signals, *This is a newsworthy topic and we are including it in the news because we think you should know about it*, then framing says, **AND THIS IS HOW WE BELIEVE YOU SHOULD THINK ABOUT THIS ISSUE.**

You can look at framing in a literal sense, as if you have an amazing photo with a lot going on in it and you want to post it on Instagram. But . . . umm . . . you can't capture all the action in the square because it doesn't fit. Now you're stuck realizing that you have to put your frame somewhere, but no matter where you put it, you're going to exclude all the stuff outside the frame. So . . . which part of the amazing photo do you center in the Instagram frame? What does it include? What colors and details does it leave out? Hopefully, you can find a piece of the photo that doesn't narrow the story too much and still manages to convey some of the details and elements that give the bigger picture, the parts you can't fit in. But that can be difficult. And now imagine you're a journalist doing this during a mass shooting. You're at the scene, you're sending updates to the newsroom, and your editor is asking you to upload a few pictures to the news site's social media accounts to give the public some quick updates.

Now imagine you're a photojournalist covering a protest, and one hundred people at the event are sitting in silent protest but ten protestors are causing a ruckus on the sidelines. Where do you point your camera? What if you point your camera in six different directions to capture different kinds of protestors, but your photo editor decides to publish only the photo of the noisy protestors? How does this framing change the way your audience sees the story?

THE FRAMING OF OPERATION IRAQI FREEDOM

Something similar happened in Iraq on April 9, 2003. Every four minutes and twenty-four seconds that day, Fox News rolled video of a crowd of Iraqis pulling down a statue of Iraqi president Saddam Hussein. CNN played the same video every seven minutes and forty-two seconds. The framing showed a crowd in a park in the capital city using a rope to topple the statue. Except the park had been mostly empty moments earlier. At the time, there had been no crowd, no sledgehammer, and no rope. Instead, Western troops—who had been toppling statues ever since they invaded Iraq in March 2003—handed a sledgehammer and rope to a few locals walking into the park. (One Marine who was there, Leon Lambert, had asked Captain Bryan Lewis, "If a sledgehammer and rope fell off the [M88 truck], would you mind?" Lewis responded, "I wouldn't mind.")

Two hundred journalists were staying at the nearby Palestine Hotel. Some saw a group of locals with a sledgehammer and rope trying to topple the statue. Those that saw the activity focused their cameras on the crowd. The activity of the journalists drew the attention of more military, which then drew the attention of more journalists . . . and so on.

Had the cameras zoomed out, they would have shown a mostly empty park with a small crowd near the statue. Had the cameras started filming earlier, they would have seen a Marine handing a sledgehammer and rope to an Iraqi passerby. Instead, the (literal) framing of the shot supported a narrative that Western troops had succeeded in bringing down an enemy regime and liberating the Iraqi people. The video footage became a symbol for the end of the war when, in reality, the war was still raging.

Source: Patrick Baz/Getty Images.

A crowd of Iraqis pulling down a statue of Iraqi leader Saddam Hussein was filmed by Western media in Baghdad in 2003 and aired as a symbol of Western victory. Some said locals wanted to pull down the statue, while others say locals were handed sledgehammers and rope by an American soldier and that an armored tank driven by American military was eventually used to bring the statue crashing down. Source: Ramzi Haidar/Getty Images.

There are at least a dozen or so commonly used story frames in journalism, according to a study by the Project for Excellence in Journalism, which looked at how often reporters used different frames. There's the **straight news account**, which follows the inverted pyramid structure and outlines the who, what, when, where, why, and how of a story. This is the most popular news frame, accounting for around one in five of all front-page news stories.

Then there's the **conflict story**, which frames the event or issue as a battle and identifies winners and losers. There's also the **consensus story** frame, which focuses more on the points of agreement around an issue or event. And there are story frames such as the **process story**, also known as an **explainer**, which helps the audience understand the way things work, and the **historical frame**, which places a current event in the context of history. There are many more story frames, but these are some of the most popular ones used in journalism.

Framing reminds us that reporting the news is about way more than just relaying facts. It's the way the facts are presented, the angle from which the story is told, and the specific words that are used to convey meaning that can entirely shift the way an issue is presented and how the audience understands it.

Here's an example of a framing decision to consider: You are covering the news of a vaccine that protects against disease 90 percent of the time. Ten percent of the time, vaccinated people will succumb to disease and die from the illness. Do you write this headline: "New Vaccine Offers 90 Percent Protection against Deadly Disease"? Or do you write this headline: "One Out of Ten Vaccinated People Will Die from Disease"? (You might go so far as to pick the frame that says "One Out of Ten Vaccinated People Will Die" . . . which takes on a different interpretation.)

These frames and headlines might be factually accurate (back to that gnarly idea that this is about so much more than just facts), but each headline tells a different story. The way the same information is presented—the framing—is different. In some headlines the framing is focused on survival; in others it focuses on the risk of dying. Readers might respond to the first frame with a positive feeling about the vaccine, to the second frame with the feeling that it's not worth their time to get vaccinated, and to the third with the worry that the vaccine itself might somehow cause death! Congratulations. The way you presented information just shifted the needle on individual behavior and public health. Your picture frame holds a lot of power.

SIDEBAR: CONTAGIOUS NEWS—THE VIENNA SUBWAY SUICIDES

IN THE EARLY 1980S, SUICIDE AND THE SUBWAY SYSTEM OF Austria's capital were not two things you would put in the same sentence. But that changed in 1984, when suicides in the Vienna subway began to increase—and newspaper reporters were blamed for the worrying trend.

The increase in suicides was dramatic. In 1983, there were zero suicides and one suicide attempt in the Vienna subway. In 1984, there were a total of eight suicides and suicide attempts. By 1987, the number increased to twenty-two, and there were sometimes clusters of up to five deaths a week. Most of those who died of suicide this way were men who were younger than the people who died of suicide in the rest of the city.

When the numbers significantly increased in 1984, the Austrian press began to report on almost every single suicide. Details of who had died, exactly how they had died, and if there had been a cluster of suicides that week would be described in vivid detail. Suicidologists started to worry about the way journalists were reporting on the devastating news. They were especially concerned about the potential for copycat suicides, or suicide contagion, where news of one person's suicide can trigger others to consider or even attempt the same.

There's a more specific name for this contagion when it's linked to writing or reporting about suicide: It's known as the **Werther Effect**, and it dates back to 1774, when German novelist Johann

Wolfgang von Goethe published *The Sorrows of Young Werther.* The novel's main character, Werther, falls hopelessly in love with a girl named Lotte; falls out of friendship with his BFF, Albert; and suffers deeply after the death of his friend Hans. Werther eventually takes his own life.

Soon after the novel was published, *The Sorrows of Young Werther* was blamed for the suicide contagion, which came to be known as the Werther Effect, or Werther Fever, and the book was banned in parts of Germany and in Italy and Denmark. Even Werther's signature fashion style—a blue coat and yellow breeches—was banned after it was reported that two thousand young men had died from suicide in a very similar way to Werther: they dressed up in his style of clothing, used a similar type of gun, and were found with a copy of *The Sorrows of Young Werther* by their side.

In 1984, Austrian scientists sounded the alarm. Stop reporting on each suicide in the subway system in such detail and the number of suicides will decrease, they said. Researchers at the University of Vienna analyzed all reports of suicide printed in two of Austria's biggest newspapers and found that journalists covering suicide wrote dramatic stories and that the suicide copycat effect was stronger when newspapers put the suicide story on the front page or included a photo of the person who had died. They said the imitation effect was also bigger when journalists included too many details of the incident, said the person who died "had everything to live for," or reported motives that were "romantic," such as when a person chose suicide to "join" a deceased loved one. This kind of reporting could influence someone who was already in a state of despair to think that suicide was their only or best option.

In 1987, the Austrian Association for Suicide Prevention launched guidelines for reporting on suicide. They suggested that reporters share information about psychological support such as counseling and write stories about people who had considered suicide but were able to overcome their crisis when they received help. Soon after the reporting guidelines were shared, suicides in the Vienna subway system dropped 75 percent. Researchers believe more responsible and less sensational and vivid reporting on suicide is the reason. In the United States, organizations such as Reporting on Suicide offer similar guidance for reporters on how best to report on suicide and mental health crises.

Even though the Werther Effect and the possibility of suicide contagion is a concern, writers don't always follow this guidance. A Netflix show called *13 Reasons Why* did many of the things experts say should be avoided when telling stories about suicide, whether fictional or real, including showing scenes of the main character's death. In *13 Reasons Why*, Hannah Baker dies from suicide and leaves behind thirteen tapes explaining the reasons why she died. In the weeks after the show first aired, Google searches about suicide increased by almost 20 percent, which meant there were up to 1.5 million more searches on suicide than usual, according to a 2017 study.

There's a flip side to the Werther Effect. The power of words and the influence of the media can be harnessed for positive change. In Mozart's 1791 opera *The Magic Flute*, the bird catcher Papageno tries to hang himself over a lost love but is helped by three spirits who remind him of his blessings. Papageno survives and gives rise to the Werther Effect's opposite, the **Papageno Effect**. (It's important to know that there is help for anyone experiencing suicidal thoughts. In the US, the National Suicide Prevention Lifeline can be reached 24/7 at 1-800-273-8255.)

As for the impact of *The Sorrows of Young Werther*, the author Friedrich Nicolai tried to undo its influence by writing a version of the story in which Werther's friend foils Werther's suicide attempt. (This angered Goethe so much that he wrote a poem about Nicolai taking a dump on Werther's grave.)

DOES NEWS INFLUENCE BEHAVIOR?

WHERE PEOPLE GET their news and how that outlet frames the news can influence the decisions they make and the way they live their lives—decisions that go beyond affecting just themselves. In 2020, during the earliest waves of the COVID-19 pandemic, researchers at the University of Chicago investigated the likelihood that a person would follow pandemic public health advice, depending on not just which outlet they got their news from, but which anchor at that outlet they liked to watch. They also looked at where COVID-19 infection and death rates were highest in the US and which news anchors were most popular in the places with the highest death rates.

The researchers found that COVID-19 infection and death rates were highest in places where one particular Fox News anchor had massive audiences. That anchor was Sean Hannity, who for months ignored the danger of the pandemic, then downplayed its severity and even advised his viewers to think of the new coronavirus as no more dangerous than seasonal flu. At one point, Hannity said that Democratic politicians were wielding the virus as a political weapon against President Trump. On the other hand, a different anchor on the same network, Tucker Carlson, had said as early as February 2020 that the new coronavirus should be taken seriously as a significant health threat. Same news network. Very different messages.

So what did the researchers find? If you watched Hannity, you were more likely to follow public health precautions, like washing your hands properly and canceling travel plans, four days *later* than people who got their news from different anchors on Fox News. If you watched Carlson, you were more likely to follow public health advice three days *earlier*.

Now, a few days may not sound like much of a difference, but the impact was huge. The researchers discovered that these personal behaviors could make a big difference to a person's chances of getting sick or even dying from COVID-19. In fact, areas where more people were watching Hannity than Carlson could experience a 32 percent increase in COVID-19 cases and a 23 percent increase in COVID-19 deaths.

But some experts disagree with this idea entirely. Changing behaviors because of news? Even watching the news to get . . . news? *Psssh*, they say. Some experts don't just disagree that where we get our news and who we get it from can drastically shift our behavior; they disagree with the idea that the main reason we watch, listen to, or read news . . . is to get information.

Hold on a second. Isn't the main reason for checking the news to get new information? Well, maybe not. This idea, that you check the news to get new info, is called the **transmission model of communication**, and it might not be the real reason people consume news!

James Carey was one journalism professor who asked himself this question for years. Truly, honestly, exactly *why* do people watch or read the news? Carey would say the transmission model is very straightforward: you turn on the TV to watch the news to find out something new. At least, that's what you *think* you're doing . . . but it's not *really* what you're doing. Carey said that if you were to dig deep and be honest with yourself, you'd find that what you are truly doing when you watch, read, or listen to the news is more along the lines of something called the **ritual model of communication**. As the word "ritual" suggests, this model of consuming news is less about new info and much more about routine and comfort. The ritual model says you watch, read, or listen to the news because you want someone to tell you the world is exactly the way you think it is and everything works the way you already think it works. Back to those cozy echo chambers. It turns out watching the news isn't always about getting new information; it's also about reaffirming an existing worldview. Humans love consistency and comfort.

The ritual model of communication is about buying into a set of beliefs, beliefs that others around you share, so that when you watch a particular news show and are fed the news in a specific way, it's almost like going to the mosque/mandir/church/synagogue/temple—you and everyone else watching that newscast or scrolling down that news website are all being preached to from the same gospel.

This starts to get a little uncomfortable. Maybe you're shaking your head in denial right this minute. *Of course people watch the news to get news*, you might be saying. But hear this out. Carey was toying with questions that we are about to sink our teeth into: Is the news really interested in providing the masses with new information and shaking things up to make the world a better, fairer place? Are we even truly interested in having our worldview shaken up? (Having your viewpoint shaken up can feel quite uncomfortable, after all.) Or is the news more invested in keeping things the way they are, that is, maintaining the status quo? And again, if we are honest, are we hoping for the news to keep us in our cozy echo chamber and reaffirm our existing worldview and tell us, *Don't worry, things are exactly as you left them yesterday. . . . Nothing will ever change. . . . Phew.*

We pick and choose where to get news, if we choose to get any news at all. A theory known as **selective exposure** says that we tune in to news that is presented in a way that matches our existing beliefs. A famous example that demonstrates this, although it might be more urban legend than factual (you can try to fact-check it if you like), is that Vice President Dick Cheney refused to enter a hotel room until the TV was first tuned to a conservative news show, the kind that agreed with his opinions. If humans are prone to doing this, how can we argue that we consume information to have our worldview challenged? It seems as if we like things to agree with us!

These are prickly and important questions. The purpose of the news and why we consume it say a lot about us, our beliefs, our societies, and why the news looks and operates the way it does today—with all the good and bad that comes with it. Sometimes, when the news sucks and polls show that public trust in the news is plummeting even further, reporters and editors are prone to say, *We're just giving our audiences what they want!* That too is a vicious cycle. Should newsroom bosses and journalists pander to what they think the audience wants, or should they decide what they think the audience needs?

In 1936, much-respected British journalist Claud Cockburn asked himself this same question. He took it to its extreme when he was in Spain and learned that the fascist general Francisco Franco was using the Spanish army to try to take down the government that had been elected by the people of Spain. Cockburn wrote a story that said the anti-fascists were victorious! They had toppled the evil, fascist dictator, and this should offer hope to freedom fighters all around the world. This was great news, he said!

Except that's not what happened. In fact, Franco was victor in the Spanish Civil War. Fascists *won* and ruled for thirty-five years. Why did Cockburn lie? Most would argue that it's not the job of a journalist to make up the news, and that telling lies crosses multiple lines and deceives and manipulates the public, which is flat-out unfair. But Cockburn would probably defend himself by saying that he was trying to do the right thing. He was cheering on the anti-fascists and making up a story that they had won in the hopes of ending fascism. He wanted to give people inspiration, to make the world a safer place. Is that an okay goal? Should he have stayed neutral in the face of fascism?

Nowadays, Cockburn's actions would get him fired from the majority of US newsrooms. But the debate continues over a journalist's role in society and whether reporters should always stay neutral in the face of injustice. There are many perspectives on this debate, and although probably all those involved would say they want the news to be truthful and trustworthy, there are different ideas about how to achieve those goals.

"ALTERNATIVE FACTS" AND THE MYTH OF OBJECTIVITY

ON JANUARY 27, 2017, Lewis Raven Wallace, a White transgender man, was suspended from his job as a reporter at the public radio program *Marketplace*. That same day, Lewis had published a personal blog about what it meant to be a journalist under a new administration that was repeating lies, demonizing Muslims and Mexicans, and making fun of disabled people. Lewis's blog landed him in deep trouble. His bosses said his writing crossed the line from journalism into activism. They asked him to take it down from the internet. So he did.

Lewis's suspension came seven days after President Trump's inauguration, an inauguration that the new president said had drawn the biggest crowds of any presidential inauguration. That simply wasn't true. Video footage and TV viewership data proved that attendance was measly. But the president and his spokespeople repeated the lie. The White House press secretary even stood behind an official podium and said, "This was the largest audience to ever witness an inauguration, period, both in person and around the globe."

When journalists challenged that statement and presented evidence showing that many more people had watched and attended the historic inauguration of America's first Black president in 2009, the president's advisor said the White House press secretary hadn't told a lie; he had given "alternative facts."

What are alternative facts, and how should reporters handle them? In Lewis's January 27 blog, "Objectivity Is Dead, and I'm Okay with It," he asked his fellow reporters to think about how they would do their jobs when those in power were creating their own versions of the truth. "Will we give voice to 'alternative facts'?" he asked. "To call a politician on a lie is our job; to bring stories of the oppressed to life is our job; to represent a cross-section of our communities is our job; to tell the truth in the face of 'alternative facts' and routine obscuring is our job."

Those lines cost Lewis *his* job. On January 30, he was fired from his position as the first and only on-air transgender reporter at *Marketplace* and one of the only out transgender reporters in all of American broadcast journalism.

In the Manhattan bistro where Lewis was fired, his boss, a White woman, told Lewis a story. In the 1980s she had been a journalism student at an American university and an activist demonstrating against the oppression of the South African government's racist apartheid regime, a regime that bulldozed Black people's homes, forbade them from being friends with non-Black people, and refused to give them lifesaving treatment in "White hospitals." But a professor told her to choose either journalism or activism; she couldn't do both. "She'd chosen journalism, she said to me with a straight face," Lewis writes in his book, *The View from Somewhere: Undoing the Myth of Journalistic Objectivity*, "as if leaving the anti-apartheid struggle was something a white person ought to be proud of in retrospect."

In his blog, and later in his book, Lewis asked if journalists should have to make that choice and what it means to be a neutral journalist in a world that is deeply unfair, where people are treated differently based on the way they look and how their body functions. Can you be neutral about racism? Should you be?

And how should reporters cover an administration that calls the press "the opposition party" and "the enemy"? he asked. What does it mean to tell both sides of a story when one side doesn't believe that people on the other side have the right to exist? How should reporters cover a president who provokes his supporters to harass and abuse journalists? And then there's that word, "objectivity," which journalism claims to be, or at least hopes to be—the concept that Lewis, in his blog title, calls *dead*. "After all, transgender people had been covered for decades with almost nothing but bias and bigotry, by supposedly 'objective' journalists," he writes, adding that he is "never neutral on the subject of my own humanity and rights."

Reporters like to say that journalism should "comfort the afflicted and afflict the comfortable," meaning that good reporting should shake things up for those who hold power and make life better and fairer for people who exist on the margins of society, such as disabled people, queer people, and people of color. (It's funny that this line has become a favorite quote in support of journalism, because the full quote comes from a fictional Irish bartender, Mr. Dooley, who is deeply critical of the press. In the 1902 novel where the line first appears, what Mr. Dooley actually says is: "Th' newspaper does ivrything f'r us. It runs th' polis foorce an' th' banks, commands th' milishy, controls th' ligislachure, baptizes th' young, marries th' foolish, comforts th' afflicted, afflicts th' comfortable, buries th' dead an' roasts thim afterward.")

This ideal, that journalism should hold the powerful to account, that it should expose corruption and make the world a better, more equal place, is shared by many journalists. It's the motivation needed to sit through hours and hours of school board meetings and city hall hearings, to ask pointed questions of people who prefer to hide behind talking points and who will sometimes lie to a reporter's face.

There are many examples of journalism that has benefited the public. TV, newspaper, and radio journalism has ousted corrupt officials, amplified the voices of organizers fighting injustice, and helped enact laws that have benefited society's most vulnerable communities. Just take a look at the Public Service category of the Pulitzer Prizes, the most prestigious category of one of journalism's most highly considered awards. The Public Service prize gives a gold medal to reporters whose journalism has made a positive difference in people's lives.

But does journalism always live up to this ideal? Or, as Mr. Dooley suggests, does journalism strengthen the power of people who already have authority? Can journalism prop up lying presidents, empower dishonest police chiefs, and protect embezzling bankers?

OBJECTIVITY AND DOUGHNUTS

Lewis argues that when journalists claim to be "objective" and "neutral," what they are really doing is reinforcing the way that things already are. He says those words are used as a cover, a way of pretending that the world is fair. Journalism that claims to be objective and neutral is actually supporting the status quo, or the existing state of affairs, especially regarding social or political issues. There's even a **status quo bias** that argues that humans love it when things stay the same; it's more familiar and comfortable that way. Because of this bias, the media can toe the line of what's mostly accepted as normal and okay, rarely including ideas that call for change in a meaningful way.

Objectivity and neutrality are not concepts that exist in a vacuum; they are ideas that exist in a world where we (and think about who the "we" is here; *who* gets to contribute to these kinds of decisions, and what do timing and history have to do with these decisions?) collectively agree what the status quo should look like, and then say, "Well, to be neutral means standing on this line in the middle of what we've agreed is normal and okay."

Ramona Martinez, a radio producer who collaborated with Lewis to create the *View from Somewhere* podcast, describes it like this: "What is considered objective or neutral is really only a matter of social agreement, or the ideological consensus of the majority or the status quo."

And this is where things get tricky . . . or should we say, this is where things get **POWERFUL**. Because social agreements have everything to do with power. The "consensus of the majority or the status quo" leaves out the minority; it excludes the voices of those who are possibly harmed by the beliefs, systems, and laws that make up the status quo, *the existing state of affairs*.

Okay. It's time for a doughnut. No, I'm serious.

One way of looking at the consensus of the majority is an idea called the **sphere of consensus**, which you can think of like a doughnut. The doughnut hole is the sphere of consensus; it contains widely accepted ideas that very few people would (openly) disagree with, such as that all people are created equal, or that every adult should have the right to vote. Journalists often assume that everyone agrees with these ideas and that it's not worth our time even debating them.

Then there's the spongy doughnut itself, called the **sphere of legitimate controversy** or the **sphere of legitimate debate**, which represents ideas that are controversial but still acceptable enough to debate, ideas such as the following: teens who are old enough to

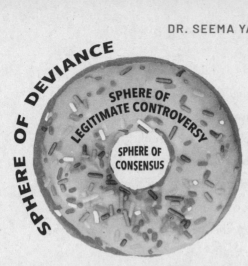

Source: Gizelka/Essentials/iStock.

enlist in the military should also have the right to vote, or people who have committed a crime should be able to vote. This spongy doughnut area is the space in which journalists are expected to stay "neutral," which can mean they include "both sides" of the argument in their reporting and keep their opinions out of the story.

Outside the doughnut is the **sphere of deviance**, where unspeakable, even unthinkable ideas live. The ideas here might be so taboo that reporters feel it's okay to never mention them. Reporters might think the ideas in the sphere of deviance are so far away from what most people agree upon that they're not even newsworthy.

But here's the thing: These spheres are not static. What was once in the sphere of *deviance* (for example, the idea that Black people in America should have the right to vote) moved to the **sphere of legitimate controversy** and eventually into the sphere of *consensus* when Black Americans were given, by law, the right to vote. It used to be completely within the sphere of consensus in the US to hit children as a form of discipline. But in 2021, fewer than two dozen states allowed children to be hit by schoolteachers. That's still a lot, but many more states used to be on the "It's okay for a teacher to hit a kid" list.

The ideas that exist in these spheres shift not only across time but also across the planet. In China and Cuba, discussions about democracy still live in the sphere of deviance—speaking openly on the topic could land you in big trouble.

These spheres are also known as **Hallin's spheres**, after Daniel Hallin, the journalist and academic who first described the idea in a book about the way reporters covered the Vietnam War. (The doughnut analogy was invented by another journalist, Brooke Gladstone, who wrote an amazing comic book about the media called *The Influencing Machine*.) Hallin said the areas in the doughnut hole and outside the doughnut—the spheres of consensus and deviance—are where journalists often trip up. For example, a reporter might simply agree with an idea that lives in the sphere of consensus—like the idea that "masculine" means "strong" and "feminine" means "weak"—without challenging that idea. A reporter might assume that if an idea lives in the doughnut hole, *everybody* in society must agree with it, so the reporter may not question the idea or check to see if it is fair or based on accurate information.

Hallin also worried that journalists would completely ignore ideas, or the people who think up the ideas, that exist outside the doughnut in the sphere of deviance. They might assume, without even realizing it, that these ideas are not worth mentioning. But since ideas usually don't stick in just one sphere, and because they often move into the doughnut and even into the doughnut hole, shouldn't we talk about them? What if the ideas that exist in the sphere of deviance right now belong to or benefit people who don't have a lot of power in society, whereas the ideas in the sphere of consensus are put there by those who already have lots of power? What if these ideas that exist in the sphere of consensus help those with power hold on to their influence?

Without really admitting it, journalists reinforce these spheres all the time. By choosing what to write about and what *not* to write about, by deciding who gets interviewed and how much space that person's words take up, journalists can subtly and sub-consciously—but sometimes blatantly—support the ideas and beliefs that occupy different parts of the doughnut. By making assumptions about what "the public" believes and agrees upon (and making huge assumptions about who exactly "the public" is—as if it's one huge group of people who are all the same) and by ignoring ideas that live outside the doughnut, journalism can help to maintain things as they already are. Journalists can support the status quo instead of speaking truth to power and making those with authority uncomfortable.

Take a look at these examples of journalism. In which part of the doughnut did these ideas live at the time they were published? In which doughnut sphere do these ideas exist now? Was this reporting objective and neutral? Was it fair? (And to whom was it fair or unfair?)

In 1942, as US president Franklin Roosevelt ordered the imprisonment of the country's 120,000 Japanese Americans, the *LA Times* supported his racist decision by writing an editorial that said, "The time has come to realize that the rigors of war demand proper detention of Japanese and their immediate removal from the most acute danger spots. . . . There is no safe alternative." A year later, the paper's editorial board continued its support of the imprisonment of Japanese Americans by writing, "As a race, the Japanese have made for themselves a record for conscienceless treachery unsurpassed in history."

Objective? Neutral? Fair? Or in support of the status quo, a status quo that endorsed racist internments? Was the *LA Times* holding the powerful to account and questioning the ethics of imprisoning innocent people based on their racial and ethnic ancestry, or was it supporting the troubling acts of an already powerful person? If the paper's editorial board was responding to the public's perception of what was fair and right . . . which public are we talking about? The Japanese American public? (Probably not, right?)

Now, there's something you should know before you answer these questions. There's a difference between a news site's editorial pages and its regular reporting. To understand this, let's start with this question: What exactly is an editorial board? The editorial board is the governing body of a news organization and is made up of people who vote on political issues and politicians. You might have seen newspaper editorials in support of, or against, your town's mayoral candidates or the country's presidential candidates. Editorials are different from regular reporting, and by regular reporting we mean the kind of journalism that claims to not take a stance on a topic. Editorials are journalism that represents the opinion of the news outlet's editorial board. It might sound strange for a news outlet to take a stand on an issue, but it's a long-standing tradition of American and Western news. Some say that editorials point back to the true history of American journalism, a history where colonizers created a partisan press to express personal thoughts and influence public opinion. Nowadays, most news organizations try to signal the separation between news reporting and opinion pieces, both on the page and in the newsroom. For example, the editorial board often sits on a different floor from the main newsroom, away from where news reporters and editors work. This can create a physical line between reporters and editors, who report the news, and editorial board members, who openly express opinions in their journalism.

Here's an example: Until the early 2000s, members of the *Dallas Morning News* editorial board—whose offices are on a different floor from the cubicles of the news reporters—wrote editorials in favor of the death penalty. The addition of a new editorial board member that year shifted the majority vote of the board to take a stance *against* the death penalty in Texas. Like other newspapers, during election seasons the *Dallas Morning News* publishes editorials that endorse or oppose people running for office. The hope is that readers can clearly see what is an editorial—journalism with an opinion—versus regular reporting that does not take a particular position.

You may have read stories in the opinion pages, or op-eds, of a news site. These are called op-eds because they used to be printed opposite the editorial page. Opinion pieces allow a writer or cartoonist to express their opinion—although that opinion should be backed up with credible evidence and the piece should stick to the same standards of fact-checking as reported news. Whereas a news journalist will rarely insert themselves into a reported piece, an opinion writer can use the first-person "I" or "we" in their work. Opinion pieces are often authored by writers who do not work on staff at the news outlet. They might be university professors or government officials with deep insights on a particular topic. Opinion pages or sections should clearly signal that they represent the views of a specific person and are not the perspective of the news outlet they are published in.

But do audiences notice these signals that try to show the separation between news and opinion? Physical newspapers often print opinions and editorials toward the back of the paper, but how do you clearly label an op-ed or editorial column on a website? The word OPINION might be missed by someone scrolling through an article.

It turns out that labeling, and the language used to label these kinds of journalism, is inconsistent, both online and in print. A 2017 study by researchers at Duke University found that only 40 percent of large news organizations labeled opinion and editorial articles in newspapers and on their websites, and that the language they used was all over the place. Especially when clicking a link on social media to a news website, a reader might land on an opinion piece and think they were reading reported news.

But some news sites did a better job in helping readers understand what kind of journalism they were engaging with. The *Washington Post*'s website, the Duke study found, used four main labels (opinion, review, analysis, and perspective) to help readers identify a news piece from an editorial. Hovering over each label offered more information about what kind of journalism they were reading.

Okay, so back to the *LA Times*' racist editorials. Now that you know the distinctions between editorials, op-eds, and regular journalism, you might take a different view on the *LA Times* backing the internment of Japanese Americans in the 1940s. *But it was the editorial board taking this racist stance, not the journalists who reported the news*, you might say. Some could argue that because the editorial board—which is separate from the news reporting department of a newsroom—endorsed imprisoning Japanese Americans, the newspaper itself could still be trusted to report fairly on lawmakers' decisions on how to treat Japanese Americans.

Racist ideas have appeared in both the reported news and

editorial pages of magazines and newspapers throughout history and today. In 1916, *National Geographic* magazine ran a full-issue article that said Aboriginal Australians were "savages" and "rank lowest in intelligence of all human beings." Three years later, the *Montgomery Advertiser* printed an editorial that said Black, Native American, and Asian people brought death-by-lynching upon themselves because they committed crimes. The *Advertiser*'s editorial board wrote, "As long as there are attempts at rape by black men, red men or yellow men on white women there will be lynchings."

When three Black men were killed by White people on September 29 and September 30, 1919, the *Montgomery Advertiser* said—without evidence—that the Black men had assaulted White women. Two of the men, Robert Crosky and Miles (or Relius) Phifer, were veterans. Phifer was killed while wearing his army uniform. The third man, Will Temple, was shot to death by a racist mob while recovering in the hospital from an earlier racist attack.

An October 1919 editorial in the *Montgomery Advertiser* blamed Black, indigenous, and Asian people for their deaths at the hands of White people. Source: Brian Lyman, "'There Will Be Lynchings': How the Advertiser Failed Victims of Racial Terror," *Montgomery Advertiser*, April 20, 2018, https://www.montgomeryadvertiser .com/story/news/2018/04/20/there-lynchings -how-advertiser-failed-victims-racial -terror-eji-peace-justice-memorial -montgomery/499656002/.

This was considered neutral and objective journalism at the time, which reminds us again that the consensus view and what is considered fair and objective shifts as months and years pass by.

The *Winston-Salem Journal and Sentinel*'s support of sterilizing disabled women without their consent in the 1940s was considered by many to be fair.

This is what one editorial in the newspaper said at the time: "The danger is in the moron group which includes a host of physically attractive individuals whose IQs are lower than a January thermometer reading. Among other things, they breed like mink." Utterly evil things to say about disabled people.

The *Winston-Salem Journal and Sentinel*'s support of North Carolina's eugenics program spread beyond its editorial pages to its reporting—the parts of the newspaper that are supposedly absent of any bias or opinion. Other papers, such as North Carolina's *Asheville Citizen* and the *Charlotte Observer*, also backed the state's sterilization program. One paper even failed to mention that at least one of its reporters who wrote about the government's sterilization program was employed by both the newspaper and the *state government*! At the time, eugenics and the forceful sterilization of people deemed to be "less than normal" was considered progressive and the right thing to do. That was the status quo. But it was inhumane.

Tom Wicker, a reporter at the *Charlotte Observer* who wrote in favor of eugenics and had a conflict of interest because he also worked for the state government, later said, "I wrote, in effect, press releases—and hoped for the best. I didn't make any distinction in my own mind between the eugenics program and feeding the hungry. I feel very badly about it in retrospect. . . . We were all kind of convinced that what our government was doing was right, that it wouldn't lie to you."

Wicker went on to have a long career as a national correspondent for the *New York Times*. Was he objective? To what standard of objectivity was he held? In 2013, the publisher of the *Winston-Salem Journal and Sentinel* apologized for the paper's support of the government's unethical program, saying, "I regret that the *Journal*, in its past, played a role in legitimizing these barbaric activities. On behalf of the *Journal*, I apologize for the paper's part in depriving these individuals of their basic human rights." But at the time, in the 1940s, the paper was considered to be printing objective, neutral, unbiased journalism.

The examples aren't always as obvious as articles and editorials in support of unethical and cruel government-run programs. Bias can be subtle. It might be the language that's used to describe poor people or the disabled, a caption under a photo of Black people peacefully protesting that uses the word "melee" or "riot" . . . or it might be the fact that some people's lives are not even considered newsworthy enough to be mentioned in the news in the first place.

In December 2020, the *Kansas City Star* newspaper apologized for "decades of coverage that depicted Black Kansas Citians as criminals living in a crime-laden world." It said there was "shame at what was missing: the achievements, aspirations and milestones of an entire population routinely overlooked, as if Black people were invisible."

In 2018, the *New York Times*' editorial board published an apology titled "Slandering the Unborn." It regretted the way the editorial board had talked about Black mothers who had become addicted to drugs in the 1980s and '90s. "News organizations shoulder much of the blame for the moral panic that cast mothers with crack addictions as irretrievably depraved and the worst enemies of their children," it said. "The New York Times, The Washington Post, Time, Newsweek and others further demonized black women 'addicts' by wrongly reporting that they were giving birth to a generation of neurologically damaged children who were less than fully human and who would bankrupt the schools and social service agencies once they came of age."

To make its point, the *Times* pointed to the "humanizing" way Americans, mostly White, who were addicted to opioids in the 2000s were covered by journalists. Same issue, addiction, but a very different way of reporting on the people affected.

Racist and blatantly biased reporting is not only a problem of past years. In 2020, when George Floyd, a Black man, was killed by a White police officer in Minneapolis, a Black reporter at the *Pittsburgh Post-Gazette* was pulled from covering the anti-racist protests that followed Floyd's death. Alexis Johnson was told by her bosses that a tweet she had posted showed bias and that she was no longer allowed to cover the protests or issues related to systemic racism.

Johnson had tweeted photos of litter-filled streets, the kinds of images included in press coverage of the anti-racism protests. Her caption called out the way the press reported on anti-racist demonstrators while letting concertgoers get away with the same behavior.

You could say that Johnson's perspective—that the press didn't fairly cover the aftermath of a racist murder and emphasized the vandalism of anti-racism protesters when concert attendees did much the same damage—lived in the sphere of deviance, and that her bosses either didn't like being called out for their editorial decisions or assumed that her perspective was so outside the sphere of legitimate controversy that she wasn't able to do her job as an "objective" reporter. They figured that Johnson was way outside the doughnut.

But Lewis and other reporters say that what Johnson's editors were pushing for is the traditional way of doing journalism, and that needs to change. The traditional way of reporting, what you might find in the *New York Times* and the *Washington Post*, for example, asks reporters to be neutral on issues that affect their survival and insists that they deny who they are and how the world treats them and their communities. Black journalists and editors make up 7 percent of newsroom staff in the US but 14 percent of the US population. Are Black newsroom staff held to a different standard from their White colleagues, who are overrepresented in the media? Would a White journalist be pulled from covering a story about the Ku Klux Klan for fear that they couldn't "objectively" cover the issue of White supremacy? Are White reporters considered inherently neutral because they live in a society where Whiteness is considered the default?

In the blog post that cost him his job, Lewis wrote,

Neutrality isn't real: Neutrality is impossible for me, and you should admit that it is for you, too. As a member of a marginalized community (I am transgender), I've never had the opportunity to pretend I can be 'neutral.' After years of silence/denial about our existence, the media has finally picked up trans stories, but the nature of the debate is over whether or not we should be allowed to live and participate in society, use public facilities and expect not to be harassed, fired or even killed. Obviously, I can't be neutral or centrist in a debate over my own humanity. The idea that I don't have a right to exist is not an opinion, it is a falsehood. On that note, can people of color be expected to give credence to 'both sides' of a dispute with a White supremacist, a person who holds unscientific and morally reprehensible views on the very nature of being human?

Alexis Johnson is a Black woman whose lived realities of the world are very different from those of her bosses, who are likely to be mostly White and male. Pretending the world is a level playing field also means pretending that her experiences of racism and sexism do not exist, that her bosses' way of seeing the world is the only way. Lewis says we should scrap this way of doing journalism, saying, "I propose that we need to become more shameless, more raw, more honest with ourselves and our audiences about who we are, and what we are in this for."

He says this could help the public trust reporters and the journalism they produce—at a time when trust in the media has been falling among some groups—instead of pretending that reporters, who are human and not robots, after all, can be neutral, and that journalism is ever objective.

INSTEAD OF OBJECTIVITY ... WHAT?

When Lewis was fired and trying to figure out exactly which rule his blog had violated, he noted that the word "objective" was not in *Marketplace*'s code of conduct or ethics. In fact, he noticed that quite a few journalism organizations had ditched that word from their guidelines. But although it was absent, it hadn't entirely disappeared. Instead of "objective," news organizations were using words like "impartial" to uphold an ideal that journalism should and can be neutral.

But we know now that the American press began as the biased mouthpiece of political parties and evolved into the sensationalist Penny Press, with its front-page stories about wild beasts escaping the zoo and unicorns flying on the moon. So when and why did journalism become obsessed with objectivity and neutrality—or at least with being *perceived* as objective and neutral?

The AP's history gives us at least one reason: focusing on facts and appealing to a variety of audiences who held different political beliefs sold more copies of the newspaper and was a business decision that helped set the AP apart from its competitors. Some historians say the news gradually became more focused on facts because that's what the public wanted. But there's another reason the news industry likely set the impossible goals of neutrality and objectivity.

Professionalizing the press—creating journalism schools and guidelines for writing professionals—was a way of attracting customers by saying, *Hey, look, we newsmakers are credible and professional.* Joseph Pulitzer—who made lots of money and gained incredible power from publishing newspapers—gave a million dollars to Columbia University to create a journalism school when he died. By training students and inducting them into the profession, journalism appeared more and more credible, even as the industry remained Whiter, straighter, and more able-bodied than the people it was supposed to serve.

But professionalizing the press was also a way of keeping the government out of journalism's affairs. By regulating itself, newsmakers could tell the government, *We've got this; you don't need to regulate us.*

If objectivity isn't the right strategy for the kind of journalism that busts open the wounds of the world to allow healing and bridge-building, then what is the strategy? What do we need journalism to be, and what role should effective journalism play in our lives?

Lewis's book, the one published after he was fired, is titled *The View from Somewhere*, a nod to a sort of central pillar of journalism that states that journalism is "The View from Nowhere." This means that journalists don't stand on any side of an argument; instead, they are impartial observers who float in some mystical place that is neither here nor there.

Holding objectivity and neutrality as ideals can lead to something called **bothsidesism**, also known as **false balance**, where a journalist feels as if they are doing everything right as long as they just include both sides of an argument. Consider this example: An iceberg melts off the coast of Greenland, earth scientists say human-driven climate change is causing sea temperatures to rise . . . and the reporter thinks, *I'd better include the voice of someone who disagrees, just to balance out the story.*

In this case, that opposing voice might be a climate change denialist, someone who, in the face of reams of evidence about humans wreaking havoc on the environment, argues that climate change is a hoax invented by the Chinese government to get Western governments to reduce their manufacturing.

False balance and bothsidesism give oxygen to a view that has been thoroughly debunked by climate scientists, who can back up their statements with evidence. A reporter intent on appearing "balanced" might include the opposing view, that climate change is not real, and treat that argument as equally valid (perhaps by including it at all, or by giving the speaker as much space in a written piece, or as much airtime on the radio or TV) as a way of saying, *But look, I covered "both sides" of the argument.*

MOVEMENT JOURNALISM

Lewis takes an entirely different stance on The View from Nowhere, which you might have guessed, since his book has the title *The View from Somewhere.* From his point of view (he admits to having one), reporters—privileged with access to sources of information, including official documents, experts, and people in power—have a duty to use that information to make the world a better place by amplifying the concerns and voices of the most oppressed people in society.

After he was fired from *Marketplace,* Lewis founded Press On, an organization that practices movement journalism. The reporters and staff at Press On say that movement journalism is "journalism in service to liberation. This does not mean turning journalists into soapboxes for activists." Instead, Press On and other organizations for movement journalists say their work focuses on injustice and the communities most badly affected by it.

People who hold a traditional view of journalism (although you could argue that the true tradition of Western news is the sensationalist Penny Press and the partisan press before it) say movement journalism is not journalism at all. It's activism. It's taking a specific stance on something—which is the opposite of staying neutral.

Lewis and other movement journalists ask: How can you stay neutral in the face of racism, homophobia, transphobia, ableism, misogyny, climate change, slavery, and other forms of oppression?

The founding mother of movement journalism might be a reporter born in 1862. Ida B. Wells was a Black woman who was born into slavery in Holly Springs, Mississippi, six months before the Emancipation Proclamation of 1863 freed enslaved people (except not many Black people were actually freed in 1863 because the law didn't apply to many states). Wells and her family were eventually freed, and she went on to work as a teacher and then a journalist at the *Memphis Free Speech and Headlight*, a newspaper that she co-owned.

Wells reported the news at a time when Black people were tortured and murdered. By some estimates, upward of 160 Black people were lynched each year during the 1880s and 1890s. Wells was both a journalist and an anti-lynching activist at a time when her survival, and the survival of her people, depended on her journalism exposing the brutal realities of barely ended slavery and the continued oppression of Black Americans.

It was Wells's own investigative journalism that discovered that 161 Black children, women, and men were lynched in the US in 1892. Her front-page report in the *Memphis Free Speech and Headlight* suggested that Black people leave Memphis and move to Oklahoma, where it might be safer. But her own survival was threatened by her work. Her newsroom was set on fire, and she was stalked and threatened. Eventually, Wells moved to New York City, where she became co-owner of the *New York Age*, a Black-run newspaper.

In 2020, eighty-nine years after her death, Wells was awarded a special Pulitzer Prize for "her outstanding and courageous reporting on the horrific and vicious violence against African Americans during the era of lynching."

This debate on the role of journalists and the best way (or ways . . . maybe there are more than one) to practice journalism continues, sometimes in a heated fashion, but mostly in an *Arggh, what are we going to do about this?* manner. What is mostly agreed upon is that large swathes of Americans don't trust the news (some won't even engage with the news) and there is much room for improvement.

LIKE EATING POOP

MORE THAN TWO hundred years after President Jefferson wrote that "the man who never looks into a newspaper is better informed than he who reads them," the problems of shrinking trust in the press and the contagiousness of false information have probably only worsened.

In 2016, Pope Francis compared consuming and sharing "fake news" to eating poop.

Yep.

In an interview with a Belgian newspaper, the pope used the slightly more polite terms "coprophilia" (meaning an interest or pleasure in feces) and "coprophagia" (the actual eating of feces) to make his case. Pointing the finger at journalists, who he claimed help spread false information, he said, "I think the media have to be very clear, very transparent, and not fall into—no offense intended—the sickness of coprophilia, that is, always wanting to cover scandals, covering nasty things, even if they are true. And since people have a tendency towards the sickness of coprophagia, a lot of damage can be done."

In 2012, a year before he was elected to serve as pope, Francis told the Italian newspaper *La Stampa*, "Journalists sometimes risk becoming ill from coprophilia and thus fomenting coprophagia, which is a sin that taints all men and women—that is, the tendency to focus on the negative rather than the positive aspects."

The soon-to-be pope perhaps had his *own* biases in mind when making these poop-adjacent comments. His interviews came in the wake of the VatiLeaks scandal, in which journalists published leaked documents and exposed alleged financial corruption inside the Vatican. Besides those scandals, the sexual abuse of children within multiple levels of the Catholic Church had already been investigated and uncovered by reporters at the *Boston Globe* and other news outlets.

SIDEBAR: JOURNALISTS UNDER ATTACK

ONE FRIDAY IN THE SUMMER OF 2018, WENDI WINTERS, A reporter at the *Capital Gazette*, called Sofia Bondi and told the eighteen-year-old that she would be featured as the *Capital Gazette*'s Teen of the Week. "Teen of the Week is a little segment she does about the teens in this area, the ones that are really going above and beyond," said Sofia, speaking from Annapolis, Maryland, where she lives and where Wendi worked. Wendi picked Sofia because the teen is passionate about ending gun violence, a problem that cuts short the lives of nine children and teens in the US every day. Sofia attends marches and advocates for gun control in the hopes that American children can go to school without fear of mass shootings.

A week after Wendi called Sofia, the pair met inside the *Capital Gazette* newsroom for the Teen of the Week interview and immediately bonded over a shared experience. It turned out that they had both attended the same protest against gun violence a while earlier. Sofia had been at the march with a placard that read "Are we next? #EnoughIsEnough" while her friends carried signs that said "Protect kids, not guns."

At the time, Wendi was mentoring a young navy cadet, and because he was also passionate about ending gun violence, she had been at the same demonstration alongside him. "We really bonded over going to the marches and speaking up about gun violence," said Sofia. "[Wendi] said that she was up front in the crowd and [the navy cadet] was by her side, crying."

When Sofia and Wendi met, they talked inside the *Capital Gazette* newsroom for 45 minutes and then Wendi took Sofia outside to snap photos and film video while Sofia talked about her belief that young people can help to make the world a safer, fairer place. Sofia asked Wendi if she could record her speech a few times, but Wendi insisted that the first try was perfect and that she had all the footage she needed. "Everything seemed really normal," said Sofia. "She walked me to my car and we said goodbye. And she just told me, you know, 'Have a nice day.'" Sofia drove home, and Wendi walked back inside the newsroom to create the Teen of the Week segment that she had told Sofia would be published in a few days' time.

Less than thirty minutes later, Wendi was shot dead. A man walked into the *Capital Gazette* newsroom and killed Wendi and four of her colleagues, including Rebecca Smith, thirty-four, a sales assistant; John McNamara, fifty-six, a sportswriter, journalist, and editor; Rob Hiaasen, fifty-nine, an assistant editor; and Gerald Fischman, sixty-one, an editorial page editor. It was the deadliest day in American journalism in almost twenty years.

At home, Sofia watched television journalists break the horrific news. The gunman had entered the exact building that she had just left. She quickly texted Wendi to check that she was okay, but there was no response.

The gunman had hated journalists for a long time. He had posted threats against reporters on social media for years, and his online messages had scared staff at the *Capital Gazette* enough that some had spoken out to say they felt that he would eventually attack them. A few years earlier, he had sued the newspaper for publishing a column about his harassment of a former high school classmate. When he lost that defamation lawsuit, he stockpiled weapons, barricaded the journalists inside the newsroom, and proceeded to kill them.

Wendi and her colleagues' deaths stunned the nation. Being a journalist might not seem like a dangerous job, not when compared with driving a taxi (the profession with the highest homicide rate in the US), but Wendi and her colleagues are among the hundreds of journalists who are attacked and even murdered around the world each year because of the work they do.

Between 1992 and 2021, more than 2,000 journalists were murdered while on assignment, 1,424 of them with a confirmed motive, according to the Committee to Protect Journalists, an organization that works to safeguard the rights of the people who gather and publish the news. Whether revealing the salacious scandals of corrupt politicians or telling the ugly truth about ordinary citizens, journalists come under fire for sharing the stories that some would prefer to remain hidden.

In some places, journalists are tortured and imprisoned for reporting the news. Countries such as Iran, Egypt, and China often top the list of the most dangerous places to be a journalist. But in 2018, the year that Wendi was killed, the US nearly topped the list of the deadliest places to be a journalist.

But why? What makes reporting the news so dangerous? Sometimes the nature of the assignment puts a journalist in harm's way. Zubair Hatami, a twenty-two-year-old video journalist in Afghanistan, was killed while covering a play in Kabul that condemned suicide attacks when a teenaged suicide bomber detonated a bomb and killed four people and injured twenty others. Christoff Griffith, a twenty-four-year-old photojournalist in Barbados, was killed at the scene of a crime in 2020 when he arrived even before the police did and the perpetrator stabbed him. But in many instances, those who attack journalists are people in positions of power who fear losing that power if journalists reveal their truths.

The danger of being a journalist speaks to the power that journalism holds and the potential it has to effect change. Many journalists, especially those covering beats such as politics, the environment, science, and crime, hope to make the world a better place by sharing information that tells hard truths, explores novel solutions, and gets people to think outside the box about the ways we live our lives and treat the planet and each other.

ACTIVITY: Visit the website for the Committee to Protect Journalists and look at the interactive maps. In which country are the highest number of journalists imprisoned, tortured, and killed? How many journalists were reported missing in your region in the past year?

HOW TO CONSUME NEWS LIKE A PRO:
FACT-CHECK THE NEWS AND CREATE YOUR MEDIA DIET

SO, HOW CAN you avoid consuming and falling for poor-quality journalism? At this point you might be thinking to yourself, **WELL, I GUESS THERE IS NO NEWS I CAN TRUST.** You might even have arrived at the conclusion that there is no point in seeking out the news in the first place. Why bother? You wouldn't be the first to think this, and you're right to ask about trust. We just have to do some work, work that huge portions of the population haven't been doing . . . but you will, because by now, freethinker, you understand how important all of this is.

The good news (pardon the pun)? Most of what is reported *isn't* false information. While agenda setting and framing can powerfully shift the way audiences see the world and understand issues, from abortion to climate change, when it comes to actual falsified facts, only 0.15 percent of news consumed by Americans is truly "fake," according to research by Jennifer Allen at the Massachusetts Institute of Technology.

This tiny smattering of fakeness is like a milliliter of pee in a ten-gallon vat of milk: it can spoil the whole lot. Researchers at Nanyang Technological University in Singapore found that once people hear that some news—even one story—is based on false information, they can be put off the whole lot and assume that nearly all news is fake news and not worth the bother, much like you might have been feeling while reading most of this chapter!

If some news really is "fake" news, and lots are framed in ways that push a particular narrative and succumb to status quo bias, should you throw it all out? Some answer this question with 24/7 skepticism. **JUST DON'T BELIEVE ANYTHING YOU READ, SEE, OR HEAR, THEY SAY. ESPECIALLY DON'T BELIEVE ANYTHING THAT A JOURNALIST SAYS.** But if much of the news is reported by credible journalists who use reliable sources and fact-check their work, perhaps the better answer is to carefully curate your media diet. You can pick news sources that challenge your worldview, examine these news sources critically, and do your own fact-checking.

CURATE YOUR MEDIA DIET

Yes, *diet*. We consume information like food. Almost half of our day, or two-thirds of our waking time—eleven hours total—is spent picking through, gorging on, and digesting content, according to the 2018 Nielsen Total Audience Report (which also found that six of the eleven hours are spent consuming video content). So much so that in 2012, author Clay Johnson took diet advice from journalist Michael Pollan, who said, "Eat food. Not too much. Mostly plants," and came up with "Seek. Not too much. Mostly facts."

But we know that humans consume news for more than just the facts, and we know that the power of the news lies in more than the retelling of only facts (which facts are included, and how are those facts framed, anyway?). Now, you might not be in the habit of seeking out news, since **BAM!**—it seems to pop up and find you no matter how hard you try to avoid it. But there is a way to take control of the information swirling around you. One way is to create a media diet. This has multiple benefits. Designing your own media diet gives you nourishing doses of information and entertainment and puts a lid on distractions so that you're not as tempted to tap every time your phone pings or an alert pops up on some screen somewhere. It also means your worldview is challenged, because you are designing a diet that exposes you to different perspectives, and this can gently guide you out of your comfort zone. This strategy also makes the best use of your valuable time and safeguards your highly sought-after attention.

Whew. Okay, we know we're asking for a lot, especially since we exist in a gargantuan and murky information ecosystem. So here are nine questions to get you started on the path to becoming an Expert in Avoiding BS and Finding Quality News.

1. WHEN AND WHERE DO YOU GET YOUR NEWS?

To really answer this properly, you'll need to do an information audit. As with mindless snacking, we might graze on information without considering what we are taking in and why. Start by asking yourself these questions: Where do you get your news? What times of the day or week do you find yourself reading, watching, or listening to news? What drives you to those news sources at those particular times? Is it boredom? A need for a particular nugget of data? Do you find yourself fact-checking something a friend texted at midnight?

You can add an extra layer to this information audit by writing down how consuming information makes you *feel*. Struggling to sleep after watching a documentary about melting icebergs at 1:00 a.m.? Late for school because you got snared in a YouTube rabbit hole of videos about the origins of goat yoga? Distracted in the middle of the day by pinging news alerts about a mass shooting in a school?

Try out apps that monitor your news consumption (and mood), such as Newstrition and Slimformation. Information can get overwhelming fast. Tracking when you consume news and how it makes you feel can help you create a media diet that keeps you informed but not stressed out.

2. WHAT'S YOUR GOAL WHEN IT COMES TO NEWS CONSUMPTION?
Make a purposeful plan.

Now that you have more awareness about where and when you consume information, as well as why you gravitate to certain sources and how different content makes you feel, ask yourself what you want to get out of the news. Do you want to feel uplifted in the evenings—or maybe avoid news altogether before bedtime? Do you want to be more informed about video games, health news, or a certain sport or team? Is understanding a local or national election really important to you?

Setting specific goals around what you need, and when and why you need it, can help you home in on which sources will help you meet those goals. That way, instead of mindlessly trawling a dozen sites, or wasting your time looking for nature news in outlets more focused on health, you can find sources that specialize in the type of news you prefer—whether that means meaty deep dives into a topic or snappy updates that take ten minutes to finish.

3. WHEN DO YOU WANT TO CONSUME DIFFERENT KINDS OF NEWS?
Create a schedule.

Now that you know *what* you hope to get out of your media diet, you can plan *when* you want to get stuck in it. Are Sunday mornings ideal for getting lost in the pages of a tech magazine that you plan to devour cover to cover? Are Thursday afternoons, when you have an hour of free time, best for doing a deep dive into the website of an international news outlet? Do you prefer thirty-minute or ten-minute news blitzes because of your attention span or schedule? It might seem like you're dedicating a lot of time to thinking about and consuming news when putting together this diet, but bear this in mind: without a plan, you can wind up spending lots more hours flipping pages and mindlessly scrolling through news sites while not getting the information you need.

4. WHICH NEWS SOURCES ARE YOU AWARE OF, AND WHICH OUTLETS AND REPORTERS ARE *NOT* ON YOUR RADAR?
Do your research.

It might be Carol Rosenberg, who has reported on the controversial prison in Cuba's Guantanamo Bay for the *Miami Herald* and the *New York Times* since 2002. It might be Dianne Solis, who has covered the immigration beat for the *Wall Street Journal* and the *Dallas Morning News* since the '90s. Maybe it's a TV reporter at your local station who you've noticed never lets politicians get away with BS and keeps asking questions until she gets an answer, or a radio anchor who does a great job of summarizing the day's sports headlines. If there are beats (the journalistic word for "topics") that are important to you—beats such as baseball, education, women's health, movies, and music—you may already know of dependable reporters who do a great job getting the news you want.

But if you are trying to expand your range of information sources, it can be hard to know where to begin. You can get started by asking well-informed friends and family where they get the news, which sources they trust, and if they know of particular reporters who do a great job covering their beats. You can also reach out to reporters on social media or via email and ask where they get their news and which of their fellow journalists they find especially credible.

Keep in mind that there's always the danger of cozying up in our little echo chambers and only getting news from people and places that back up what we already think of the world. One way to avoid this is to check a few different news sites to compare how they are reporting on a particular topic. Say you're interested in how your country is responding to climate change, and so about twice a week you check news sites A and B for info on what's being done to fight it. You can also check sites C, D, and E, though maybe less frequently, to compare how they cover the same issue. Are the reporters at these sites presenting information differently from what you've been reading on sites A and B? Is what they are saying challenging you? Which sources are the reporters using? How does the framing of the stories differ? You might want to add a new outlet to your diet for a week or two to make these comparisons so you can decide which is best suited to you.

5. DO YOU GET MOST OF YOUR INFORMATION FROM ONE MEDIUM?

Think about the strengths and weaknesses of different media.

A story that lacks good video content might not appear on TV, or it might appear as a brief update when you are really in search of an in-depth explanation. A story that lacks good audio might not find its way to radio or a podcast. The emphasis on visuals to drive the news is known as the **visual bias**, and it applies to print news too. It's why some stories go viral while other equally important stories aren't featured on the front page or home page of an outlet and never come to your attention. Another bias to keep in mind is **narrative bias**, which applies to news in all its forms—print, TV, and radio. It's a bias that can lead reporters to look for patterns across stories and try to tidy up the ending of a complicated story to make it fit a pattern.

What are the strengths and limitations of different media, and is your current diet skewed toward a particular medium? Are you missing out on learning about some issues because you get most of your news from video, audio, or print? Consider mixing things up a bit and comparing how a story is reported not just across different outlets but across different media.

6. ARE YOU GUZZLING NEWS WITHOUT ASKING QUESTIONS ABOUT WHAT YOU'RE CONSUMING?

Chew slowly: read, watch, and listen to news critically.

Read with a pen—at least when you're reading a printed story. Circle the sources—are they mostly men, or all men? Whose voices are included in the story and whose voices are missing? Consuming news with a critical eye (or ear) means asking questions about who reported the news and which perspectives the story frame centers and excludes.

7. ARE THE WORDS, PHOTOS, AND VIDEOS ACCURATE?

Do your own fact-checking.

Journalists fact-check their stories, either themselves or with the help of a fact-checker, as part of the reporting and editing process. This can involve highlighting every fact, from the names of places and people to numbers and quotations, and searching the original data source for each one. You can take a broader approach when someone sends you a "news" article that you're not too sure is news by asking yourself these questions: Are other outlets reporting this news? Is the source of this news usually reliable? Does the story contain links to its data sources? Does it mention the names of real people who were interviewed, and can you check that these people exist? Check the date the story was published and take a look at websites, such as Snopes.com and Politifact.com, that research frequently shared articles to see if they are based on accurate information.

Reverse image search by going to Images.Google.com or TinEye.com to find the original source of a photo. For video, use tools such as Amnesty International's YouTube DataViewer or download the InVID browser extension. These allow you to search for the original source of a video and pull out key frames for a closer look.

8. HOW IS YOUR NEW MEDIA DIET WORKING OUT?

Test, test, and reassess.

Try another audit a month or two into your new media diet. Is your plan meeting your goals? If you think tweaks are required, repeat steps two to four.

9. REMEMBER, "CLICKS HAVE CONSEQUENCES."

This might sound like a very personal plan, but how you consume news isn't only about you. It's a two-way relationship, and your media diet affects . . . the media. Clay Johnson, who wrote *The Information Diet: A Case for Conscious Consumption*, says, "If we want to make media better, then we've got to start consuming better media." He also reminds us that "clicks have consequences" because which channels you tune into, which online stories you click, and how much time you spend on specific YouTube videos feeds an algorithm that tells news outlets which news is popular and which isn't. There's much more on these algorithmic rabbit holes in the next chapter.

ALGORITHMIC BANANAS

IT BEGAN WITH a banana for breakfast. Then Leanne Ratcliffe was peeling and munching on a few more bananas throughout the day. Nothing too interesting about this, right? Probably not enough to make you click on a blog post titled something like "Girl Eats One Banana for Breakfast!" Definitely not captivating enough to make journalists write headlines about Leanne and her boring one-banana-for-breakfast diet.

But then Leanne started to eat bananas for breakfast, lunch, *and* dinner—up to thirty bananas a day. She said she was on a frugivorous (that's the fancy word for fruit-based) diet and was loading up on almost all her day's calories from just one food source. The Australian blogger began writing about her diet and posting photos, posing in crop tops and shorts that showed off washboard abs and a trim waist, standing in her kitchen holding . . . you guessed it . . . bananas. LOTS of bananas. Leanne insisted that if you wanted to be healthy, you should follow her example and load up on bananas too.

In 2009, Leanne launched a website, 30BananasADay.com, and posted to social media accounts, including one with the handle @freeleethebananagirl to push for a diet that was more and more extreme. "Eat a monkey diet where most of your carbohydrates and calories are coming from whole ripe fruits supplemented with about ½-2 pounds of lettuce greens every other day (or every day if you choose) and less than a handful of nuts a day," her website says.

It wasn't only bananas. Some days Leanne ate bananas *and* two whole pineapples or half a dozen mangoes. Other days it was mostly bananas . . . as many as fifty-one bananas in twenty-four hours. Okay. Now THIS is getting WILD! "Monkey diet"? Two whole pineapples for lunch? **FIFTY-ONE BANANAS A DAY?** That's one banana every twenty-eight minutes! Now you're interested, right? Now you want to read more!

Leanne posted photos of herself lying on grass, surrounded by dozens of bananas. Her posts were clicked and liked and shared and reshared. Tens of thousands of people followed the Banana Girl across her social media sites. Journalists around the world began to write about the Banana Girl with the skinny waist and the stacks of banana crates in her kitchen.

Leanne didn't start out as a mega-influencer with thousands of followers and international headlines about her diet. She became a mega-influencer by pushing more and more extreme content, the kind of content that was so out-there, so outlandish and bizarre, that you just couldn't help but click, like, and share. *Excuse me, but WHO eats fifty-one bananas a day?!* **CLICK.** *And she looks like that?* **LIKE.** *Omg, she ate how many mangoes today?!* **SHARE.** It's as if your fingers are held hostage by your brain and your brain is overloaded with chemicals that have you on high alert. You're interested. You're curious. You can't help but . . .

CLICK.

LIKE.

SHARE.

Okay, so you might be lying on the couch, still in your pajamas, using only the muscles that make your thumb go *swipe swipe.* But your brain! Your brain is on high alert! It's pinging and zinging and surging with activity! Leanne's extreme banana diet and attention-grabbing posts exploited the algorithms of social media sites—algorithms designed to reward people when they post extreme, attention-grabbing things. The reward for Leanne? More **CLICKS, LIKES,** and **SHARES** encouraging her to share even wilder, more extreme content. Your reward? A brain buzzing with chemicals triggered by posts and comments, eyeballs glued to the screen, thumb swiping and swiping and swiping. Those brain chemicals, by the way, well, they make you feel **AMAZING!**

More on the brain stuff in a minute, but first, algorithms: What exactly are they? An algorithm is a set of step-by-step instructions that tells a person or a machine what to do and how to do it. *Whisk the eggs with the sugar till smooth, then add a few drops of vanilla essence and carefully fold in the flour.* Yup, a cupcake recipe is an algorithm. When it comes to social media, algorithms give a set of step-by-step instructions (written in computer code) to a platform such as TikTok, YouTube, or Instagram, telling it how to do things like arrange content on your timeline or recommend posts or videos.

Algorithms can be basic. For example, a social media algorithm might be designed to put the newest content at the top of your feed and dump the oldest content at the bottom. That's it—all that algorithm is taking into account is what time a photo or video was posted and maybe which accounts you follow. But an algorithm might be much more complicated. An algorithm could put slightly older but more popular content at the top of your feed. It might even bury some content so that your chances of seeing it are miniscule. On the other hand, an algorithm could promote dangerous posts. Even the kinds of posts that spread false information about a perilous new virus. (Remember Peter Lee Goodchild?)

Why would a social media platform manipulate your feed? Social media giants such as YouTube, Reddit, TikTok, and Meta, which owns Facebook (which owns Instagram), say their algorithms are designed with your happiness in mind. They care about *you*, they say. They want to keep you entertained, and to do that, their algorithm designers make decisions about what you like and don't like. They design algorithms that consider your behavior and online activity. A lot of what is coded into the algorithms is kept secret by the companies, but if the algorithms could talk, we think they'd say something like *Hmmm, based on this user's age and zip code, and the posts they've previously clicked, liked, and shared, we should show them a LOT more content about . . . rabbits and surfboards.*

The algorithm might run on a machine, but it was programmed by people who coded it to decide how to order content by the likelihood that you'll enjoy and engage with it and stay on the platform for hours. They want you to **CLICK, LIKE,** and **SHARE** over and over and over again.

What's in it for them? The $85 billion that Facebook made in 2020 didn't directly come from you . . . did it? Did you pay to sign up for Facebook? No. Did you enter credit card details to watch YouTube videos? No. Does it cost you money to *swipe swipe* on TikTok or Instagram? No. So where do the billions of dollars that the largest social media companies make come from?

Your attention! **CHA-CHING!** Your brain energy + your eyeballs + your time = $$$! You are not making money for spending time on social media, for being forced to look at ads or swipe past promotions, but huge social media companies are raking in billions of dollars by capturing your attention. That's why they work so hard to design secretive algorithms that will keep you on their platforms even at the expense of things like your health, your focus and attention, or world peace. The more time you spend swiping and liking, the more posts your eyeballs absorb and your brain engages with, the more accounts you follow and comments you write, the more money flows into the pockets of social media bosses. That's because they sell your attention. They tell advertisers, *The average TikTok user spends forty-five minutes a day on the app. Cha-ching!* Or, *More than three billion people are active on social media.* Or, *The average internet user spends close to two and a* *half hours of each precious day on social media! So you need to pay us more to advertise your products to our users.*

Social media platforms that make money from advertising are fighting for your attention because your attention is making them millions of dollars every minute.

CLICK.

LIKE.

SHARE.

CHA-CHING!

None of this would be so bad if what kept humans online were posts about sunsets and clumsy kittens, or carefully reported stories written by journalists and verified by fact-checkers. But it turns out that to keep you online for as long as possible, social media platforms boost the content that wins the most engagement. And guess what that content is? It's negative stuff. Tweets that contain words about negative emotions, things like **"THIS IS A DISGRACE!"** and **"OMG I AM SO DISGUSTED!"** or **"WTH?! THIS IS EVIL!,"** are 13 percent more likely to be retweeted than posts with positive emotions, according to a study by researchers at New York University.

Platforms like Facebook and Twitter know this. Their staffs monitor what trends and what flops. They don't seem to care so much about the content of that stuff, just how well it does or doesn't do at keeping people online. And what keeps people online is content that makes you feel strong emotions. That's why in 2016, Facebook staff added five new ways to react to posts: ♥, HAHA, WOW, SAD, and ANGRY, so you could do more than just "like" content. They want you to FEEL things. In 2017, they even rejigged the Facebook algorithm to make reactions to posts five times more influential than "likes" in terms of how content was ranked.

Posts that attack groups of people based on their identity also do really well. These kinds of posts are said to promote tribalism, which means they make people feel a strong sense of loyalty and belonging to what they consider their own identity group. (More on this in the extremism part of this chapter.)

Over the years, leaked documents from inside the company formerly known as Facebook and now called Meta have revealed how staff there hoped that content that sparked lots of reactions and high emotions would keep eyeballs on the app and thumbs scrolling along timelines for longer. Facebook scientists even confirmed what many had been worried about all along when more internal documents revealed that Facebook posts that provoked the ANGRY reaction were more likely to spread false information and hate.

We often talk about algorithms as if they are mysterious, shadowy creatures shrouded in cloaks of cryptic code. Some even try to argue that algorithms are neutral. But they're not. Algorithms are a series of step-by-step instructions that *humans* designed, and humans are not neutral, no matter how much we like to think we are. Every computer engineer, data analyst, and content moderator sees and experiences the world a certain way, and this colors their interactions with the world and with the algorithms and social media platforms that they design. It was people working at Facebook who decided the best way to keep your eyeballs glued to your feed was to make the algorithm promote content that had received lots of attention. If it turned out that what attracted attention was anger-fueling, hate-spreading misinformation, then so be it. *Cha-ching!*

Facebook's *own* research found the platform worsened disagreements between people. In a 2018 presentation, Facebook staff said, "Our algorithms exploit the human brain's attraction to divisiveness." They warned that, "if left unchecked," the platform would give users "more and more divisive content in an effort to gain user attention & increase time on the platform." This revelation came two years after another disturbing finding, which, again, came from inside Facebook. A 2016 report said, "64% of all extremist group joins are due to our recommendation tools." Facebook's "Groups You Should Join" and "Discover" algorithms were nudging people towards extremism. In another presentation, Facebook staff admitted, "Our recommendation systems grow the problem."

Social media algorithms can act like rabbit holes that lead you into a swamp of quicksand. First the rabbit hole takes you deep, deep down into a murky underworld of falsehoods and hateful ideas, and then the quicksand traps you there while more and more misinformation is shoved at you. But that content, instead of getting buried, gets boosted and spotlighted by algorithms that receive a metaphorical pat on the back for keeping you online no matter the cost to your brain or the world.

How is that? One way to explain how algorithms can trap you in a corner and feed you endless streams of similar content can be explained using a car crash analogy. Once you've been lured in by those highly emotional posts, once you've hit LIKE or SHARE, or—better still, from Facebook's perspective—added an ANGRY or SAD emoji, that's when the algorithm knows to feed you more of the same. Evan Williams, who co-founded Twitter and worked at Google, says it's like driving down the highway and looking forward but then turning your head when you spot a wreck on the side of the road. You try to get a good look at what on earth happened because that most valuable of commodities, your attention, has been hooked. When it comes to social media, whatever grabs your attention is what the algorithm will keep feeding you. *Oh, you turned to look at a wreck? Here's another one! Annnnd here! Look at another wreck! We're not done yet, here's a wreck! But you LIKE wrecks, don't you? Here, look at another one. And another. And two more! You're welcome!*

All this to keep your eyes glued to their platforms. The algorithms are clamoring to hook your attention.

The advertising itself—the thing social media bosses are selling to rake in billions of dollars a year—is hyper-targeted advertising. That means you often see the ads that are most likely to interest you. Love to hike on the weekends? Funny how a new pair of trail shoes keeps popping up on your timeline, isn't it? Have a taste for noodles? How come that new Japanese cookbook keeps flashing across your screen? Creepy, right?

If you think companies are listening to you when you're staring into the fridge saying, "Mmmm, I would die for noodles right now," they're not exactly spying on you in *that* way. But they are tracking your movements and behaviors in a different way. With every second you spend online, with every click, like, and share, streams of information about you are spotted and stored. Not only that, but sometimes social media apps collect this data alongside other information about you that comes from your real-life activities, like when you buy a backpack using a discount card in a store. Bit by bit, data point by data point, companies build up a digital picture of who you are, what you like, what grabs your attention, and what makes you spend money. If you're thinking, *How dare they?!*, well, for the most part, you agreed to it. You said they could collect and even share your information when you clicked "accept" on the terms of service and privacy policies when you signed up for your social media accounts and store discount cards . . . remember?

Because the inner workings of social media algorithms are mostly kept behind locked doors, we rely on leaked documents from disgruntled staffers and the work of data scientists to figure out how they might work. Some say that social media companies probably don't have the capacity to create a very detailed digital map of every single user, that they mostly shove us into pools of users according to our similarities. Here's the pool for fourteen-year-olds who watch makeup tutorials and live in the Northern Hemisphere. Here's the pool for sixteen-year-olds who like cooking content and live in the Middle East. Others who have worked for some of the social media giants say it's much more detailed than that. They argue that even the people around you can influence this digital picture of who *you* are.

Ever notice how that protein bar your friend eats but you think tastes like chalk and moldy chocolate keeps popping up on your timeline? If your phone is often in the same location as another phone, social media companies can connect the dots. They make a web of your contacts to map your social circle, the people you hang out with both in real life and online. You are seeing some ads because your friend's phone has been detected next to your phone and their interests, habits, and likes are being added to your digital picture. You hate those chalky protein bars but now they're popping up on your feed, and so, without realizing it, you end up having a conversation about protein bars with your friend, who tells you, "If you don't like the chocolate flavor, you should try the peanut butter bars instead."

CHA-CHING.

Social media companies might know what your best friend eats and how often you hung out with them this week, and BAM! Just like that, you start to see ads for your best friend's favorite protein bar when you scroll through your timelines. Your social media behavior, your phone data, the way you shop in real life, the places you visit, and who you spend time with can be used to influence your thinking and actions.

CHA-CHING. CHA-CHING. CHA-CHING.

YOUR BRAIN ON SOCIAL MEDIA

AND YOUR BRAIN, well . . . It's not *your* fault that it's lured in by social media apps. Your brain is being manipulated, its chemistry and electrical wiring studied under a microscope, its inner workings exploited by social media bosses desperate to cash in on your attention. The people behind many large, money-hungry social media algorithms sell your time and attention to the advertisers: *Look, this person spends two whole hours on our social media platform every single day! Three hours on Sundays!* These engineers need to understand your brain because they need to know how to hook your attention and keep you online.

One thing social media designers understand well is your brain's reward system. These are parts of the brain that make you feel cozy and lovely and gushy in response to triggers like yummy food or a nice, warm hug. If you want to get technical and sound extremely impressive, the proper name for one of the brain's most important reward pathways is the mesolimbic dopamine pathway, which is connected to the ventral tegmental area, or VTA, and the nucleus accumbens. Bleh. Basically, these are parts of your brain, buried deep inside, that give you feelings of reward and pleasure. Say you get a new puppy that just loves to snuggle on your chest and look up at you with big brown puppy eyes. When the puppy blinks at you, one part of your brain's reward system (the VTA) makes a chemical called dopamine, also known as the happy hormone. Because of the puppy eyes looking straight into your eyes, the happy hormone dopamine gushes from your VTA to another part of your brain's reward system, the nucleus accumbens. The dopamine flows via the . . . you guessed it . . . mesolimbic dopamine pathway. As the dopamine gushes, it sends a signal that communicates something like this inside your brain: **OMG, AN AMAZING THING IS HAPPENING RIGHT NOW! LOOK AT THE PUPPY! REMEMBER THIS! LET'S CUDDLE PUPPIES EVERY DAY!**

The brain's reward centers are connected to other parts of the brain, parts that control what you remember and how you act. That way, you'll remember the things that made you feel good and you'll repeat whatever you were doing that released the dopamine in the first place so you can feel good over and over again. Sounds amazing, right? It is . . . except when the feel-good trigger that's making dopamine flow is the flashing button on a slot machine, or an addictive drug, or a food that is yummy but you can't stop eating. In cases like these, the slot machine/addictive drug/yummy food causes dopamine to flow, which makes you feel lovely, but then you can end up gambling/taking drugs/eating too much over and over again, even when it's bad for you, because your brain is chasing the dopamine surge and the pleasant feelings it gives.

Brain scans of heavy social media users can look similar to those of people addicted to drugs or gambling. Scientists still aren't sure if these brain changes last a long time or if they disappear when a person takes time away from social media and maybe reads books instead. Speaking of addictive drugs, the way they affect the brain teaches us something else about social media. Some drugs can reprogram the brain so that the reward centers and pathways become less sensitive to dopamine. For example, addictive drugs that cause dopamine to flow can mess up the circuit so that you need larger and larger amounts of the drug to get the same amount of dopamine flowing and the same good feelings. And by making the brain circuits less sensitive, things that used to make you feel good naturally—a cuddle from a friend, hitting a home run in baseball, that puppy looking into your eyes—don't feel as good anymore because the brain's reward system is out of whack and needs a lot more dopamine to get the same effects.

But it's not only some drugs that can reprogram the brain's reward circuits. Social media and being online can reprogram the brain too. That's because one of the amazing things about human brains is also the thing that makes them vulnerable to the worst aspects of social media. It's a phenomenon called **neuroplasticity**, and it explains how our brains can adapt and change under the influence of outside factors. Like how your brain changed when you learned to ride a bike. Or how your brain changes when you learn a second or third language, or when you study for an exam and cram so many new facts that your head starts to hurt. That's neuroplasticity—your brain adapting and growing new connections—at work.

So . . . what if you don't need to memorize so many facts because you can outsource your memory to your social media account? Like . . . *Let me upload a video of my favorite band to my page so I can remember this concert tomorrow.* Are you one of those people busy focusing their phone camera on the guitarist at the concert, watching them play from behind the lens? Scientists have been studying people like you. They want to know: Does using social media as an external memory bank change your brain? Is social media changing the way we experience and even enjoy the world?

There's a kind of memory called **transactive memory** that helps you decide what you need to store in your brain versus what information is not important enough to remember. Humans have probably been using transactive memory for as long as we've been around. You use transactive memory when you're watching football and don't really understand the play but you *do* remember which cousin knows everything about college football and so you text them to ask what just happened. Or when you call your friend to check how long it takes to cook a perfectly soft-boiled egg because you know she's a culinary queen and you don't need to waste precious brain space with information about eggs. You knew who to call because you remembered who or what those information sources were and where they were located. That's transactive memory at work.

Because social media presents the world as super fast-paced and filled with endless, ENDLESS! streams of new and absolutely-critical-to-remember, wow-this-is-such-unique-and-important-MUST-take-NOTE-of-THIS! information, scientists have wondered if social media is changing our transactive memory and if we're outsourcing a ton more of our remembering to places that are not our brain. Is social media changing the way we remember things like concerts, movies, vacations, and trips to the museum?

In one experiment, people were asked to do two things old-school style, like back in the day before there was social media. They were given instructions to watch a TED Talk and to go on a self-guided tour of a touristy place. The first group was told to absorb the experience and not share thoughts or photos on social media. Another group was told to watch the talk and go on the self-guided tour with a mind for sharing some of their experiences on social media later. Here's what happened: Those who watched the talk and went on the tour without taking photos or videos or sending tweets along the way had stronger memories of their experiences later on than those who were busy recording parts of the talk and tour so that they could upload content. It's almost as if the last group was outsourcing memories to their social media feeds instead of storing the sounds, smells, and sights in their brains. Scientists say that when we outsource our memories onto our feeds, we're using social media platforms as a "crutch," meaning we signal to our brains *Hey, no worries about storing memories of this concert/museum trip/weird lobster ice cream for sale at the seaside. I can search for the memories on social media later.*

This particular study was published in 2018, but it confirmed what many studies on social media and memory had already discovered: recording and sharing experiences on social media might lessen the memories you store in your brain and make it harder to remember details later. What was that song at the concert that made everyone cry? What was that artifact at the museum that had the longest line but looked like a weird lump of clay? Did you really eat lobster ice cream at that weird shop by the sea, or did you sniff it and refuse to eat shellfish mixed with sugar? (You could always check your social media account to find out what you did!)

Other experiments have found that taking photos of museum objects made it more difficult for visitors to remember details of what they had seen. Another study found that taking photos might leave you with better visual memories but fewer memories of the sounds and smells that you were hearing and sniffing while you were busy snapping photos.

Why does this happen? It all comes back to that valuable thing everyone is fighting for: your attention. Taking photos and sharing them while you're in the middle of a concert means you're multitasking—trying to concentrate on getting the lyrics right as you sing along, *and* zooming in *and* focusing, *and* trying to get a great shot, *and* uploading a post or making sure you can livestream the concert to people in your social network who are stuck at home. Multitasking messes with your concentration, which isn't great for absorbing the details about how the guitarist is killing that riff or how your friend force-fed you lobster ice cream and you nearly barfed on the beach.

You might think that all that time spent on social media, switching between tabs, checking DMs on one app while sending ten-second videos on another and checking the group chat on another and keeping up with notifications on a new app, makes your brain better at multitasking. But that divided attention comes at the expense of solid concentration. Scientists discovered that people who spend lots of time on social media are easier to distract than those who spend less time on social media. The person who isn't checking for notifications or switching between apps is better at staying focused.

Social media bombards you with new content constantly as the next new things—a fifteen-second video, a twenty-second dance, sixteen brand-new photos!—flash before your eyes. Researchers say this can even shrink the part of the brain that is responsible for keeping you attentive and focused.

There are particular worries about younger users, whose brains are still developing. In 2021, Facebook's plans to launch a version of Instagram called Instagram Kids for people younger than twelve was leaked by *BuzzFeed News*. "We have identified youth work as a priority for Instagram," said an internal Instagram post that was discovered by journalists. The backlash to that news was intense, so much so that Facebook quickly said it was delaying its work on Instagram Kids because of the criticism about how it might hurt the mental health of the very young. There were even comparisons to the tobacco industry's efforts to hook children into becoming lifelong customers/addicts.

Then came more revelations. Leaked Facebook documents meant only for the eyes of employees uncovered that the company knew about a link between using Instagram and suffering from depression and anxiety. Facebook's own research showed the app caused teenaged girls in particular to scrutinize their faces and bodies, and that over time this was encouraging eating disorders and mood changes in some. A few apps have banned the kinds of beauty filters that slim cheeks, straighten noses, widen eyes, plump lips, and generally morph faces into a standardized idea of what is beautiful, as if there's only one way to look "pretty." But other apps continue to let users distort waists and hips, lighten skin, or slim noses to fit a trend.

If social media is potentially hurting our brains, we should just use it less, right? That's what some say, but let's be real. Now that we know how dopamine and the reward pathways work, we understand why it's so hard to resist the urge to check for notifications, to not refresh the app in case there are new posts or messages, to not give in to the sweet, sweet temptation to swipe for fresh content just one more time.

Social media constantly bombards us with shallow rewards. **NOTIFICATION! PING! DOPAMINE! LIKE! PING! DOPA-MINE! NEW FOLLOWER! PING! DOPAMINE!** This can reprogram your brain to want more and more of the things causing dopamine to flow and making you feel great: **CLICKS. LIKES. SHARES.** More attention-grabbing content that makes you happy, sad, surprised, angry.

This cycle of dopamine and emotion is what can make it seem

impossible to put your phone down, to stop scrolling, to stop refreshing your computer browser for new updates every nine seconds. It can make it unbearable to stop switching between tabs on your laptop or phone. In fact, scientists have measured excitement levels in the brain and body and discovered we get little zings of excitement when we switch tabs to look at things that are not related to the work we're supposed to be doing! (You won't be surprised to find out that the same excitement is not seen when we switch back to the tab that has the assignment we were supposed to be working on.)

Social media is still young, but scientists have already discovered a few ways that the first two decades of these apps have changed our inner mechanics. They're not certain whether these are life-long changes or short-term ones, but they have seen changes to the parts of the brain responsible for memory, the parts responsible for our ability to focus and multitask, and even the part responsible for our thumb's sense of touch and movement, which is likely in response to all that swiping.

But let's not forget about the benefits of using social media. Friends on every continent, the instant sharing of ideas and feedback, feeling connected to people whom you might never have met offline. And there are social media apps other than the Big and Obvious ones we've focused on here. There's Goodreads, where people share book reviews and set reading goals for the year. Instead of Nextdoor, a neighborhood social media app meant to connect residents but with a sordid history of racist comments about Black neighbors, there's Front Porch Forum, which connects people who care about their community. (Nextdoor has been described as

"Twitter for old people" and "A home for racial profiling.") We'll talk more about these smaller, usually less money-hungry apps in a moment, but before we do, let's dig into the bigger apps, get back to algorithms, and unravel how social media can steer you deep down into dark and murky corners of the internet.

INTO THE RABBIT HOLE

BY NOW WE understand your brain's sensitivity to the constant pings and rapid-fire, shallow rewards of social media (**PING! DOPAMINE!**). We know how this cycle pushes users to post more "interesting," more "out-there" content, and we know that some social media algorithms boost content that riles us up and rouses intense emotions inside us, especially anger. We also know that this formula (dopamine + pressure to get more clicks and shares + addictive algorithms) can cause you to endlessly swipe and scroll until your thumb and neck ache. But what does any of this—the stuff that's happening between your thumb and your brain and the mysterious lines of code—have to do with hate crimes, a divided society, and even riots to overturn the results of a fair election?

Even though we know how social media helps spread false information, often directing people to "news" that is really false information, it's important that we map the connection between what's happening inside our brains and what unfolds online. How is it that a regular armchair swiper in search of healthy eating information and fitness inspiration can fall down a rabbit hole into extreme, hateful, and dangerous content? How does a journey that begins with curiosity about an excessively fruity diet lead you down a path that goes from 🍌🍌🍌🍌🍌 to 卐 卐 卐 卐?

Does that sound outrageous? To go from bananas to swastikas in a matter of hours? It is outrageous, but it's exactly what can happen on some social media sites. Journalists and scientists have tracked what happens to social media users on apps such as Tik-Tok and have found that what can start with an innocent search one day can land you in a dark hole of the internet watching disturbing content the very next day. There are reports of social media guiding users as young as thirteen years old toward content that encourages terrorism. This has landed some teens in jail and on terrorist lists because platforms have exposed them to hateful content that has radicalized them—pushing them toward extremist views about Black people, women, the disabled, Muslims, Jews, immigrants, and other groups.

In 2019, a sixteen-year-old boy was the youngest person ever convicted of planning terrorist attacks in the UK. Notebooks in his bedroom listed the synagogues and schools in his hometown that he planned to burn down. There were handwritten notes that said a "race war was inevitable." No one begins life hating people for their religion. Over a period of years, probably beginning with a far-right Twitter account he had followed since age thirteen, the boy was radicalized via social media and websites, including a far-right message board where he learned how to make explosives.

Teenagers are even starting up and leading extremist movements. A fifteen-year-old in England was discovered to be the mind behind what experts described as an "extreme right pro-terror" organization called the British Hand, which is made up of members who are mostly teenagers, some of them unable to even spell the word "fascist" but posting disturbing messages about killing people who were not White.

In Estonia, the "commander" (his description) behind a neo-Nazi group that spread to include members in the US and across Europe encouraged the group to bomb government buildings. The "commander" turned out to be thirteen years old.

A fourteen-year-old was arrested in Germany in 2020 when police discovered that he was making plans to attack a mosque and synagogue. And in the US, Kyle Rittenhouse, seventeen, shot three men, killing two of them, at a protest after police in Wisconsin shot a Black man named Jacob Blake. Lawsuits say the teenager followed a far-right Facebook group that posted content urging members to get guns and attack people protesting the police shooting that left Blake paralyzed.

These are just a few of the teenagers radicalized on social media in recent years. The radicalization happened as they scrolled through phones and laptops inside their homes. Now, let's pause for a second, because what's really the role of social media in this? Nazis existed before social media, and racism is hundreds of years old! Here's the thing: Social media holds the power to lift extreme ideas—ideas that mostly exist on the sidelines of society—and shove them into the mainstream. Think back to those algorithms. They are designed to boost engagement, not positivity. So when a hateful post about disabled people is getting a ton of engagement (clicks, likes, and shares), it can rapidly spread that idea to a lot more people than before the creation of social media. Social media holds the power to radicalize people who might otherwise not have been exposed to disturbing, dangerous ideas. It also uses sound and color to reward clicks, likes, and shares, something that psychologists say can make scrolling on social media feel like playing a game or even a slot machine. There's also the personal boost that happens when a thing you post gets lots of comments and likes. Social media can shower users with feelings of importance. It's easy to fall into an affirmation trap based on other people's judgement and to then feel the need to keep posting more of the same.

But again, bananas to swastikas? From one innocent search to an extremely dangerous idea? Let's retrace the step-by-step instructions of the secretive lines of code to unravel how social media can lead you down a rabbit hole.

Remember those recommendation algorithms, the ones that feed you video after video and post after post? They were designed to bring in the big dollars by keeping you online for a long time, and now, they are pushing you toward extreme content. That's because one way of keeping you online longer is to send you down a rabbit hole related to the content you were originally enjoying. Eventually that content might be further and further removed from your original search. You might wind up falling down a topsy-turvy rabbit hole that goes down and right and left and right again, curving and swinging in dark directions. That's how you might go from watching banana videos to watching videos saying Whiteness is the "pure race." Seriously.

But *you* would never click on a video like *that*! Sure, you didn't mean to. Maybe you didn't even need to click—the video just autoplayed for you. You certainly didn't type "reasons racism is great" into the search bar. You simply started off watching videos or scrolling through posts about, let's say, diets and fitness. But here's how the rabbit hole becomes deeper and murkier. The way this slippery slope twists and turns is based on the way we think some social media algorithms work ("think," because algorithms are mostly kept secret by big social media companies and the little we know about them comes from upset employees who have leaked information and from data scientists who try to reverse engineer how these slippery systems operate).

Let's begin down the rabbit hole.

We live in an image-obsessed society, so you search for healthy eating inspiration.

Up pops a list of videos. First on the list, a short video with a bright thumbnail and two million views. Must be good! It's about a girl who says she stays healthy by eating mostly bananas. Yum. **CLICK.**

Three minutes pass; the video ends. On the right-hand side of your screen is a list of related videos, and overlying the video you just watched are clickable links. One reads, "Get started now! Here's how I kick-started my weight loss journey!" **CLICK.**

Six minutes later, the video ends. More recommended videos on the right. More clickable links with recipes and advice. One says, "Here's why your last diet didn't work!! GUARANTEED WEIGHT LOSS!" **CLICK.**

You watch four more videos, maybe six . . . Who's counting? One video mentions this idea that what we put into our bodies and what we put into the soil is connected, that heavily processed foods and chemical fertilizers are a bad way to live.

You're thinking about this blood-soil connection and miss the chance to click on a recommended video. Instead, a video autoplays. This one is about eating a "pure diet."

You watch two more videos on autoplay; each argues that living on a farm is a much better idea than living in the city. You watch a teenaged influencer in England pluck carrots from the ground while two goats bounce around her knees. She chops the carrots in the field and makes a huge salad.

The next video lists "12 reasons to eat a purely vegetarian diet." It has six million views. You watch till the end and click on a recommended video, one about cooking. Two teenaged influencers in Germany prepare a meatless casserole and talk about "blood and soil." "We grew these veggies ourselves," they say, holding up bunches of parsnips. Thousands of comments gush gratitude at how the cooking videos have changed people's lives.

Another chatty cooking video. **CLICK.** This time the duo cooks spaghetti squash. (They didn't grow these vegetables; they bought them at a local farmer's market.) They don't exactly say who their idol is, but when the next video autoplays . . .

It's a newer video by them, this one with close to half a million views. The cooking duo talks about the connection between a "pure diet" and a "pure race."

See where this is going?

The influencers don't need to say that Adolf Hitler was vegetarian (you'll get to those videos eventually, thanks to the platform's recommendation algorithm), but while searching for fitness inspiration and clicking on a few cooking videos, you've landed in a sinister corner of the internet, one with videos liked by millions and commented on by thousands of people who believe Whiteness = purity.

Hitler's vegetarianism might have been disinformation, by the way, a publicity stunt by his chief minister of propaganda, Joseph Goebbels. A quick fact-check brings up a book written by Hitler's chef that lists sausages, pigeon, and turtle soup as some of the fascist leader's favorite dishes. But the claims that Hitler was vegetarian line up with the slogan "blood and soil," or *Blut und Boden* in German, a motto of the Nazi Party, which promoted farm life and linked genetic and racial purity (blood) to a land meant for White people (soil). This idea did not die in 1940s Germany. It is still circulating on social media, where apps sometimes boost or recommend this content because of the engagement it wins. In 2017, when White nationalists and fascists rioted at a "Unite the Right" rally in Charlottesville, Virginia—where 32-year-old anti-fascism protester Heather Heyer was killed by a White supremacist—the fascists chanted the phrase "blood and soil" to proclaim the US as a place only for White people.

Alt-right movements and the ideas they spread are being promoted on social media platforms, including YouTube and Reddit. Both YouTube and Reddit use algorithms that boost posts that win lots of attention and interaction. We already know why and how algorithms boost that content. And here's that booster effect again: While ideas of White nationalism and purity are considered absurd and outrageous in many places, we can find them being promoted on social media. That's because platforms driven by cash-hungry algorithms take White supremacist ideas that usually (but not always) linger on the sidelines and shove them to the tops of feeds and into "For You" and "Discovery" pages where many people stumble across them.

It's not just racist ideas being shared, and it's not just YouTube and Reddit helping them spread. After lots of complaints, TikTok eventually banned videos promoting eating disorders, but even then, an investigation by *Guardian* journalists in 2021 found that within twenty-four hours of watching videos linked to one of TikToks's most popular hashtags—#WhatIEatInADay, which is listed in videos that have a total reach of nine billion views—users were taken to content with the hashtags #IWillBeSkinny and #Thinspo and confronted with videos pushing extreme diets.

The reporters also found twenty-two TikTok hashtags promoting disordered eating *after* the ban. Among these were #SkinnyCheck with a million views, #Size0 with 1.4 million views, and #ThighGapWorkout with 2.6 million views. Clicking on #Skinny (1.7 billion views) takes users to weight-loss videos, including some where girls talk about starving themselves for days. The hashtags #WeightLossProgress and #CalorieDeficitSnacks encourage viewers to eat dangerously small amounts of food. Sixty percent of TikTok's one billion users are ages sixteen to twenty-four. That's why people were especially worried about the impact this was having on the hearts, bones, and overall health of people whose organs were still developing.

The journalists also discovered that despite the ban, when users typed #Thin into the search bar, TikTok's own search feature suggested harmful hashtags. This even included #Thinspao, a misspelling of #Thinspo. Misspellings were used as a way to get around TikTok's ban of #Thinspo.

TikTok said it uses a combination of human moderators and artificial intelligence to enforce the ban. So let's talk about those human moderators. An internal TikTok report discovered by news organization the *Intercept* in 2020 showed that TikTok moderators were told to carefully select which videos to feature on the highly influential "For You" feed. This is a place where TikTok users find posts by people they don't follow. Getting posts onto this feed gives accounts a huge, algorithm-powered boost.

So what can you do to up your chances of getting your video featured on the "For You" page? Be skinny and able-bodied. TikTok moderators were told, according to the leaked instructions, to hide videos by "ugly, poor, or disabled" people and people who had an "abnormal body shape . . . (not limited to: dwarf, acromegaly) . . . ugly facial looks . . . or facial deformities." A spokesperson for TikTok told the *Guardian* that these instructions were just an attempt to protect these users from bullying.

If the social media moderators were controlling appearance and deciding what was beautiful and what was ugly, the platform was also controlling political views and deciding what was an okay thing to believe and what was not. TikTok moderators were also instructed to delete videos promoting Taiwan's independence from China, an idea that infuriates the Chinese government, which believes Taiwan belongs to China.

The thing is, you might be happily scrolling through TikTok very much *not* looking for pro-Chinese-government content . . . so how do you wind up watching posts that argue against Taiwanese independence? (Take a guess.)

Say you're looking to get up to speed on some political stuff that's going on in the world and hoping to land on news that's well-reported and accurate. Well, you might start off looking at that stuff, but according to experiments by researchers at the Lowy Institute, if on a Monday you watch some of what they call "neutral" political stuff on TikTok, then expect to watch videos promoting racist or far-right beliefs by Tuesday. That's how intent the algorithms are on keeping you hooked online and how poorly the content is moderated, they said. This, despite TikTok's statement that it uses people and AI technology to take down inaccurate or harmful information.

We already know that recommendation algorithms mainstream ideas that (usually) live on the outskirts of society. But you might come across those same ideas IRL, say while attending an anti-racism march attended by neo-Nazi counter-protesters, so what's the big deal about coming across them on social media?

IRL, humans tend to shut out ideas that sound extreme. Say you hear an extreme idea from a friend or family member. They might even add, "I heard this wild thing . . ." or "I saw this awful thing . . ." And you would say, "Yeah, that's absurd." But when the idea is presented not by a person but via a social media feed or discovery page, it doesn't come with a "I heard this wild thing . . ." heads-up. In fact, online, the extreme idea is often presented as something that lots of people are talking about, even one that hundreds or millions of people "liked," shared, and commented on. Now you're less likely to say, "That's absurd," and you could be more likely to look at this extreme, absurd idea like something worth considering. All of a sudden, the idea of a really restricted diet or two chatty guys cooking vegetarian food and talking about the idea of a "pure bloodline" might not seem so out-there. And even if it seems absurd at first, you're noticing that millions of people have watched and liked the content, or written comments endorsing the ideas.

This comes back, again, to the hunger to hook your attention. The platforms, experts say, don't care about your well-being. What they are programmed, designed, and incentivized to chase is engagement—those precious clicks, likes, and shares. If the content getting the most comments and clicks is about what women should look like and how it's atrocious for women to be fat—as happened on Reddit in 2014 and again in 2015—then those angry, hateful, misogynistic posts will be upvoted and made visible to more people, creating a vicious loop. Tribalism? Check. Disgust and anger? Check. Lots and lots of engagement? Check. (And *cha-ching*.) Now these ideas about women's bodies are no longer on the fringes; they've been shoved to the tops of feeds. (In the case of Reddit, these 2014 and 2015 hate campaigns meant that online attacks against women festered for months and turned into IRL attacks against women too.)

Why don't the platforms just delete fascist content and block the White supremacists? They do, in some cases—even banning the president of the United States from Facebook for two years for stoking an insurrection in 2021. But attempts to block individuals aren't that helpful, say experts. Here's why. Those bans usually focus on just a handful of people who are pushing the most extreme content, ignoring how easy it is for many regular people to get sucked into the hate. A study of 100 million posts on two

Reddit forums (r/fatpeoplehate and r/[redacted-because-it-is-so-bad]) found that what ended the problem wasn't banning people; it was shutting down the forums where they gathered to spread extremist views. These forum shutdowns happened in 2015, and they went beyond anything Twitter and Facebook had done.

Shutting down toxic communities without banning individual users had this effect: Some who had posted offensive material left Reddit. We don't know what they did—they might have hopped onto another platform and acted just as badly. But some stayed, and of these people, many didn't post hateful things elsewhere on the site. In fact, their number of hateful posts decreased by 80 percent. Experts say there was less hate because the echo chambers of hate had disappeared. This is one approach to making social media a safer place for everyone, but it was a too-late approach given that the attacks had raged online and IRL for two years.

IT DOESN'T HAVE TO BE THIS WAY!

SOCIAL MEDIA ISN'T going anywhere. It has a mind-blowing power to connect people and boost ideas, ones that are great for humanity and ones that are terrible. But we can see its danger when it pushes all sorts of beliefs—ones that question the humanity of already marginalized people—to hook our eyeballs, all in the interest of bigger paychecks for the social media bosses and at the expense of users' health and world peace.

And here's another thing. Radical ideas aren't always bad; in fact, sometimes they are great. Being angry online can be an important and effective way to speak out against misogyny, anti-Semitism, racism, and other injustices. Sometimes, radical ideas that spread on social media promote democracy in places run by dictators, like in 2010 and 2011 when young people in Tunisia took to the streets after connecting on social media. They gathered to protest police brutality and demand better jobs and living conditions. More protests led to more social media posts, including videos and photos that showed horrific injuries inflicted by police, which pushed more people to take to the streets in protest. Or like in Egypt in 2010 when Wael Ghonim, a young Egyptian man, posted "We are all Khaled Said" on Facebook. He was referring to the brutal beating of a twenty-eight-year-old Egyptian who was killed by police. Thousands protested on the streets and encouraged others to join them, using Facebook and Twitter to share information.

The same platforms that boost videos about fascism can also bring together anti-racist organizers who correct dangerous false information. For every platform rewriting history or deleting posts about Taiwanese independence, there is a platform helping ordinary people overthrow tyrannical governments. And the same platforms that push extremely unhealthy diets or spread the idea that a pure diet is linked to a pure race also bring together survivors of eating disorders who find support and community online.

Things get dangerous and ugly when negative, tribal emotions spread and spread and get thrust to the tops of timelines and feeds. And with billions of humans spending hours on social media a day, and with all these threads we've talked about—mainstreaming hateful ideas, endorsing racism, encouraging violence against some groups of people, rewarding engagement with colorful emojis and playful sounds—it's easy to make the brain-belief-behavior connection and map how fringe ideas morph into real-life attacks.

But it doesn't have to be this way, and it isn't this way in every corner of the net. *An Illustrated Field Guide to Social Media* lists tons of apps that connect people around the world based on shared beliefs, locations, or just the desire to share ideas and get to know others. These apps don't put profits first. They don't boost hateful content just because it's winning lots of clicks and likes. They don't hesitate to say *bye-bye* to harmful users. While most of them need to make a basic amount of money to keep the platform going, they don't put profits ahead of people.

Many are struggling in the shadows of the big, profit-hungry platforms, but they are not giving up in their quest to connect people *without* resorting to algorithms that promote hate. *An Illustrated Field Guide to Social Media* was created by researchers at the Knight First Amendment Institute at Columbia University and the University of Massachusetts Amherst. You can check out some of the alternative apps in the guide, but what else can you do to protect your brain, your self-esteem, and your attention from the worst effects of social media?

Figure out how social media makes *you* feel. We've talked lots about results from experiments and studies about mental health and self-esteem. But what does being online and checking the apps do to your mood, mental health, and feeling of self-worth? Keep a diary to record your emotions after using social media to track if the overall effects are good or bad. Are there certain sites you enjoy more than others? Any that leave you feeling not-so-great? Writing down your feelings can help you make the connection.

While you're at it, take a week or two to monitor how often you use social media. Some apps, such as Instagram, keep track of the minutes you spend on them, but for others you can take note for yourself. Once you know how much time you spend on social media, you can take control of your schedule and decide if, as with your news diet, you want to set aside certain times of day to check for engagement, new content, and messages. Taking note of the time can prevent you from mindlessly scrolling for hours and losing track.

As with the offline world, it's impossible to avoid hate speech. But when you come across offensive content online, there are a few things you can do. One option is to report it so it's flagged to the platform. You can also block the accounts sharing the stuff, and on some apps you can block certain words.

You can also vote with your feet. If there are apps that seem to ignore hate speech and false content or even boost dangerous content when it's spreading like wildfire, or if there are apps that you notice from your mood diary leave you feeling crappy, take a break from them and consider spending less time there.

Which brings us to a final piece of advice . . . maybe the most difficult point of all. After you've figured out how much time you spend on social media and how it makes you feel, consider setting a time limit and spending some time off the apps and reading a book, or taking conversations you've seen online into real life. Social media has firmly planted its feet in our lives. It's not going anywhere, and it offers amazing connections and information, but it's important that you control its effects on your time, mood, and health.

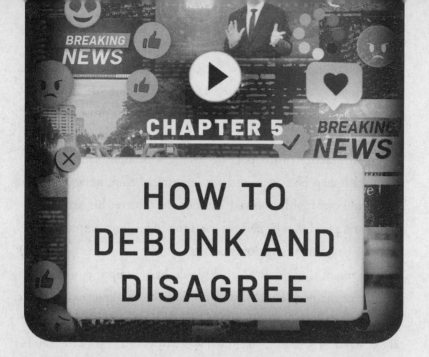

CHAPTER 5

HOW TO DEBUNK AND DISAGREE

IS THERE A VACCINE AGAINST BS?

IN THE EARLY 1700s, a deadly virus was spreading through Massa-chusetts, wiping out entire indigenous communities and killing thousands of colonizers and the people they enslaved. There was no vaccine for the variola virus, which causes smallpox. Infection meant a one-in-three chance of dying a painful, disfiguring death.

An enslaved man known by the name Onesimus had a solu-tion. Onesimus was given to a White man, Cotton Mather, in 1706, a human "gift" from the Puritan minister's Boston con-gregation. Because smallpox was killing so many people, Mather asked Onesimus if he had suffered the disease. Onesimus said something like "Yes and no."

To explain his complex answer, Onesimus described what had

happened to him as a child in Africa. A thorn, dipped in the pus of a sick person's smallpox sore, was scratched into his arm. The exposure caused a mild version of the disease that protected him from future bouts of severe or even deathly infection. It was a common practice in his part of Africa, Onesimus said, a technique that had been repeated for centuries before he was born. Onesimus apparently showed Mather the scar on his arm from the thorn, proof that he had received the lifesaving treatment that came to be known as **variolation**.

You might think that Mather would have jumped at a chance to protect the people of Massachusetts from smallpox using this advanced African technology. Nope. Mather was a racist and an enslaver. He said Onesimus was "thievish," "wicked," and "immorigerous," meaning rebellious.

A few years later, when a smallpox epidemic ravaged Boston, Mather paid closer attention to Onesimus's scientific acumen. He had even heard of a similar technique used in Turkey. In 1716, Mather wrote a letter to the Royal Society of London describing the method that Onesimus had shared, and in 1721, as the smallpox outbreak killed Bostonians, he wrote a letter to the city's doctors describing variolation. But most of them paid little attention because the scientific knowledge had come from a Black man.

One doctor read the letter and tried it out. Dr. Zabdiel Boylston used Onesimus's variolation method on his son as well as two people whom he had enslaved. White doctors were outraged that the ideas of a Black person were being taken seriously, and someone actually threw a grenade into Mather's house, punishment for sharing the idea in the first place. But variolation kept Boylston's son safe, and it worked on the two people he had enslaved. Over the following months, the doctor used Onesimus's technique on 242 people. As the viral epidemic spread over two years, only 2 percent of those Boylston treated with variolation died from smallpox. The death rate among Bostonians who had not been variolated was seven times higher.

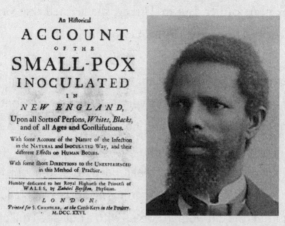

Onesimus, an enslaved African man, played a crucial role in the invention of vaccines by sharing an idea that protected Bostonians from death and disfigurement caused by smallpox. Source: "A Slave's African Medical Science Saves the Lives of Bostonians During the 1721 Smallpox Epidemic," *Washington Informer*, January 31, 2019, https://www.washingtoninformer.com/a-slaves-african-medical-science-saves-the -lives-of-bostonians-during-the-1721-smallpox-epidemic/.

Decades after Onesimus purchased his freedom from Mather, another smallpox epidemic raged. It was 1777, the Revolutionary War was being fought, and General George Washington, who remembered the suffering of smallpox from his own illness as a teenager, used Onesimus's method to protect his troops.

Three thousand miles away in England, Lady Mary Montagu, a poet and aristocrat, had made a similar discovery. Visiting

Turkey in the 1700s, she noticed how the locals had flawless skin. "I am going to tell you a thing, that will make you wish yourself here," she wrote in a letter to a friend back in England. "The small-pox, so fatal, and so general amongst us, is here entirely harmless." Montagu's skin was deeply pitted, her eyelashes had fallen out, and red rings circled her eyes ever since she survived smallpox years earlier. But in Turkey, she learned that variolation saved lives and protected the beauty of the locals.

> There is a set of old women, who make it their business to perform the operation, every autumn, in the month of September, when the great heat is abated. People send to one another to know if any of their family has a mind to have the small-pox; they make parties for this purpose, and when they are met (commonly fifteen or sixteen together) the old woman comes with a nut-shell full of the matter of the best sort of small-pox, and asks what vein you please to have opened. She immediately rips open that you offer her, with a large needle (which gives you no more pain than a common scratch) and puts into the vein as much matter as can lie upon the head of her needle, and after that, binds up the little wound with a hollow bit of shell.

Montagu's discovery was built upon by the English scientist Edward Jenner, who switched the pus of smallpox sufferers for a different infectious source: cowpox sores on the hands of milkmaids. Jenner used an idea derived from Mary Montagu and

Onesimus to develop the first smallpox vaccine in 1796. (The Latin word for cow, *vacca*, gave us the term "vaccination.") To this day, smallpox remains the only infectious human disease that has been successfully eradicated from the earth—thanks to Onesimus, Mary Montagu, and Edward Jenner. (Guess which of the three received all the credit?)

As fascinating as all this is, what does it have to do with protecting our brains from BS? In the 1960s, an American psychologist applied this medical thinking about preventing disease in our bodies to preventing our brains from being swayed by falsehoods.

William McGuire thought that if disease can be prevented by giving a small and weakened dose of a bug, such as smallpox or cowpox, to a person, then maybe we could protect people from believing falsehoods by exposing them to a small and weakened dose of a lie.

Vaccines work by giving the immune system a heads-up about an incoming invader. By offering the body a small or weakened piece of a virus or bacterium, they allow the immune system to "study" the threat and get ready to fight off a future infection. One way the immune system prepares is by making antibodies. Antibodies are large proteins that seek out invaders, latch on to them, and defend the body against attack.

The US had recently been at war with North Korea in the hopes of quelling the rise of communism, and McGuire was worried that Korean forces would take a page out of the Soviet Union's disinformation playbook and brainwash Americans. So he wondered if small, weakened doses of a lie would help Americans develop "intellectual antibodies." McGuire called his BS vaccine

inoculation theory. It's also known as prebunking. It wouldn't protect against bugs, but it could, McGuire thought, protect a person from believing in propaganda and disinformation.

For example, if you believe that a terrible tragedy at a concert where people were crushed to death occurred because crowd safety wasn't taken seriously by the concert organizers, but then someone comes along and tries to convince you that the concert was actually a satanic ritual and the deaths were planned, then McGuire hoped his method of developing intellectual antibodies would help you hold on to your original belief.

You'd still hear the false counterarguments: *It was a satanic cult; how else can you explain how so many died in the same area?* Or, *What the police are saying doesn't add up. They're trying to cover up that it was really a satanic ritual. Blah blah.* But because of the "intellectual antibodies" made using McGuire's technique, you'll stick with your belief that crowd safety was poorly managed and concerts are generally safe and not places of satanic worship. McGuire was interested in helping you hold on to that original belief, the one that you had formed based on good evidence.

But how did it work? McGuire said a "vaccine" against false information, the kind that would help you produce "intellectual antibodies," did two things: First, it issued a threat that served as a warning that false information was headed your way, almost like an alarm that rings to say "Incoming BS! Watch out!" Second, it made you think of responses to challenge the false information that you were about to hear. (McGuire called these responses "counterarguments.")

The warning makes you pay attention to how vulnerable your

beliefs might be. You might start thinking about what you know and *don't* know about satanic cults and concert safety. McGuire ran experiments that found noticing the vulnerabilities of your original belief can trigger a strengthening of the belief. *What do you mean someone's going to tell me to watch out for Satan worshippers at the gig next week? I've been going to this band's shows for years.*

This brings us to the second element of the BS vaccine. The threat warning makes you come up with responses, or counterarguments, to the incoming false information. You might think, *Okay, so I'm going to be told that when bad things happen at concerts, it's because of pre-planned satanic rituals blah blah. But this information is untrue because the evidence points to poor crowd control and not a cult.*

The threat warning prompted you to develop responses to the incoming false information. Together, the threat warning and the counterarguments strengthened your belief that concerts are generally safe from satanic worship. They made you more resistant to persuasion. Noticing the very thing we don't like to address—the vulnerability of our beliefs—can help us develop resistance to persuasion.

A modern way to use inoculation theory has been developed by John Cook, a researcher in Australia, who suggests this four-step prebunking method. First, lead with the facts if the facts are clear, pithy, and sticky. Keep things simple and fit them into a story. Second, warn just once that some BS is incoming. Third, explain how the myth is spreading a lie. Fourth, finish by reinforcing the first fact a second time and making sure to provide an alternative explanation for whatever the BS is claiming to explain.

Inoculation theory has been used to help people say no to cigarettes and say yes to safer sex. In the case of teen smoking, high school students "vaccinated" junior high students against smoking. First the junior high school students were told, *Hey, did you know peer pressure is really persuasive and actually makes a lot of people start smoking?* After the warning came the chance to role-play a scenario where the junior high students were called cowards by older students for not trying a cigarette. The younger students could practice how they might successfully react to the peer pressure. Students who received the psychological vaccine—in the form of the warning and role-play—were 50 percent less likely to become smokers than students who were not immunized against peer pressure to start smoking.

In the case of preventing teen pregnancy, sexually transmitted infections, and drug use, programs that used inoculation theory had success rates of 30 to 70 percent, meaning up to 7 out of 10 people were less likely to engage in harmful behaviors after receiving the psychological vaccine.

McGuire's research began not because he was particularly concerned about smoking or teen pregnancy, but because he was worried about how ridiculously easy it is to convince humans of anything . . . even that brushing our teeth could be bad for us. It is easy to dupe us because we like to form a belief, latch on to it, protect it, and NEVER practice defending it.

Challenge your beliefs! Practice defending your beliefs! That's what McGuire recommended and what modern-day scientists who study critical thinking recommend too.

If only. Too often we go out of our way to safeguard our

beliefs and *not* question them. We surround ourselves with people who think just like us and with books and news programs that only reaffirm our beliefs. Any hint of a challenge makes us feel attacked—even though it's a *belief* that's being challenged, not our humanity. So we stick to our cozy echo chambers.

It's exciting to know there is a scientific method—a BS vaccine!—that can protect us from falling for lies. But what if McGuire's findings were put to *bad* use and the inner workings of our susceptible brains, the ways we establish and clutch on to our beliefs, were exploited? And what if some of your existing beliefs are based on wrong information and actually *do* need to be challenged and updated? We don't want to be resistant to all persuasion! Some instances of questioning and testing can be helpful.

You probably won't be surprised to know that it didn't take long for inoculation theory to be exploited by advertisers intent on selling all kinds of products. It's been used to sell alcohol, cigarettes, and more. Even worse is the way governments have used inoculation-theory-like strategies to manipulate people whose beliefs the government dislikes. One example is China's attacks on Uighur Muslims, which have been going on for decades.

The attacks on the World Trade Center in the US on September 11, 2001, gave rise to widespread Islamophobia in many parts of the world, including China, where government officials used the attacks to justify the persecution of Muslims. And then there were massacres like the 2009 Ürümqi Massacre, the 2009 Shaoguan incident, and the 2014 Kunming attack, all of which led to Muslims being interrogated and spied upon. Chinese officials especially targeted people in the Uighur and Kazakh ethnic groups, most of whom are Muslim. Starting in 2014, more than a million Uighurs and Kazakhs, nearly all of them Muslim, were sent to secret "reeducation camps" where government workers inoculated them against Islamic beliefs.

Sanitized tours of the camps were given in an attempt to convince foreign leaders and journalists that the camps were more like boarding schools and less like concentration camps. Except attendance was not optional; Muslims were detained in the camps, and surveillance video showed hundreds of blindfolded men with their heads shaved and hands tied behind their backs. It's the largest imprisonment and persecution of religious and ethnic minorities since the Second World War.

What happens inside the camps is described by human rights lawyers as "mass brainwashing" and systemic indoctrination. Imprisoned Muslims are made to drink alcohol, which their faith prohibits, and told that their religion is backward and wrong.

Techniques to manipulate people's beliefs are invaluable for those who want to control others—even brainwash entire groups of people that the faith they were brought up in is evil. There are many more examples like this, including the Nazi Party's indoctrination of German citizens that Jews, LGBTQI people, and the disabled—among others—were inferior and did not deserve to live. There are modern-day examples too, such as how some American lawmakers, with help from journalists, pushed a false narrative that Black people commit crimes at higher rates than White people. You can see the results of this effort by taking a look at who is behind bars in American jails and prisons. It is overwhelmingly and disproportionately Black people and other minoritized groups.

But just because these kinds of techniques have been used for evil doesn't mean we can't use them in our quest to resist false information. In fact, ever since McGuire introduced and proved the concept of inoculation theory, philosophers, psychologists, and political scientists from all around the world have been expanding on his techniques.

Andy Norman, an American philosopher, coined the term **cognitive immunology** to help us think of the brain as having its own defense system. He imagines an entire "mental immune system" where doubts and reservations zip around your beliefs, acting like antibodies and white blood cells, except instead of protecting you from infection, these doubts and reservations act like antibodies that protect you from "mind parasites." Mind parasites are bad ideas and false information that you want to keep out.

While you want to keep the mind parasites out, you don't want to block the entry of good ideas. You might hold beliefs that *need* to be challenged and changed. We all fall for lies at some point, and sometimes they stick in our brains for years and years. Doubts and reservations about beliefs are good for you. Listen to those doubts, test your beliefs, and see if they stand up to the challenge.

Do you believe all the same things now that you did when you were eight years old? Hopefully not. Hopefully, you have greatly expanded your beliefs based on all the things that you have learned since then. Unfortunately, we're plagued with "mental disruptors," says Norman. These disruptors get in the way of updating our beliefs and letting good ideas in—kind of the flip side to McGuire's theory, which was focused mostly on resistance to persuasion.

One example of a mental disruptor is a fixed mindset. It's a sign of a broken mental immune system. Being set in your ways and saying, "I believe what I believe and you'll never make me change my mind!" is not a great way to experience the world. A fixed set of beliefs means you limit your growth and learning. Maybe many of your beliefs are based on good information and are worth protecting. But if they can't stand up to a challenge, how great can they be?

We are expanding the idea of what a mental vaccine against false information could look like, based on the work of researchers such as McGuire and Norman. How can we protect ourselves from persuasion by false information while staying open-minded enough to let in new ideas, even uncomfortable ones that challenge our existing beliefs?

"Rumor vaccines" aren't literal vaccines in syringes, of course. No one is going to poke you in the butt cheek or arm to immunize you against BS. But being given a heads-up about incoming threats to your beliefs, noticing your vulnerabilities, learning to be okay with doubts and reservations, challenging your beliefs, and forming counterarguments to false information boost the "intellectual antibodies" needed to keep you safe. It's like how vaccines against flu give you a smidgen of the flu virus (an inactivated version) so your body can make protective antibodies and prepare for future attacks.

And just the way mass vaccination programs immunize lots of people against disease to achieve **herd immunity**—a high level of protection across a large group, also known as **community immunity**, which stops disease outbreaks—rumor immunization using a BS vaccine could protect millions of people by stopping the viral spread of false information. If each of us were better at telling apart fact and falsehood, if each of us were more comfortable with challenging our beliefs, assessing new information, and updating what we believe, we might slow down or even stop the massive spread of false information from one person to another.

Inoculation theory was used to protect people against false information during the COVID-19 pandemic. But instead of using inoculation theory to protect against pandemic disinformation specifically, psychologists at the University of Cambridge used a different approach. They created a computer game that uses inoculation theory to protect more broadly against the many *ways* that people are duped, just like what we said about learning the five FLICC strategies and then using a logic-based approach to fighting lies.

We learned about some other methods for making lies believable and viral in chapters one and two. They included using language to trigger strong emotions, such as rage or disgust; using photos and videos out of context, or editing the photos and videos; and fabricating information in lots of other ways to manipulate people.

The *Bad News Game* gives you, the player, the chance to put these deceitful tactics into action! You can unleash Twitter bots and fake experts, manipulate photos to spread false information, and even pose as the editor of a newspaper. Your goal is to spread false information far and wide and to mislead as many people as possible (all within the safety of the game world). But at the same time, you must keep a close eye on your "credibility score."

If your score drops, it means people are less likely to believe the false information you are spreading, and you lose the game. **WAH WAH WAH.**

The *Bad News Game* exposes players to the many ways that people can be duped. In a study of fifteen thousand people, those who played the *Bad News Game* were less likely to be swayed by false information in real life. Spreading disinformation in the game gave players mental immunity against disinformation in the real world. The *Bad News Game* worked like a psychological vaccine against BS.

The creators of the *Bad News Game* also made a game called *Go Viral!* that takes five minutes to play. They wanted to see how long a five-minute "dose" would last in protecting players against BS, and they discovered that it protected a person against misinformation (to some extent) for up to three months. After that . . . a booster shot was needed.

Source: getbadnews.com/en.

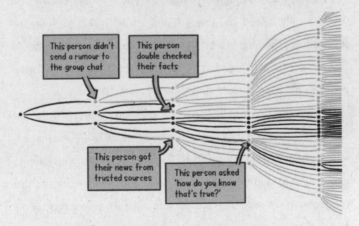

One savvy person can stop a dangerous lie from going viral and "infecting" others. This diagram from the World Health Organization shows how individuals can make a big impact in stopping the spread of false information when they know how to spot lies and myths that are spreading like wildfire. Source: WHO page on infodemics, https://www.who.int/news-room/spotlight/let-s-flatten-the-infodemic-curve.

SIDEBAR: CRITICAL ~~THINKING~~ *FEELING?*

WE'RE TALKING ABOUT IMPORTANT THINGS LIKE FACTS and biases, mental shortcuts, and the impact stories make on our brain chemistry. So what do feelings have to do with any of this serious stuff?

Some even say we need to leave our emotions OUT of this whole business of critical thinking, since critical thinking focuses on carefully collecting evidence, listening to arguments, analyzing information, and using all these moving parts to guide our beliefs and actions. They argue that reasoning and evaluating need to happen independently of our feelings. Some say that feelings make us act in irrational ways and believe in things that aren't true.

But not everyone agrees. First, are you a robot? Because if you're a fully flawed and lovely human, then trying to separate feeling from thinking is a bit like separating words from a book. The two are tangled together in ways that you can't unravel. That's probably because thinking and feeling belong together.

If you were told that in 2020, one in seven children in America were not sure where their next meal would come from, and that 2.5 million children were houseless that year (that's one in thirty American children), and then you were asked to consider solutions to the problems of childhood hunger and houselessness, you'd likely feel sad, angry, shocked, and possibly disturbed and disgusted. Even as you thought critically about the information and weighed possible solutions, you'd have feelings about the millions of children facing these horrors. Probably very strong feelings.

While critical thinking can lead to feelings, the opposite can also be true. Intense feelings about a topic can help us understand the importance of an issue and apply our critical thinking skills. And anyway, ignoring or avoiding feelings is useless. Ever felt angry and had someone say to your face over and over, "Don't be angry! Just relax!" Ugh, it's the most annoying thing ever. Just hearing that can drive you to fury!

So instead of brushing our feelings under the rug, we can add critical *feeling* to our critical *thinking* tool kit. Critical feeling has been around for as long as humans have existed, but the first person who is said to have documented it is Confucius, the Chinese philosopher born in 551 BC, who gave us teachings like this: "Wheresoever you go, go with all your heart." Confucius was all about heart, about using feelings as a guide.

Confucius. Source: Public domain.

Confucius suggested looking inward to consider if what you feel at a given time is appropriate, and that if it is appropriate for the time, place, and topic, then you should lean into those feelings to explore what they have to teach you.

Understanding our emotions can guide us to think deeply about issues. Our feelings can even act as alarm bells that remind us when we are stepping out of our comfort zone. For example, say a friend asks why you're not vegetarian, and you recall bits of a study that argued that ethical farming and moderate amounts of meat in your diet were actually good for the environment because . . . But wait; you can't really remember the main argument and this cool info-graphic they used to explain everything . . . so you get mad. "Ugh! Why are you always being high and mighty about your diet and giving me a hard time just because I like chicken wings on game night?!" Umm, those are some emotions you're exhibiting. What are they? Frustration? A bit of anger? Maybe those emotions are signs that your evidence base for eating meat isn't quite as robust as you'd like it to be, and now you're thinking about the holes in that particular study and considering that you might need to go back to the drawing board to reconsider your beliefs and possibly update them. Yeah, it's a bit awkward to sometimes doubt and go back on what you believe, but it's always okay to look at the evidence again and update the strength of your beliefs.

Recognizing and admitting to yourself that you felt frustrated and a bit angry—instead of pushing those useful feelings away—can help you grow as a person (and hopefully help you to feel less annoyed the next time someone asks why you insist on eating chicken wings).

PREBUNKING VERSUS DEBUNKING

INOCULATION THEORY IS sometimes called **prebunking**, because it gives a heads-up about false information *before* the falsehood goes viral and lands on phone screens, computer screens, TV screens, airwaves, front pages of newspapers . . . basically everywhere.

Debunking is different from prebunking. Debunking is when false information is explained to be wrong *after* people have already been exposed to the lies. For example, say you read on social media that COVID-19 vaccines made using messenger RNA (a small piece of genetic code) interfere with a person's DNA. That's not true, but you only hear that it might be untrue *after* you've heard the lie. At that point, it might be too late to correct your beliefs, according to some scientists who argue that you're more likely to stick with what you first heard.

They say that's because of a problem called the **continued influence effect**. The continued influence effect is when fact-checking *after* a person has been exposed to false information turns out to be ineffective. It can happen because the inaccurate information they saw *first* continues to influence their beliefs and perspectives, even though someone has tried to correct them.

Another thing that can happen when you try to correct someone's beliefs is the backfire effect. We learned about this problem in chapter two. The backfire effect is when telling someone their belief is based on wrong information causes them to dig their heels in even deeper in defense of the false belief! Not only that, but the backfire effect can also lead people to reject the correction *and* create counterarguments to push back against the truth!

Thankfully, some scientists say the backfire effect does not happen as commonly as we might fear. (They say it's more likely a person will push back against what you are saying without actually creating counterarguments to the truth.) But it's important to keep in mind that the obvious approach to correcting someone—telling them their belief is based on false information and shoving more facts at them—is not the most effective approach. It can literally backfire.

Could debunking false information help the false information spread? Some scientists warn that repeating a falsehood so that you can debunk it gives the false information a platform and more oxygen. But others share evidence that careful debunking, done properly (more on exactly how to do that in the next pages), can help lead people away from false information that might otherwise incorrectly guide their beliefs.

In fact, when it comes to online news, studies have found that debunking false information can be more effective than prebunking. When researchers at the Massachusetts Institute of Technology ran an experiment with nearly 3,000 people, the results shocked them. Giving people a heads-up that an online news headline was false did not help them avoid falling for the falsehood. That was the opposite of what the scientists were expecting. They thought a warning *before* the post would be more helpful. Instead, when a warning came *after* the false online news, readers were nearly five times more likely to understand that the information was not to be believed. Debunking beat prebunking.

But why were people better guided by fact-checks that came *after* the false information? Two reasons come to mind. Letting people read the news and come up with their own impression first and then adding a label that says "sorry, this is false" acts as feedback. Studies have found that offering feedback helps correct information stick. Then there's something called the **concurrent storage hypothesis**, which is another way of saying that humans are capable of holding false information *and* corrections in their minds at the same time. Sticking a label that says FALSE before a lie won't necessarily put someone off reading the news in the first place. It might even make them feel as if they are being coerced to stay away from that particular headline or story. But allowing them to read the news and *then* informing them it contains false information can nudge them toward reconsidering what they just read and could help them update their beliefs.

Sigh. If only our brains were less complicated. Given all you now know about the weird and wonderful ways in which our brains work, the cognitive biases and heuristics (mental shortcuts) that can trip us up even as they try to help us out, and the many ways false information can be made to look credible (not to mention the powerful tools that help lies go viral), you might want to throw your hands up and say, "There's no way to fight this mess!"

But there are powerful ways to counter false information and successfully encourage people to challenge their beliefs.

HOW TO DISAGREE

CAM PUT HER phone facedown on the desk. Another day, another shooting. This time in a school, which put her on edge as she packed her bag for Tuesday's classes. What made it worse was that every time there was a shooting, her mom repeated this same lie: mass shooters are people with mental illness. Cam had checked the evidence and seen that most mass shooters are not mentally ill and that this lie hurts people who really do suffer with conditions like depression or schizophrenia. She thought of her best friend, who had a severe anxiety disorder, and wondered how he was feeling knowing his condition was being used as an excuse to explain a terrible person's behavior.

Dozens of text messages passed between Cam's and her mom's phones as they paced in their rooms on opposite sides of the house. Cam was incredulous that after years of warning her mom about the poor quality of the "news" she watched, her mom was still falling for false information. On the other hand, Cam's mother believed her daughter was naïve and unable to separate fact from fiction. She told Cam to protect herself from brainwashing by the "mainstream media."

Neither daughter nor mother dared to bring the conversation up at dinner. This was their new thing: argue over text and try to keep the peace when talking in person. But the tension was so thick you could cut it with the steak knives Cam's mom was setting on the table.

Their text messages were tense enough, crammed with all-caps words and too many exclamation marks. Their once loving relationship, which consisted of watching reality TV together and obsessing over who was kicked off the latest talent shows, deteriorated into an angry sequence of texts every time there was a mass shooting. Which was all too often. Both worried that a conversation might spark an all-out shouting match, and they were already exhausted from staying up to watch the nightly news—on very different channels—to understand the reaction to the latest tragedy.

Cam called her aunt, a college professor, to vent about her heartache. "I'm really worried about Mom because if she can believe this lie about mental illness and shootings, then what conspiracy theory will she fall for next?" She felt she understood that her mom was like so many other people who were sucked in by daily TV shows that fed them misinformation and disinformation. But she didn't know how to get her mom to question what she was watching.

Cam had been texting and emailing her mother links to news stories about mass shootings and what can be done to prevent them. She had hoped that by sharing fact-checked reporting that was debunking the lies about people with mental illness, she would protect her mother from falling for false information. But Cam's aunt reminded her that it was possible to have an open, calm discussion—in person—and air out their views.

"You say that, but you don't really know how it is!" Cam said, squeezing her lips together at the end of the sentence and wishing she herself had sounded a little less irate. "I don't know how I can help her see that she's being brainwashed. You don't get it. It's like this *every* single time!"

"Deep breath, Cam," said her aunt. "Let's start with this: Talking with your mom about this topic is not going to be a one-and-done conversation. It's going to be a process."

"You mean we're going to need to talk about it a bunch of times?" said Cam.

"Exactly. There's a lot of tension between you two right now. Heck, there's a lot of tension between everyone. The entire country is on edge. We're all feeling unsettled. So for you two to reach any kind of consensus, even miniscule shifts in understanding, you're going to have to start with reconnecting and building back your relationship."

"I mean, our relationship isn't bad or anything," said Cam, quietly. "It's just the news she's watching and the lies she repeats. She doesn't know how to fact-check. It's so annoying."

Cam's aunt made several *uh-huh*s and *mmm-hmm*s as her niece spoke. "Just have a conversation with your mom where you're not going straight to the thing that gets you both extremely heated," she said.

Cam replied, "Wait, you're saying I should go down and ask her if she wants to watch the new reality TV show we've been taping? Because I don't know if I can have a fake conversation like that when I'm so upset and she's thinking I'm too ignorant to understand her perspective!"

"I'm not saying ignore the elephant in the room. You can even address it up front and say something like, 'Mom, I know you're ignoring those news articles I sent you, but it's okay, and I miss making our trays of TV snacks. Can we just sit and watch the show together?'"

"That seems so fake! We're not talking about a disagreement over a *movie*! This is literally a life-and-death issue. You can't make it sound like conspiracy theories are benign and maybe a bit stressful when you see how much damage they are doing."

"I agree, and I'm not downplaying the seriousness of this at all, but imagine a situation where you talk to your mom and you get straight to talking about the news. How do you think that would go?"

"I honestly think we'd both end up shouting and then both end up sobbing. That's why dinners are so quiet on days like this." Cam paused. "I can't believe this is happening to us. Disagreements have never gotten *this* bad. We're so close."

"It's really hard, and I'm sorry you're going through it," said her aunt. "I know you're aware that you and your mom are not the only ones, not that it's any consolation. But researchers have been studying polarization for years and looking for ways that we can have difficult conversations when people are extremely opposed to each other's ideas and beliefs. Can I tell you some of the things they've learned and share some advice for dealing with situations like this?"

Cam was all ears.

THE TEN STEPS FOR EFFECTIVE DISAGREEMENTS

PICK YOUR BATTLES

The first piece of advice, even before diving into the trove of strategies for tackling difficult conversations, is to ask yourself these questions: Is it safe for you to challenge this person's belief? Is it worth your energy? Do you have enough time for a meaningful conversation? Is this the right place to have this difficult discussion? Can this person even be engaged in a conversation in your current environment? (For example, you might be on a busy train, in a store, at a stressful family dinner, or at school.)

Next, think about the content of the discussion. Is this person or group sharing beliefs that challenge the right of marginalized people to live freely or even exist? For example, are they saying inaccurate things about the intellect of Black people, or the traditions of Muslim people, or the rights of queer people?

You might take these things into account and decide not to engage in a discussion. Walking away from a polarized conversation does not mean you are weak or that you have been defeated. Context is important. If two people are in line for movie tickets and saying Islamophobic things, the young Muslim woman who is standing behind them wearing a hijab (and therefore appearing visibly Muslim) might choose to stay silent. She's alone. She can't spot any other visibly Muslim people, and no one else is making eye contact with her or causing a stir about the conversation. On the other hand, she might say, "EXCUSE YOU? WHAT DID YOU SAY?!" The decision is hers and ideally is based on her ability to stay safe while countering the pair's incredible ignorance.

A young cisgender straight man from a wealthy family who is set to inherit the family business might play things differently. At a family dinner, his uncle, who is head of the family cake business, says he would never employ bakers who had served time in prison or jail. "Absolutely not," the uncle says. "Those people are beyond redemption, and they are dangerous to the frosting industry." A chunk of potato gets stuck in the young man's throat and he splutters and coughs. All eyes are on him. Should he challenge his uncle or let the ignorance go unchallenged? The stakes are different for him.

If you are a person who was formerly imprisoned and you approach the uncle to inquire about job vacancies, and he says to you, "Get out of here! I don't like your kind!," not only has he violated the law in many parts of the world, but you, a formerly incarcerated person who happens to be a brilliant baker, are unlikely to sway his belief in one brief encounter. Given the harshness and ignorance of his beliefs, you might take a swift mental shortcut that leads you to think, *Oh, this man might think everyone who has spent time in prison is a violent person. If he thinks that I'm violent, he could attack me and think he's justified in protecting himself. Time to leave.*

Context is key, and so is your safety. In Cam's case, it's her mother whom she is in disagreement with, and she's invested enough in that relationship to want to make a change. She also has the time and space to engage in a series of discussions, which leads us to the next piece of advice.

PREPARE FOR MORE THAN ONE CHAT

It's unlikely that one brief conversation will put to rest a deeply emotional and difficult debate. If Cam approaches the conversation thinking, *This is my one and only chance to convince Mom that she is totally wrong!*, she is setting herself up for failure. Cam and her mother's first talk after a period of avoiding one another might focus on a topic that is not immediately about school shootings and gun control (maybe they'll talk about lasagna or Cam's new poem) while showing their love and respect for one another. Like Cam says, it would feel fake to avoid the elephant in the room, but they could bring up the issue of gun control laws and say, "Let's talk about that a bit later. Right now, I just want to hear about how you are doing. . . ."

This opens the door for more conversations instead of shutting down communication forever. This initial conversation can be used to set the tone, reestablish boundaries, display compassion and empathy, and get ready for following discussions that really get to the heart of the disagreement.

ASK QUESTIONS, THEN LISTEN (LIKE, *REALLY* LISTEN)

Shifting a tense disagreement where all parties feel attacked to a productive and healthy conversation that can move toward resolution requires listening. Not listening as in "Yeah, yeah, I hear what you're saying, but . . ." We're talking about deep, active listening. The kind where you shut up while the other person is talking and listen to every word they share.

Sounds easy, but think of the last heated disagreement you were in, the time when your heart was beating fast, you were starting to sweat, and you could feel your muscles tense and your blood pressure rise. Were you really listening to the other person? Chances are that while they were speaking, you were stockpiling all the things you were about to say to prove to them that they were utterly wrong. If you were actively listening, you would not be thinking about what you were going to say next. You would be listening carefully to everything the other person was saying.

This is difficult. Like, really, really difficult. Imagine someone saying, "Ugh, ice cream is just the most disgusting food," and having to listen—without judgement—and ask questions. Imagine. It feels almost impossible. But if you were to jump in and say, "What is wrong with you?! Ice cream is the most delectable delicacy on the planet, and you are wrong wrong wrong wrong wrong!," you'll never understand how or why they came to hold such a belief.

An active listening technique called **looping** can be helpful. Looping, short for "completing the loop of understanding," shows the other person that you really are listening to what they are saying. Here's how it works. You ask the person you're disagreeing with "Why on earth would you hate ice cream?" and you give them time to answer. They say, "I just don't like it." You give them more space, and they say, "And this one time, when I was six or seven, I ate vanilla ice cream and I had explosive diarrhea." Instead of responding with "But that was *one* time and it was ages ago and why would you hate *all* ice cream forever and ever just because of that *one* time . . . !", you take a deep breath and use looping to say, "So it sounds like you got really sick from eating ice cream once and you haven't liked it since then. Is that right?" And they might respond, "Well, yes, and this other time I was on a trip and the hostess gave me a small tub of ice cream straight out of the deep freezer, and it was so cold that the ice cream burned my lips and tongue and I had blisters that lasted two weeks."

You've now garnered a new piece of information. The other person might not have even been willing to share this new context had you not looped back on their first story about getting sick. To continue looping, you might say, "Wow, I'm sorry to hear that you were injured from eating ice cream." Because it's obvious that you are truly paying attention, they might even add, "It's not just that. Both those times I didn't even *want* ice cream. I was forced to eat it by my dad, and I hate being forced to do anything." Now they have added even more context that helps you better understand why they believe what they believe. You've come to a place of deeper understanding, and they feel listened to, which helps them share more. Looping creates a feedback loop of empathy, comfort, and sharing.

Looping is powerful because you're echoing back important pieces of the conversation and checking in that your understanding is correct. But more than that, looping shows the other person that you are paying attention to what they are saying and feeling.

Never underestimate the impact of being heard. So much of the time, we are in conversation with people who have a million things ricocheting through their heads. We all do it. We're concentrating, but then our attention drifts to the puppy wagging its tail across the street and the mac and cheese we plan to eat for dinner and . . . "Hmm, what was that you were saying . . . ?"

Other times, especially in challenging conversations, we're stuck in our own heads, thinking of what we'll say next that could convince the other person that they are wrong and we are right. (This is called **stockpiling thoughts**.) Meanwhile, the other person is talking and possibly sharing key information that could help bring the conversation to a place of understanding.

Looping forces you to focus. It helps the person you're speaking with feel that they are in conversation with someone who cares. On the flip side, not being properly listened to can have all sorts of negative effects. Feeling ignored or unheard can make people defensive, reluctant to share, even anxious. They might cross their arms, stare at the ground, and start to disengage from the conversation. None of that is helpful for resolving a disagreement.

Something interesting happens when you create space for people to share more: They begin to notice their own inconsistencies. They even admit to them. "Huh, I guess getting sick a couple of times from eating ice cream doesn't mean all ice cream is bad. Maybe . . . I might give it a try again . . . when no one is forcing me to eat a double scoop of vanilla bean!"

Asking open-ended questions and making the other person feel like they are being listened to can help them open up, which can stop you from falling into the assumption trap. There can be a temptation to make assumptions about a person based on one belief they hold. ("I bet this ice cream–hating person also thinks puppies are evil, and I bet they eat sardines for breakfast!")

But you'd be basing those assumptions on just one thing that they have shared. Sometimes this kind of mental shortcut might be useful: *People who oppose the use of fossil fuels often support tax cuts for those buying an electric car . . . maybe.* But other times, assumptions can lead you down a dangerous path.

By asking questions and listening deeply, without butting in or rolling your eyes or cutting them off while they answer, you can gather information. This information, about why they believe what they believe, will be crucial later on in the conversation.

Before we get to that part, remember what we learned in chapter two. Challenging a belief can feel, to the holder of that belief, as if you are attacking *them* as a person. Saying "OMG, but ice cream is the food of the gods!" can feel like an attack on *them*, not only a challenge to one belief that they hold. Once a person feels under attack, they double down on their belief and close themselves off from listening to any conflicting information that you might want to share.

Does all this mean you should never challenge someone? Definitely not. But the goal is to have a debate about the issues in a way that never feels like an attack against the person. You want to guide them to a place where they feel they are choosing to question, examine, and change their perspective *themselves*.

In Cam's case, after reestablishing her relationship with her mother, she might say, "I know this topic gets emotional for us, Mom, but I do want to understand why you believe this false information about mental illness and mass shootings, especially school shootings, which freak me out so much. I feel like I can't talk to you about something that makes me really, really anxious. Can you say more about what you believe?" The tone of Cam's voice and her body language are making time and space for her mother to answer. This can help her mom feel that it's okay for her to share her thoughts and that Cam is paying attention in a caring way. If Cam uses the looping technique, studies find that Cam's mother is much more likely to share information and make more interesting points, which can help the pair reach a place of understanding, even if they choose not to agree about everything.

Over time, broad questions and deep listening can help soften tension and help people understand that they are not under attack. A conversation about polarizing topics can start to feel more like an interesting and thought-provoking chat and less like a confrontation.

USE THE PRINCIPLE OF CHARITY

You can be charitable or uncharitable when listening to someone's point of view. For example, if a person screws up their face and says, "This tastes like pond water," while slurping on a hemp protein-wheatgrass-algae smoothie, an uncharitable response would be, "OMG, do you drink pond water? How do you know what pond water tastes like?" The charitable approach would be to think the smoothie drinker is speaking figuratively, not literally, and that the green goo tastes gross.

The **principle of charity** is a critical thinking idea that says you should assume the best possible interpretation of a person's argument. (This is an example of a time when making an assumption can benefit everyone.) When someone states an argument that you could interpret as logical *or* illogical, the principle of charity encourages you to assume the logical interpretation, so long as it's reasonable to do that.

Going even further, you can take their argument, put it into its strongest possible form, and *then* evaluate its strengths and weaknesses. The goal of this principle is to take on a default position that the person you are in conversation with is a smart, rational truth-teller and not an ignorant, irrational liar. The principle of charity helps you avoid making the assumption that every argument you hear is silly and full of falsehoods.

One way of practicing the principle of charity is to use a version of the looping technique. Here, you repeat the other person's argument back to them to make it clear that you are listening, but you also edit their argument a little to express it in the strongest possible way. So if they said, "People who buy puppies from pet shops are cruel and they hurt animals," you could think for a moment about how to strengthen their argument and respond like this: "What I'm hearing you say is that buying a puppy from a pet shop is possibly unethical, maybe because it's hard to tell which pet shops buy puppies from unscrupulous people who overbreed dogs in puppy mills, and because animal rescue shelters are packed with dogs that need adopting. Am I on the right track?" The other person might even listen to you and say, "Yes, that's actually what I meant. Thanks for putting it so clearly."

Next, you take this argument, which is now packaged in its strongest possible form, and you figure out which parts you do agree with, if any. You follow this by telling your conversation partner—who is now saying that all pet shops should be permanently banned—what you've learned from their argument so far. You might say, "You know, you're making me think about all the things that could go wrong with pet shops selling puppies. I usually think of them as selling cute dog outfits and treats for kittens, but some do sell puppies, and I'm curious where those animals come from and how a person shopping for a dog would know if a dog in a pet store came from a puppy mill." Then, and only then, would you point out any errors in the argument and state your disagreements.

There are at least three other principles related to the principle of charity that philosophers say we can keep in mind to reach a place of agreement with other people. The **principle of cooperation** says that most of the time, when stating an argument, people are trying to be as clear, honest, and helpful as possible because they want to be understood by other humans. The **principle of rational accommodation** says that in order to increase the chances of agreement between each other, humans tend to assume, "Hmm, this person is saying something weird and I'm not too sure it makes sense, but I'm going to go with the idea that they know what they're talking about and listen some more before butting in." There's also the **principle of coherence**, which helps us zoom in on the most logical points in whatever our conversation partner is saying. All these charitable principles can keep us on track for a conversation that pushes us to expand our thinking and respond with empathy and compassion when we disagree with an argument.

ASK FOR EVIDENCE

One way scientists recommend cooling down a heated debate is by asking this question: What information and evidence did you use to form your point of view?

Remember when we learned how the human brain in all its glory can get a little carried away when it comes to estimating its capacity? The Dunning-Kruger effect and the illusion of explanatory depth are biases that lead us to think we know more about a topic or issue than we really do. To uncover these biases, you might start off with the looping technique by saying, "Okay, so I hear you when you say you don't believe more laws to keep guns out of dangerous people's hands is a good thing. Is that correct?" Wait for an answer. Then you might follow up with "Can you explain how current gun laws work and why you think they don't need to be changed?"

As we now know, in study after study, scientists have found that people who feel very strongly about something often overestimate their understanding of the issue. But after trying to explain the inner workings of the college financing system, or climate change, or tax policies, and coming up against their own lack of understanding, they start to veer away from the strong feelings they once had. They no longer strongly support or oppose a particular belief. Realizing they know less than they thought lessens the polarization and softens the extreme beliefs.

Once Cam and her mother's conversation is off to a good start, Cam might ask her mother to talk about the ways in which gun control works. She might ask her mother to describe what a person has to go through to become the owner of a gun. Cam's mother might ask her similar questions, and the two could find themselves agreeing on how the process operates, which could help them reach a place of mutual understanding. They started off at loggerheads about gun control, mental illness, and shootings, but now they've found they at least agree on how the system of gun control functions.

LOOK FOR COMMON GROUND

Which brings us to another strategy: in the middle of a disagreement, search for something you can agree on. This might seem really strange, since we're talking about situations where people hold opposing beliefs, but take Cam and her mother's example. Both are upset. Both believe different things about why mass shootings come to be, but both want the same thing: a safe society where teens like Cam are not petrified about going to school. That's their common ground. Focusing on that—the thing they share and not only the things causing them to butt heads—can help them on their way to resolving the conflict.

The common ground might not always be obvious. A parent refusing to vaccinate their baby because they incorrectly believe that vaccines cause autism might feel they have nothing in common with the pediatrician strongly recommending vaccination. But the parent and the pediatrician share a common goal: they both want the baby to grow into a happy and healthy adult. They currently hold opposing views about the best way to do that, but realizing they have reached consensus on one thing—the health of the baby—can open up the situation to more sharing of thoughts and concerns.

There's a saying by the thirteenth-century Sufi poet Moulana Jalal al-Din Muhammad Rumi that reminds us of this: "Out beyond ideas of wrongdoing and rightdoing, there is a field. I'll meet you there."

DON'T SHAME PEOPLE

It's important to ask about a person's understanding of a topic (or lack of understanding) without making them feel small and ashamed. The last thing you should do here is make them feel bad for realizing that they know less about gun control laws than they thought they did.

That's because shame and humiliation make us feel miserable and misunderstood. Trying to shame people into doing or believing something is a strategy that's been tried and tested for everything from lowering teenage pregnancy rates to getting people to quit smoking. It doesn't work.

In a study of nearly 2,000 Americans, Italians, and South Koreans, people were asked to rate how ashamed they would feel if they became infected with the coronavirus that causes COVID-19. In all three countries, the more people felt ashamed about becoming infected, the less likely they were to report their infection status to health authorities or to friends and family. Feeling ashamed meant people were even less likely to follow public health guidelines about things like wearing a mask and avoiding physical contact with others.

Shame and humiliation do not make us behave well. In fact, when it comes to conflict, these emotions can rapidly escalate an already bad situation. Journalist Amanda Ripley studied the kinds of conflicts that get deeper and uglier over the years, never coming to an end. She found that feelings of shame and humiliation make conflict much, much worse. Ripley calls humiliation a fire starter when it comes to conflict because of how quickly it can accelerate an already bad situation.

DON'T POUR FACTS ONTO POLARIZED CONVERSATIONS

It's tempting to shove facts at a person whose beliefs are based on false information. "But sixteen studies have shown that what you are saying is wrong . . . " is almost a guaranteed way to shut down a conversation. Some scientists even say pouring facts onto a polarized conversation is like pouring kerosene onto a fire. The flames burn brighter.

Why don't facts fix everything? Asking someone to question their beliefs can feel to them as if you're asking them to question their identity. We choose what to believe based on more than facts, even if we don't admit this. The views of those around us, of our family and friends, play a big role. Then there's the fact that we can be resistant to information that disagrees with our beliefs. "Oh, you want to disagree with me that ice cream tastes like garbage?! Well, everyone in my neighborhood hates ice cream and we can't all be wrong, so you must be wrong!"

Facts might seem like neutral packets of information, but these packets are loaded with context: Who created the fact? Which institutions lie behind the research that developed the fact?

No human is 100 percent neutral or objective. Even the algorithms and automated systems that computer scientists make are filled with human biases. And speaking of scientists, haven't researchers made mistakes before? Didn't we think for centuries that lambs grew on trees and the earth was flat? If facts are constantly being updated and the key to progress is changing your mind as new information becomes available . . . then how much weight should we put on facts anyway?

Keep these questions in mind when you're tempted to pour facts onto a polarized conversation. And remember, people's past experiences can act as a filter that influences how they see the world and how they will receive the facts you throw at them.

One problem with assuming that facts fix everything is the presumption that "Oh, this person just believes that climate change is a hoax because they haven't seen the gazillion studies that prove climate change is real."

PAUSE.

Do you really think this is the case? Often, people *will* have seen tons of data saying climate change is real and will *still* believe that they are right in thinking this data is false and that climate change is a hoax.

Thinking "Well, obviously this person just needs more data thrown at them to see how wrong they are" is an approach called the **knowledge deficit model**. It's the typical way we share information, especially in the world of science communication. The knowledge deficit model is at play when scientists say, "I'm giving a talk to the public today about climate change, so I'm going to find all the new evidence showing it's real, translate it to the right level for this audience, and hope that changes their minds so that they believe climate change is real."

SIGH.

The knowledge deficit model has a lot of . . . deficits. It ignores what we know about the biases in our brains, the way beliefs are tribal, and how facts are not enough to change our minds. Sadly, even though the knowledge deficit model has been shown to be quite ineffective, it continues to be used, especially for science communication. (It's almost as if the scientists are ignoring the facts about how useless the model can be. . . .)

Hitting people over the head with facts and drowning them in data is boring for them and frustrating for you. Facts don't fix the problem of polarization. Something that has been proven to work in shifting perspectives and helping people to change their minds is stories.

HARNESS THE POWER OF STORIES

Remember Sara and her little stray dog, Mimi? Remember the scans that show how our brains light up like Christmas trees when we hear a story, and how dull our brains look when we hear blah-blah facts? Since our brains are biologically wired to respond to stories, use that. Use stories. This doesn't mean sidelining facts and data. It means incorporating them into a story that connects with your audience and convinces them to question and even change their beliefs.

Savvy politicians do this. They don't call it storytelling; they call it **deep canvassing**. It's a strategy that helps build support from voters around specific issues, especially controversial ones.

Deep canvassing does the opposite of making a person feel pressured to change their mind. Instead, it uses a person's own life story to guide them toward shifting their perspective. For example, instead of jumping straight into a conversation about the rights of LGBTQI people and saying to a voter, "Where do you stand on gay marriage? Are you pro or against? We think you should be pro!," the canvassers might ask, "Can you think of a time when someone who was different from you was kind and open-minded when you really needed it?"

By opening up the conversation this way and listening without judgement to the person's own story, the canvassers can pivot the discussion back to LGBTQI people and issues such as gay marriage. They might say, "That time you really needed someone different from you to understand who you are and not make assumptions is not that different from LGBTQI people asking to be treated the same way as everyone else. . . ." Researchers at the University of California, Berkeley, studied this using immigration as an example and found that instead of feeling pushed to change their mind, a person in this situation might start to make the connection between their story and another person's story. Reaching this place of connection and understanding on their own leads them to reconsider their beliefs. In fact, the Berkeley researchers found that people who were engaged in conversations using this deep canvassing strategy favored more compassionate and inclusive immigration policy for many months after they'd had the discussion about their own life story.

Deep canvassing may not feel like storytelling in the traditional "Once upon a time, there was a refugee . . ." kind of way, but by bringing a large and complex topic—immigration—down to the experience of one child or one family, and by nudging another person toward empathy by asking of a time when they relied on kindness, we see radical shifts in perspective take place.

It turns out that stories dampen defensiveness and lessen that awful feeling of being pressured to change your mind. Stories allow a person to experience a change of heart and mind independently.

NO ONE-SIZE-FITS-ALL APPROACH

Finally, these nine strategies can help, but you don't have to use all of them all of the time. There isn't a magical one-size-fits-all approach to de-escalating tense conversations about controversial and polarizing topics. You might find yourself taking different approaches at different times over different topics. For example, if Cam was thinking of having a conversation about school shootings and mental health with a friend whom she sees for only an hour a week, she might decide not to have the conversation at all. Cam might make a mental calculation that it's not worth her time and effort to engage with this person on a difficult topic. If it was her swimming coach who muttered conspiracy theories about school shootings and mental health during warm-ups, Cam might switch to a different coach or she might decide to begin a series of conversations because she knows she'll see the coach at least twice a week. But since it's her mother and she's invested in this relationship, Cam will try out a few of these strategies to help navigate the difficult conversation.

WHAT IS GOOD CONFLICT?

ON THE FACE of it, you might think that Cam and her mother's situation is 100 percent terrible and unfortunate and that their lives would be so much better if they just agreed about everything. But not seeing eye to eye with someone is not a negative thing in and of itself. Disagreements aren't all bad, and they don't have to turn into angry and upsetting fights. In fact, conflict can be an opportunity for growth and a chance to test your empathy and listening skills.

Journalist Amanda Ripley spent four years investigating gang violence, nasty divorces, neighborhood feuds, and even the Middle East Peace Process and came away with this conclusion: we need *more* conflict—not less! In her book *High Conflict: Why We Get Trapped and How We Get Out*, Ripley says, "Living without conflict is like living without love."

Sounds weird, right? Likening conflict to love seems bizarre until you realize there are different kinds of conflict. There's high conflict, which is the kind of conflict that likely comes to mind as soon as you hear the word "conflict." In high conflict, people blame each other, shame each other, and bring up old grudges instead of dealing with the issues really at hand. High conflict leaves everyone feeling bruised and a solution feeling way out of reach, if not impossible.

Ripley discovered that certain feelings reign supreme during high conflict. Certainty and rigidity are central to high conflict, which burns stronger when a person is fixed in their way of thinking and feels that they are the only one who is right.

On the other hand, there's good conflict. Good conflict is a healthy and productive disagreement where two people who are arguing with one another ask questions and really listen to the other person's answers. There's still friction, and things can still get a little intense during good conflict, but there's no blaming and shaming. Among the characteristics of good conflict that Ripley noticed are humility, passion, and an understanding that even when you feel right about a subject, the world is a beautiful mess full of complexity and contradiction.

In both good conflict and high conflict, stress hormones surge, the heart pounds, and blood pressure rises. But in good conflict, these physical effects subside after a short time. In high conflict, stress hormones flow chronically, the conflict stays on the person's mind 24/7, and the person ends up losing sleep and even getting sick.

HIGH CONFLICT	GOOD CONFLICT
• One or all sides don't want to find a solution	• All sides want to come to an agreement
• People want to fight	• There's curiosity
• Lots of assumptions are made	• Lots of questions are asked
• Feeling happy when bad things happen to those on the "other side"	• Feeling sad when bad things happen to those on the "other side"
• Violence is more likely	• Broad thinking
	• Violence is unlikely

Features of high conflict and good conflict. Source: Adapted from the original in *High Conflict: How We Get Trapped and How We Get Out*, by Amanda Ripley.

We sometimes find ourselves trapped in high-conflict situations. So how do we get unstuck? Listening to the other person or group is key to getting untangled, says Ripley. In her four-year deep dive into high conflict, she found that people in a relationship where they felt understood by their partner said an argument actually made them feel *better*! They could be in complete disagreement with the other person but still feel happy and understood. Arguing was a way of getting things off their chest and expressing an opposing opinion. And because they felt listened to and understood, they still felt loved. In fact, feeling listened to increases trust and can help a person share more interesting thoughts during the conversation.

Another key to avoiding high conflict is to keep an eye out for conflict fire starters. One of these is feelings of shame and humiliation, which we mentioned already as a surefire way of making people *not* do the thing you want them to do. Ripley found that shame and other fire starters, including corruption, quickly accelerate conflict and can shift good conflict into the unhealthy zone.

People who live their lives always seeing conflict as a bad thing to be avoided at all costs are likely to implode, says Ripley. There's no way to live a fun and full life without running into disagreements, but those disagreements don't have to escalate into high-conflict situations. You can have healthy conflict, the type of conflict that helps you learn, broaden your perspective, and evolve into a better person.

SIDEBAR: THE SOCRATIC METHOD (AND THE SAD FATE OF SOCRATES)

THE MAN PACED THE STREETS OF ATHENS BAREFOOT, speaking to anyone who had interesting ideas about life and the world. Sometimes he would fall so deep into thought that he would stand in a trance for hours, swaying in the rough woolen overcoat that he wore year-round.

In the fifth century BC, Greeks in Athens spoke with Socrates because he helped them understand the meaning of their lives. He interrogated their values and beliefs, the way they behaved in their relationships, their political ideologies, and every aspect of being human, not because he believed there was one right way to live a good life, but because he felt passionately that debate and discussion could help people live a happier, more fulfilled existence.

Some liked the philosopher and enjoyed his genuine curiosity. "A life not examined is a life not worth living" is a quote attributed to Socrates. But others felt that humans were happier without asking deep questions about life. Some Athenians despised Socrates' incessant questioning and the way it made them feel utterly confused about their values and second-guess important decisions they had already made. Speaking with Socrates could be a discombobulating experience.

Socrates believed that reasoning, not the recitation of facts, was the best way of seeking truth. He asked his students to propose a point of view that he would question, asking why they held that belief and what it meant to live life that way. Socrates would scratch at the surface of his students' statements to find their philosophical roots. When the students tripped up or *umm*ed and *ahhh*ed, Socrates kept quiet, giving them room to think more deeply. He didn't claim to have the answer or to be an expert on any topic; he didn't even say there *was* a right answer, only different ways of looking at *your* truth.

One of his students, Plato (the guy for whom platonic love is named), took copious notes during these conversations and wrote many books about what came to be known as the Socratic method, or Socratic dialogue. Socratic dialogue aims for "productive discomfort," the kind of pondering that makes you shift in your seat and furrow your brow a little while your friend says, "But *why* do you think that?"

The Socratic method uses two kinds of reasoning, inductive and deductive reasoning, which were discussed in chapter two. Deductive reasoning relies on facts, such as "The definition of vegan includes not eating meat." Inductive reasoning relies on evidence, which leads to conclusions like "I've only ever seen white sheep in my life; therefore, all sheep are white."

In the Socratic method, everyone involved in the conversation is responsible for pushing the dialogue forward through questioning. Everything is open-ended with no expected result or winning argument.

One person can be the leader or teacher and the other the student, but both are participating equally and the teacher is not considered "a sage on the stage." In fact, Socrates believed that understanding his own ignorance was the basis of his wisdom. He said he knew nothing but could help draw out other people's ideas just as his mother, a midwife, helped babies be born.

This kind of learning through examination and excavation is considered to be a superior form of thinking. Rote learning, the kind that relies on pure memorization of lists of facts, uses the lowest level of thinking. It tests the skill of recall, but it doesn't get deep into ideas and perspectives. The Socratic method is not about repeating facts. It's about adding your perspective to the facts and sharing what you think about them in a way that reveals your assumptions and motivations.

The Socratic method is a type of good conflict, because there is still tension and high stakes but there are none of the features of high conflict. Everyone feels listened to and no one feels under attack.

Here's an example of Socratic dialogue between two friends.

FRIEND 1

What are you up to later?

FRIEND 2

I thought I might go over to Ali's house. Watch that movie he's always going on about.

Oh. How come?

Ugh, I shouldn't have said anything. Why do you hate him so much? Did he do something to you?

Have I said I hate him?

Well, maybe you haven't said it, but I feel like you judge me for being friends with him.

Do you think it's okay for me, as your friend, to ask about your other friends?

Sure.

Why do you think I ask about Ali?

I mean, you care. I get that. You don't want me getting hurt again.

Do you think there's a reason why I ask about him specifically?

I'm thinking about that time he stood me up and then ghosted me for two days and I ended up imagining that something really, really bad had happened. . . . I remember how upset you were after that. You said a good friend wouldn't make me worry.

Why do you think he would do that?

I dunno. He seems to find it easy to not worry about what other people might be thinking. Like, I don't think it registered with him that I would be worrying about his safety while he was out having fun.

How did that make you feel?

Worried at the time, obviously! You remember that. I kept texting you like, "What if x, y, z has happened?"

Yes, you were imagining all these worst-case scenarios because you were scared.

It was the same time that girl from the other high school had gone missing.
Remember that?

Oh my God, yes! My dad was so paranoid.

He made me keep the location thing on my phone activated 24/7. I forgot this happened at the same time. Why do you think he didn't just text you to say he was okay?

Like I said, he doesn't always think about other people's feelings.

And that made you feel . . . how?

Definitely neglected. Like I wasn't that important to him. I thought, well, maybe he's texting other friends but just not me.

Would you treat him like that?

You know I wouldn't! I wouldn't treat you that way either.

I know. You're a *very* attentive friend. Did it make you feel sad that he didn't text or anything?

I guess. Annoyed, weirded out. Sad.

Why do you stay friends with him?

I don't know! We've been friends since middle school. That's a long time.

It is. That's at least four years you've known him.

Yeah. And I'm loyal. I don't just ditch people because they acted badly once.

Were there other times that Ali made you feel sad or neglected?

<silent>

I don't want to make you feel more sad thinking about it, but I'm curious why you stay friends with him.

Like I said, loyalty. I've known him a long time.

How do you like friends to treat you and make you feel?

Obviously, I hate worrying about people, so there's that. Just let me know you're okay, even if you can't hang with me.

Yeah, that sounds important to you. And to me, to be honest. I hate going through worst-case scenarios in my head. What else?

I like the way Xin remembers *everything* I tell her. Like, yesterday she said, "Isn't today your favorite aunt's birthday?" and I was like, "How do you even remember me telling you that?!"

Haha, sounds like she made you feel listened to. Right?

Her memory is amazing!

How did you feel when she came out with that?

I felt like she's a loyal friend, you know? Like, what's important to me becomes important to her.

That's a nice way to be treated.

The questions lead. The conversation follows.

The Socratic method is not about deciding what is right or wrong. It's about demonstrating the messiness and uncertainty of the world. It takes you to the murky in-between world that exists between right and wrong. Critical thinking happens because of the questioning. Friend 2 reaches a place of realization about what's important to them in a friendship and how they want to be treated by their friends.

You've probably had conversations similar to this one. But by incorporating the methods of Socratic dialogue, you can delve even deeper into understanding why someone behaves a certain way or believes the things they do. Using the Socratic method, Friend 1 isn't interrogating Friend 2. They are leading them through a natural conversation, asking questions, and listening well enough to respond with follow-up questions. Imagine if the conversation *were* happening in a more traditional teaching style, with one friend telling the other, "Here is a list of friendship qualities and traits that are important. Let's go through them and memorize them together. Now rank them in order of . . ."

Boring. The kind of learning that happens via the Socratic method is said to be deeper and more long-lasting because the person in the conversation realizes important things for themselves. A friend made them feel neglected; that made them feel sad. Another friend remembered things that were important to them; that made them feel cared for and heard. They arrived at these conclusions themselves because a friend was asking questions and connecting their responses to new questions, encouraging them to go deeper with their answers so that if they said, "I was neglected," the friend might follow up with "And how did that make you feel?"

Sadly for Socrates, all those years of making the people of Athens feel that their ideas and decisions needed deep probing, and that some of their political beliefs were potentially nonsense, caught up with him. His fellow citizens charged him on three counts: being a menace to society, corrupting the youth, and heresy (even though Socrates followed all the religious practices of the time).

Socrates' friend Crito bribed the prison guards to let the philosopher escape. But Socrates decided it was immoral to run away. He also chose not to apologize for the behaviors that had led to his trial, because he felt that standing by his principles was the right thing to do.

In 399 BC, a jury of five hundred Athenians found Socrates guilty and sentenced him to death. He drank the poisonous herb hemlock, which paralyzed his breathing muscles.

HOW TO BS-PROOF YOUR BRAIN

WHAT HAPPENS WHEN the person being challenged is . . . *you*? What happens when someone says, "You know that thing you just mentioned? I think you're wrong because . . ."

How do you respond?

Your first instinct might be to say that you're a very open-minded person, or even that you enjoy a bout of intellectual sparring. But think about the last time someone said something that challenged your perspective. Did you feel uncomfortable? Did you feel attacked? Did you reflexively say "What? No!" and disagree with them disagreeing with you?

In the busy world of information disorder, where we're bombarded with solid evidence and not-so-solid evidence all at the same time, we have to take steps to check in on our own beliefs. While inoculation theory and sophisticated rumor vaccines might protect us from falling for false information in the first place, there will always be times when existing beliefs need dusting off and updating.

Now that we've talked about how you can challenge *other* people's beliefs, here are eight steps to BS-proof your brain and boost your own mental immunity against falsehoods and fixed beliefs.

UPDATE, UPDATE, UPDATE

Step one is to regularly update your beliefs. This means not being fixed in your thinking and being willing to take a close look at new evidence on a topic, whether it's climate change or satanic cults at concerts, and checking if the new evidence shifts your understanding and therefore your standing on the topic.

BELIEFS ARE NOT BINARY

But it's important to keep this second step in mind: beliefs are not absolute binaries, meaning you don't always have to be "for" or "against" something. The world is complex, and you can hold a perspective that takes into account those complexities. You might, for example, believe genetically modified foods are safe to eat but want better regulation of the companies that make them. You might think renewable energy is a great idea but have concerns about the way indigenous people's land is used to mine for the minerals needed to make rechargeable batteries for electric cars.

BELIEF LEVELS

Don't feel pressure to believe everything to the same extent. Beliefs come in levels, meaning you can assign a confidence level to each belief you hold. Do you think vaping is safe and an effective way to quit cigarettes? One day you might answer "yes" and give that belief a confidence level of 90 percent. But then you might read a report that finds there are a lot of unanswered questions about some of the chemicals in the liquid cartridges of vape pens. You might update your belief based on this new evidence, still favoring the use of vaping to help people quit cigarettes but changing your belief confidence level. Maybe it drops from 90 percent to 70 percent. And because you're not fixed in your thinking, you'll come back to this when new evidence emerges to update your belief again . . . and again . . . and again.

KNOW YOUR BIASES

While it's pretty easy to call people out on their biases, it can be harder to figure out your own. Many of our biases are implicit or unconscious, so we don't even realize that we passed the jar of honey with the stuck lid to a male friend, in the hopes that he can open it, instead of to the female friend sitting next to him who happens to be a bodybuilder. Why not hand the jar to the woman?

A good place to start is by acknowledging that you, yes, you, are biased. Then, because implicit biases are hidden by definition, you can use an online test, such as Harvard University's Implicit Association Test, to figure out what you need to work on.

Something to be mindful of when interrogating your biases: This is important work, but it's *your* work. If the online implicit bias tests tell you that you hold inaccurate beliefs about disabled people, for example, don't go to your disabled friends and ask them to educate you. That is not their labor. It's yours. (Also, if you are reading this and realizing that you don't have any disabled friends . . . think about your biases and ask yourself why that is.)

GET COMFORTABLE WITH BEING WRONG

Updating our beliefs, recognizing our biases . . . all this can be uncomfortable work. You might have lived fifteen full years on this planet thinking that genetically modified foods are dangerous to your DNA, only to be humbled by the evidence that this is not true. THAT'S OKAY! It's okay to be wrong! In fact, it's healthy to get comfortable with being wrong. It keeps you humble and mindful of all the times that you've been wrong. That, in turn, keeps you alert for all the future times you will be wrong again.

Getting comfortable with being wrong also means you'll lean in instead of getting defensive when someone challenges your point of view, which can prevent you from letting in new questioning and new data. Being comfortable with being wrong can also make you kinder and more compassionate when talking with someone who is clearly wrong about something, because you'll tell yourself, *Been there, done that; I've been wrong about a ton of things myself.*

DOUBTS ARE YOUR FRIENDS

We like to be sure of things, as close to 100 percent certainty as possible, even though the world doesn't work that way. But trying to squash doubts and reservations can be dangerous. That's because they can serve as red flags that tell you, "Hey! Here's a thing we maybe need to question some more before we arrive at a belief!"

For example, say you've always argued that people who do not have a home become houseless because of something they did, such as not being able to hold on to a job, or not being good at managing their finances.

Then one day you see a woman who is houseless telling a man in a suit that she used to work at his real estate firm but was fired after she complained about harassment from a manager. *Ping.* Doubt creeps into your head. *Maybe . . . bad things happen to people and that results in them losing their jobs and financial stability. Maybe ending up without a home is not about personal failure at all.* Hold on to that doubt! Don't squash it because it goes against your existing point of view. Use that doubt to ask yourself questions about why you believe what you believe about people who are houseless. Use it to get some data to help you understand why people end up houseless. Or talk to a friend (using the Socratic method) to interrogate your beliefs and now your doubts. Doubts and reservations are your friends. Listening to them will strengthen your mental immune system.

USE THE SOCRATIC METHOD

Andy Norman, the philosophy professor who wrote the book *Mental Immunity: Infectious Ideas, Mind Parasites, and the Search for a Better Way to Think*, calls the Socratic method a "mind inoculant," meaning this type of dialogue protects you from being fixed in your beliefs and from being easily persuaded by weak evidence. It's harder to get away with thinking something like "Houseless people end up without a home because they did something wrong" if a friend is using the Socratic method to ask you deep questions on that topic.

This kind of dialogue can protect you from falling for false information. Researchers found that people exposed to online misinformation and disinformation about vaccines weren't equally vulnerable to believing the false news. Some people were protected from believing the lies. Protection came in the form of real-life conversations. Say a person saw a tweet that made another false claim, such as "people with mental illness are a danger to themselves and society and are most likely to commit mass shootings." If the person reading that tweet took the information off-line into real-life conversations with trusted friends and family, they were less likely to believe the falsehood and more likely to understand that mental illness is very common, affecting nearly one in five teens and adults, and that people living with mental illness need care and help and should not be treated as if they are a danger to society.

THINK FOR YOURSELF

While you need a group of trusted friends and family around who will help you explore your beliefs and doubts, you don't want to fall into the trap of **groupthink**. Groupthink happens when people believe the same things as others in their group because they don't want to stand out, be accused of being different or wrong, or rock the boat in any way. Groupthink can be dangerous. It can lead people to hold strong views based on inaccurate information just because that's what people in their circle believe.

Don't underestimate its power. In the past, groupthink has allowed for disgusting and inhumane things to take place, all under the guise of "Yes, it seems severe, but we all think it's okay to persecute this particular group of people, and because so many of us think it's okay, it must be okay." (Just check the history books for details of the Vietnam War's escalation, the space shuttle *Challenger* tragedy, and the horrors of Pearl Harbor to see how groupthink has resulted in millions of human deaths.)

Protect yourself from groupthink. To avoid it, encourage your circle to share lots of ideas, to hear everyone out, and to recognize that often it's not the best ideas that win; it's the loudest ones. Look out for times when you nod your head and go along with everyone else's thinking just because it's the easiest thing to do.

EPILOGUE

HI, CRITICAL THINKER!
SO . . . WHAT NOW?

YOUR BRAIN IS probably processing some dizzying thoughts right now. Thoughts like:

A free press is essential for a healthy society and for keeping us in the know, but . . .

News organizations are highly imperfect, reporters are not neutral, and tons of biases seep through our news feeds and into supposedly fair and objective news stories every day.

Some governments silence the press and attack and imprison journalists for publishing facts, so the public sees a distorted version of the truth, making it difficult to know what to believe.

*The information universe is huge and complex,
and contagious information spreads constantly,
infecting millions with myths, hoaxes, and false
and polarizing beliefs.*

*Social media is abuzz with addictive
algorithms that push content creators toward
extremist views and lead users deep
into dangerous rabbit holes.*

*Being aware of the existence of false information
can make us wary of believing anything, even the
fact-checked, carefully reported stuff.*

This is the messy world we live in. A world where some of the most respected news organizations began as government propaganda machines and still support systems of power . . . even as they hold (some of) those in authority to account and land corrupt officials in prison.

A world where people profit from spreading disinformation that hurts millions, and where lies are packaged to appear more believable and memorable than the truth. A world where people push back to protect beliefs based on lies when you try to correct them!

It is all. So. Confusing.

Before you read this book, you may have thought the safest way of surviving the messy world was this: Just don't believe anything. Be skeptical 24/7 about absolutely everything you read, see, hear, smell, feel . . .

Well, that's one way of living. It's an exhausting, depressing, bewildering, headachey, not-so-efficient way of sorting through information overload. But overarching skepticism about absolutely **EVERYTHING** is not the answer.

If total skepticism isn't the solution, then what is?

The answer is YOU.

Yes, you. You with your brilliant, complicated, messy brain. A brain that loves mental shortcuts and forms beliefs based not only on facts but on feelings and friends and the very human need to belong.

That brain of yours might be harboring a few biases, but it's now brimming with the skills of critical thinking, media literacy, and digital literacy. Those are just fancy phrases for the knowledge you've absorbed while reading or listening to the sentences on these pages. You can poke and pull at your biases now; you can challenge and fact-check a statement presented to you as The Truth. You can spot a sneaky algorithm nudging you toward BS. Because now you hold the tools to navigate the information universe more confidently and smoothly.

You will trip up. One day you will find yourself taking a left turn at the corner of Fake Experts and Cherry Picking or getting stuck at the junction of Person-You-Trust-Says-Something-False-But-Convincing. You might even find yourself saying **ARGGHHHHH** as you slip down the ravine of Conspiracy Theories and land face flat in Blatantly False Territory. You will ride the Heuristic Highway and argue with a friend when they challenge one of your biased beliefs. And you will become annoyed when these things happen. But that's okay. Dust yourself off, critical thinker. This is all part of your journey.

Even as social media platforms are revamped and renamed, as algorithms advance and disinformation spreaders find new ways to push lies, you have the foundation for your lifelong journey of truth seeking. Because now you know that beliefs are not yes/no, black/white switches. Beliefs are dimmer knobs, and you have the power and the knowledge to crank up the dial on the strength of a belief based on new evidence. Evidence that you gather when you challenge the ideas presented to you as "facts." Evidence that you collect as you climb out of your echo chamber and thoroughly and thoughtfully ask questions of others and of yourself.

This journey requires pit stops and fuel breaks. You'll have to regularly reevaluate your beliefs, push yourself out of your echo chamber, ask lots of questions, and remain open to different perspectives. But far from feeling like a chore, it will become a habit that opens up the world—and your mind—in a million fascinating ways. Bon voyage.

GRATITUDE

MY NAME MIGHT be on the cover of this book, but without the support of the following people, there would be no book.

HH Lilly Ghahremani, I curtsy before thee, ma'am. While it's highly likely, but currently uncorroborated, that we are related through a lineage of Persian princesses, what *can* be fact-checked is my deep, deep gratitude for you. Thank you for wholeheartedly, enthusiastically, and lovingly diving into every project with me and for being the OG of Literary Hustling. There's so much more to come, including, perhaps most importantly, lilac hats on the beach. I love you.

Justin Chanda: Thank you for believing in me; for believing in the mind-bending, world-changing, lifesaving power of words and sentences; and for conspiring with myself and Lilly in the belief that books can save us from ourselves. And thanks for tweeting about your frustrations. Without that tweet, there might be no *What the Fact?!*

To my fellow Emerson Collective "Recover and Renew Fellows," aka the Pandemic Fellows: thank you for your kindness, inspiration, and support while I was working on this book.

Massive thanks to Patrick, Amy, Megan, Cassia, and the entire Emerson Collective for supporting my research on information inequity and news deserts.

To the John S. Knight Journalism Fellowship at Stanford University and most especially the class of 2017: I love you all so much. Even if you weren't hell-bent on saving local news and inciting the fury of demagogues and autocrats, I would still be awed by your kindness and tenacity.

My deepest gratitude to the sagacious and generous Megan Marelli for the title of this book. Thank you for sharing your brilliance.

Melisa Basol: I'm so grateful for the ways in which you show up for me. Thank you for your friendship and for all of your support.

Vianey: Thank you for your diligence and astuteness during the fact-checking process. I am grateful for your friendship and intellect.

Mum, you took me to libraries and left me in the care of librarians, which turned out to be the best thing ever. Thank you for filling my life with books, relishing in the beauty of sentences, and pacing around the flat with a thesaurus in your hands, reading aloud words like "diatribe" and "jeremiad." I write books because of you.

Dalvin, you unknowingly snapped me out of my first and hopefully last bout of writer's block. You are a creative catalyst. Thank you for the gift of your friendship.

To all the journalists out there, especially the underpaid and underappreciated local news reporters who sit for hours at city hall meetings, hound prevaricating elected officials with vigorous questions, and weep into heavily redacted FOIA-requested documents: Thank you for your work. Especially you, Cassandra Yarelli Jaramillo. You are an inspiration.

SOURCES

INTRODUCTION

AI Impacts. "Information Storage in the Brain." AI Impacts. Updated November 9, 2020. https://aiimpacts.org/information-storage-in-the-brain.

Lee, Henry. *The Vegetable Lamb of Tartary; A Curious Fable of the Cotton Plant. To Which Is Added a Sketch of the History of Cotton and the Cotton Trade.* London, 1887. https://play.google.com/books/reader?id=IeBCAAAAIAAJ&pg=GBS.PP6&printsec=frontcover&output=reader&hl=en.

BBC. "Coronavirus: Technicians Held in Peru over False 5G Covid Links." June 12, 2020. https://www.bbc.com/news/world-latin-america-53021239.

Los Angeles Times. "Medicos Meet (Radiophobia)." June 3, 1903. https://www.newspapers.com/clip/10421078/medicos-meet-radiophobia-1903/.

Centers for Disease Control and Prevention. "What Is Radiation? The Electromagnetic Spectrum." CDC. Updated Dec. 7, 2015. https://www.cdc.gov/nceh/radiation/spectrum.html.

Centers for Disease Control and Prevention. "Ultraviolet Radiation." CDC. Updated August 25, 2016. https://www.cdc.gov /nceh/radiation/ultraviolet.htm.

Borrego-Soto, Gissela, Rocío Ortiz-López, and Augusto Rojas-Martínez. "Ionizing Radiation-Induced DNA Injury and Damage Detection in Patients with Breast Cancer." *Genetics and Molecular Biology* 38, no. 4 (October–December 2015): 420–432. https://doi.org/10.1590/S1415-475738420150019.

Reuters. "False Claim: Pictures Link Bird Deaths to New 5G Mast in the Netherlands." April 28, 2020. https://www .reuters.com/article/uk-factcheck-starlings-netherlands /false-claim-pictures-link-bird-deaths-to-new-5g-mast-in-the -netherlands-idUSKCN22A3D9.

Guardian. "Cyanide in Fruit Seeds: How Dangerous Is an Apple?" October 11, 2015. https://www.theguardian.com /technology/2015/oct/11/cyanide-in-fruit-seeds-how-dangerous -is-an-apple.

CHAPTER 1

Robinson, Olga, and Marianna Spring. "Coronavirus: How Bad Information Goes Viral." BBC, March 19, 2020. https:// www.bbc.com/news/blogs-trending-51931394.

Extreme Virus Lab. "Critical Reading of COVID-2 'Advice' Letter." Extreme Virus Lab, March 12, 2020. https://www .extremeviruses.org/sarscov2-blog/2020/3/12/critical-reading -of-covid-2-advice-letter.

Kasprak, Alex. "'Uncle With Masters Degree' Gets Facts Wrong in Coronavirus 'Announcement.'" Snopes, March 5, 2020.

Updated March 23, 2020. https://www.snopes.com/news/2020/03/05/uncle-coronavirus/.

Griffith, Janelle. "He Thought the Coronavirus Was 'a Fake Crisis.' Then He Contracted It and Changed His Mind." NBC News, May 18, 2020. https://www.nbcnews.com/news/us-news/he-thought-coronavirus-was-fake-crisis-then-he-contracted-it-n1209246.

Brito, Christopher. "Brian Hitchens, Who Downplayed Coronavirus, Now Warns Others After Contracting It." CBS News, May 19, 2020. https://www.cbsnews.com/news/brian-hitchens-coronavirus-florida/.

McGraw, Elizabeth. "What Is a Super Spreader? An Infectious Disease Expert Explains." *The Conversation*, January 30, 2020. https://theconversation.com/what-is-a-super-spreader-an-infectious-disease-expert-explains-130756.

Wang, Qiyao, Zhen Lin, Yuehui Jin, Shiduan Cheng, and Tan Yang. "ESIS: Emotion-Based Spreader-Ignorant-Stifler Model for Information Diffusion." *Knowledge-Based Systems* 81 (June 2015): 46–55. https://doi.org/10.1016/j.knosys.2015.02.006.

Varol, Onur, Emilio Ferrara, Clayton A. Davis, Filippo Menczer, and Alessandro Flammini. "Online Human-Bot Interactions: Detection, Estimation, and Characterization." *Proceedings of the Eleventh International AAAI Conference on Web and Social Media* (March 27, 2017): 280–289. https://ssrn.com/abstract=3324593.

Duell, Mark. "London Attack: Muslim Woman Trolled on Twitter." *Daily Mail*, March 24, 2017. https://www.dailymail

.co.uk/news/article-4342438/Trolls-blast-Muslim-woman-seen-walking-attack.html.

Richardson, Hayley, and Ellie Cambridge. "Muslim Woman Slams Trolls Who Accused Her of 'Casually' Walking Past Westminster Terror Victims as She Reveals She Helped." *The Sun*, March 24, 2017. Updated March 25, 2017. https://www.thesun.co.uk/news/3172279/muslim-woman-slams-trolls-who-accused-her-of-casually-walking-past-westminster-terror-victims-as-she-reveals-she-helped/.

Bluestein, Greg. "The Story behind the #EbolaInAtlanta Hoax." *Atlanta Journal-Constitution*, June 4, 2015. https://www.ajc.com/blog/politics/the-story-behind-the-ebolainatlanta-hoax/6nx0WvNBJu28IsxcNbqDmM/.

Timberg, Craig, and Shane Harris. "How Did Russian Agents Use Twitter at Key Moments in the 2016 Election?" *Washington Post*, July 20, 2018. https://www.washingtonpost.com/technology/2018/07/20/russian-operatives-blasted-tweets-ahead-huge-news-day-during-presidential-campaign-did-they-know-what-was-coming/.

Booth, Robert, Matthew Weaver, Alex Hern, Stacee Smith, and Shaun Walker. "Russia Used Hundreds of Fake Accounts to Tweet about Brexit, Data Shows." *Guardian*, November 14, 2017. https://www.theguardian.com/world/2017/nov/14/how-400-russia-run-fake-accounts-posted-bogus-brexit-tweets.

Lockhart, P. R. "How Russia Exploited Racial Tensions in America during the 2016 Elections." *Vox*, December 17, 2018. https://www.vox.com/identities/2018/12/17/18145075

/russia-facebook-twitter-internet-research-agency-race.

Jowett, Garth S., and Victoria O'Donnell. "What Is Propaganda, and How Does It Differ from Persuasion?" *Propaganda and Persuasion*. 4th ed. Sage, 2006. http://www.ffri.hr/~ibrdar /komunikacija/seminari/Propaganda%20&%20persuasion %20-%20difference%20(Chapter1).pdf.

Poole, Steven. "Before Trump: The Real History of Fake News." *Guardian*, November 22, 2019. https://www.theguardian .com/books/2019/nov/22/factitious-taradiddle-dictionary -real-history-fake-news.

Aikin, Scott F. "Poe's Law, Group Polarization, and the Epistemology of Online Religious Discourse." *SSRN* (January 23, 2009). https://ssrn.com/abstract=1332169.

Caramanica, Jon. "Tiger Beat: Still Squeaky Clean After All These Years." *New York Times*, April 16, 2011. Updated April 24, 2011. https://www.nytimes.com/2011/04/17/weekinreview /17tigerbeat.html.

Onion. "Barack Obama 'Tiger Beat' Cover Clinches Slumber Party Vote." *Onion*, June 19, 2007. https://www.theonion .com/barack-obama-tiger-beat-cover-clinches-slumber-party -vo-1819569174.

Caramanica, Jon. "Tiger Beat: Still Squeaky Clean After All These Years." *New York Times*, April 16, 2011. https:// www.nytimes.com/2011/04/17/weekinreview/17tigerbeat .html?referringSource=articleShare.

Simon, Scott. "Sexiest Man Alive Gets 'The Onion' Taken Seriously." NPR, December 1, 2012. https://www.npr.org /2012/12/01/166293306/the-onion-so-funny-it-makes-us-cry.

Pham, Nga. "Haunting 'Nepal Quake Victims' Photo from Vietnam." BBC, May 4, 2015. https://www.bbc.com/news/world-asia-32579598.

Ethical Media for Active Citizenship. "Media Disinformation." Ethical Media for Active Citizenship. Accessed February 4, 2022. https://ethicalmediatraining.eu/training/activities/media-disinformation/.

Giella, Lauren. "Fact Check: Did Megan Fox Author COVID Anti-Mask Post on Instagram?" *Newsweek*, February 22, 2021. https://www.newsweek.com/fact-check-did-megan-fox-author-covid-anti-mask-post-instagram-1571082.

Heil, Emily, and Paul Farhi. "Fake Copies of the Washington Post Handed Out in D.C." *Mercury News*, January 16, 2019. https://www.mercurynews.com/2019/01/16/fake-copies-of-the-washington-post-handed-out-in-d-c/.

Cook, John. "23 Ways to Mislead." YouTube, October 8, 2020. https://www.youtube.com/watch?v=gecDy9wDuCs.

Wilson, Sharon (@Txsharon). "Frackademia Gate: #Fracking Industry Funding Favorable Science." Twitter, July 23, 2012. https://twitter.com/Txsharon/status/227405542509924352?s=20.

O'Connor, Anahad. "How the Sugar Industry Shifted Blame to Fat." *New York Times*, September 12, 2016. https://www.nytimes.com/2016/09/13/well/eat/how-the-sugar-industry-shifted-blame-to-fat.html.

Brandt, Allan M. "Inventing Conflicts of Interest: A History of Tobacco Industry Tactics." *American Journal of Public Health* 102, no. 1 (January 2012): 63–71. https://doi.org/10.2105/AJPH.2011.300292.

Oreskes, Naomi, and Conway, Erik M. *Merchants of Doubt: How a Handful of Scientists Obscured the Truth on Issues from Tobacco Smoke to Climate Change.* New York: Bloomsbury Publishing, 2011.

Cook, John. "A History of FLICC: The 5 Techniques of Science Denial." *Skeptical Science*, March 31, 2020. https://skepticalscience.com/history-FLICC-5-techniques-science-denial.html.

Beaujon, Andrew. "Trump Claims He Invented the Term 'Fake News'—Here's an Interview with the Guy Who Actually Helped Popularize It." *Washingtonian*, October 2, 2019. https://www.washingtonian.com/2019/10/02/trump-claims-he-invented-the-term-fake-news-an-interview-with-the-guy-who-actually-helped-popularize-it/.

Adams, Paul C., and Barney Warf, eds. *Routledge Handbook of Media Geographies.* New York: Routledge, 2021. https://doi.org/10.4324/9781003039068.

Poole, Steven. "Before Trump: The Real History of Fake News." *Guardian*, November 22, 2019. https://www.theguardian.com/books/2019/nov/22/factitious-taradiddle-dictionary-real-history-fake-news.

Browne, Thomas. *Pseudodoxia Epidemica, or, Enquiries into Very Many Received Tenents and Commonly Presumed Truths.* London: Printed by T. H. for E. Dod., 1646; Ann Arbor: Text Creation Partnership. http://name.umdl.umich.edu/A29861.0001.001.

Diamond, Edwin. *Behind the Times: Inside the New New York Times.* Chicago: University of Chicago Press, 1995.

Kennedy, Lesley. "Did Yellow Journalism Fuel the Outbreak of the Spanish-American War?" History.com, August 21, 2019. https://www.history.com/news/spanish-american-war-yellow-journalism-hearst-pulitzer.

Merriam-Webster. "Factitious." *Merriam-Webster Online Dictionary.* Updated December 14, 2021. https://www.merriam-webster.com/dictionary/factitious#h1.

BBC. "'Post-Truth' Declared Word of the Year by Oxford Dictionaries." November 16, 2020. https://www.bbc.com/news/uk-37995600.

CHAPTER 2

Guy-Evans, Olivia. "Wernicke's Area Location and Function." Simply Psychology, July 28, 2021. https://www.simplypsychology.org/wernickes-area.html.

Dickerson, Kelly, Peter Gerhardstein, and Alecia Moser. "The Role of the Human Mirror Neuron System in Supporting Communication in a Digital World." Edited by J. Michael Williams. *Frontiers in Psychology* (May 12, 2017). https://doi.org/10.3389/fpsyg.2017.00698.

Renken, Elena. "How Stories Connect and Persuade Us: Unleashing the Brain Power of Narrative." NPR, April 11, 2020. https://www.npr.org/sections/health-shots/2020/04/11/815573198/how-stories-connect-and-persuade-us-unleashing-the-brain-power-of-narrative.

Wallentin, Mikkel, Andreas Højlund Nielsen, Peter Vuust, Anders Dohn, Andreas Roepstorff, and Torben Ellegaard Lund. "Amygdala and Heart Rate Variability Responses from Listening to Emotionally Intense Parts of a Story." *Neuroimage* 58, no. 3 (October 2011): 963–973. https://doi.org/10.1016/j.neuroimage .2011.06.077.

Smith, Jeremy Adam. "Five Surprising Ways Oxytocin Shapes Your Social Life." *Greater Good*, October 17, 2013. https:// greatergood.berkeley.edu/article/item/five_ways_oxytocin _might_shape_your_social_life.

Zak, Paul J. "Why Inspiring Stories Make Us React: The Neuroscience of Narrative." *Cerebrum*, February 2, 2015. https:// www.ncbi.nlm.nih.gov/pmc/articles/PMC4445577/.

He, Allison. "The Dunning-Kruger Effect: Why Incompetence Begets Confidence." *New York Times*, May 7, 2020. Updated April 12, 2021. https://www.nytimes.com/2020/05/07/learning /the-dunning-kruger-effect-why-incompetence-begets -confidence.html.

Mercier, Hugo, and Dan Sperber. *The Enigma of Reason*. Cambridge, MA: Harvard University Press, 2019.

CHAPTER 3

Jefferson, Thomas. Thomas Jefferson to John Norvell, Washington, June 14, 1807. In "The Letters of Thomas Jefferson 1743-1826." From Revolution to Reconstruction and Beyond (website). Accessed February 6, 2022. http://www.let.rug.nl /usa/presidents/thomas-jefferson/letters-of-thomas-jefferson /jefl179.php.

"An Account of the Conversation, Behaviour, and Execution of William Anderton, Printer Who Was Condemned at the Old Baily, on Thursday the 8th of June, for High Treason, and

Executed for the Same, at Tybourn on Friday the 16th of June, 1693." Printed by John Wallis near the Green Dragon in Fleet Street, 1693; Ann Arbor: Text Creation Partnership. https://quod.lib.umich.edu/cgi/t/text/pageviewer-idx?cc=eebo;c =eebo;idno=a25014.0001.001;page=root;view=text.

National Park Service. "5. The Origins of Hydroelectric Power." Discover Our Shared Heritage Travel Itinerary Series. Updated January 13, 2017. https://www.nps.gov/articles/5 -the-origins-of-hydroelectric-power.htm.

Herschel, John. "Great Astronomical Discoveries." *New York Sun*, August 25–31, 1835. Lost Museum Archive. https:// lostmuseum.cuny.edu/archive/great-astronomical-discoveries -newyork-sun.

Dunlop, Doug. "The Moon Hoax of 1835: Great Astronomical Discoveries." Smithsonian Libraries and Archives, August 28, 2013. https://blog.library.si.edu/blog/2013/08/28/great _moon_hoax_1835/#.YducUhPMKNI.

Young, Kevin. "Moon Shot: Race, a Hoax, and the Birth of Fake News." *New Yorker*, October 21, 2017. https://www .newyorker.com/books/page-turner/moon-shot-race-a-hoax -and-the-birth-of-fake-news.

Williams, Julie Hedgepeth. "The Founding of the Penny Press: Nothing New under 'The Sun,' 'The Herald' or 'The Tribune.'" Paper presented at the Annual Meeting of the American Journalism Historians Association, Salt Lake City, Utah, October 6–9, 1993. https://files.eric.ed.gov/fulltext /ED360650.pdf.

Mitchell, Robert. "'A Carnival of Death' on New York's Streets:

The Newspaper Hoax that Panicked a City." *Washington Post*, June 13, 2017. https://www.washingtonpost.com/news/retropolis/wp/2017/06/13/a-carnival-of-death-on-new-yorks-streets-the-newspaper-hoax-that-panicked-a-city/.

Museum of Hoaxes. "The Central Park Zoo Escape." Museum of Hoaxes. Accessed February 4, 2022. http://hoaxes.org/archive/permalink/the_central_park_zoo_escape/.

Stites, Tom. "A Quarter of All US Newspapers Have Died in 15 Years, a New UNC News Deserts Study Found." *Poynter*, June 24, 2020. https://www.poynter.org/locally/2020/unc-news-deserts-report-2020/.

Tracy, Marc. "A Paradox at the Heart of the Newspaper Crisis." *New York Times*, August 1, 2019. https://www.nytimes.com/2019/08/01/business/media/news-deserts-media-newspapers.html.

Henry, Mike. *What They Didn't Teach You in American History Class*. Landham, MD: Rowman & Littlefield, 2014. https://books.google.com/books?id=wOQjAwAAQBAJ&printsec=frontcover&source=gbs_ge_summary_r&cad=0#v=onepage&q&f=false.

Pasley, Jeffrey L. "The Two National 'Gazettes': Newspapers and the Embodiment of American Political Parties." *Early American Literature* 35, no. 1 (2000): 51–86. http://www.jstor.org/stable/25057179.

Thompson, Susan. *The Penny Press: The Origins of the Modern News Media, 1833–1861*. Northport, AL: Vision Press, 2004.

National Park Service. "The First Ride." Pony Express National

Historic Trail. Updated January 30, 2021. https://www.nps .gov/poex/learn/historyculture/the-first-ride.htm.

myMailHouse. "Who Knew: The Pony Express." *myMailHouse* (blog). Accessed February 4, 2022. https://blog.mymailhouse .net/the-pony-express.

Worrall, Simon. "Why the Short-Lived Pony Express Still Fascinates Us." *National Geographic*, June 23, 2018. https://www .nationalgeographic.com/history/article/why-the-short-lived -pony-express-still-fascinates-us.

Crawford, Amy. "How the Associated Press Got Its Start 175 Years Ago." *Smithsonian Magazine*, May 2021. https://www .smithsonianmag.com/arts-culture/associated-press-turns -175-years-old-180977462/.

Komor, Valerie S. "AP at 175: A Photographic History." *AP Images Blog*. February 14, 2021. https://apimagesblog.com/historical /2021/1/30/ap-at-175-a-photographic-history.

Ritchie, Donald A. *American Journalists*. New York: Oxford University Press, 1997. https://books.google.com/books?id =rfhQEAAAQBAJ&printsec=frontcover#v=onepage&q&f=false.

California Trail Interpretive Center. "First Transcontinental Telegraph." California Trail Interpretive Center. Accessed February 4, 2022. https://www.californiatrailcenter.org/first -transcontinental-telegraph/.

Library of Congress. "Today in History—May 24." Library of Congress. Accessed February 4, 2022. https://www.loc.gov /item/today-in-history/may-24/.

Kielbowicz, Richard B. "Electrifying News! Journalists, Audiences, and the Culture of Timeliness in the United States, 1840–1920."

Time & Society 28, no. 1 (2019): 200–230. https://doi
.org/10.1177%2F0961463X16634724.

Dodson, Brian. "Plug Pulled on the World's Last Commercial
Electric Telegraph System." *New Atlas*, July 17, 2013. https://
newatlas.com/last-telegraph-message/28314/.

Scanlan, Chip. "Birth of the Inverted Pyramid: A Child of
Technology, Commerce and History." *Poynter*, June 20, 2003.
https://www.poynter.org/reporting-editing/2003/birth-of-the
-inverted-pyramid-a-child-of-technology-commerce-and
-history/.

Abadi, Mark. "The Ninth US President Died on This Day in
1841—Here's How Newspapers Reacted." *Business Insider*,
April 4, 2017. https://www.businessinsider.com/william-henry
-harrison-death-newspaper-reaction-2017-4#north-carolina
-standard-raleigh-north-carolina-7.

McCombs, Maxwell. "A Look at Agenda-Setting: Past, Present
and Future." *Journalism Studies* 6, no. 4 (2005): 543–557.
https://doi.org/10.1080/14616700500250438.

Kleis Nielsen, Rasmus, Meera Selva, and Simge Andı. "Race and
Leadership in the News Media 2020: Evidence from Five Mar-
kets." Reuters Institute, July 16, 2020. https://reutersinstitute
.politics.ox.ac.uk/race-and-leadership-news-media-2020
-evidence-five-markets.

United States Census Bureau. "Race and Ethnicity in the United
States: 2010 Census and 2020 Census." United States Census Bureau, August 12, 2021. https://www.census.gov/library
/visualizations/interactive/race-and-ethnicity-in-the-united
-state-2010-and-2020-census.html.

Robert, Yola. "How the Vision of This Female Founder Has Created Unrivaled Access for Black Voices in Media." Forbes-Women. *Forbes*, June 14, 2021. https://www.forbes.com /sites/yolarobert1/2021/06/14/how-the-vision-of-this-female -founder-has-created-unrivaled-access-for-black-voices-in -media/?sh=76270e9f5626.

Schumacher-Hodge Dixon, Mandela. "How to Get Your First Million Users, with Morgan DeBaun, CEO & Founder of Blavity." *Mandela SH Dixon* (blog). October 27, 2016. https:// mandelash.medium.com/how-to-get-your-first-million-users -with-morgan-debaun-ceo-founder-of-blavity-643a472f6490.

News Leaders Association. "ASNE's 2018 Diversity Survey Results—Data Tables." News Leaders Association. Accessed February 4, 2022. https://members.newsleaders.org/diversity -survey-2018-tables.

PBS. "Freedom's Journal." PBS. Accessed February 4, 2022. http://www.pbs.org/blackpress/news_bios/newbios/nwsppr /freedom/freedom.html.

PBS. "Robert Sengstacke Abbott (1870–1940)." PBS. Accessed February 4, 2022. https://www.pbs.org/blackpress/news_bios /abbott.html.

Schlabach, Elizabeth. "The Influenza Epidemic and Jim Crow Public Health Policies and Practices in Chicago, 1917–1921." *The Journal of African American History* 104, no. 1 (2019): 31–58. https://doi.org/10.1086/701105.

Pitz, Marylynne. "The Pittsburgh Courier Chronicled History of Black Americans." *AP News*, March 6, 2021. https://apnews .com/article/race-and-ethnicity-pittsburgh-newspapers

-education-5d57379df13e4fa0d1969d52ff1a5273.

Chicago Defender. https://chicagodefender.com/.

Goodnough, Abby, Monica Davey, and Mitch Smith. "When the Water Turned Brown." *New York Times*, January 23, 2016. https://www.nytimes.com/2016/01/24/us/when-the-water -turned-brown.html.

Carmody, Steve. "GM May Soon Get Back on Flint Water." Michigan Radio, June 13, 2018. https://www.michiganradio .org/politics-government/2018-06-13/gm-may-soon-get-back -on-flint-water.

Murembya, Leonidas, and Eric Guthrie. "Demographic and Labor Market Profile: City of Flint." State of Michigan Department of Technology, Management and Budget, April 2016. https:// milmi.org/_docs/publications/Flint_City_Demographic _and_Labor_Mkt_Profile.pdf.

Shultz, David. "Was Flint's Deadly Legionnaires' Epidemic Caused by Low Chlorine Levels in the Water Supply?" *Science*, February 5, 2018. https://www.science.org/content /article/was-flint-s-deadly-legionnaires-epidemic-caused-low -chlorine-levels-water-supply.

Dingle, Adrian. "The Flint Water Crisis: What's Really Going On?" American Chemical Society, December 2016. https:// www.acs.org/content/acs/en/education/resources/highschool /chemmatters/past-issues/2016-2017/december-2016/flint -water-crisis.html.

Leonnig, Carol D. "Increase in Miscarriages Coincided with High Levels of Lead in DC Water, Study Finds." *Washington Post*, December 9, 2013. https://www.washingtonpost.com

/politics/increase-in-miscarriages-coincided-with-high-levels
-of-lead-in-dc-water-study-finds/2013/12/09/22b4fe72-60f9
-11e3-8beb-3f9a9942850f_story.html.

Bock, Eric. "Pediatrician Who Uncovered Flint Water Crisis
Recounts Experience." *NIH Record* 73, no. 9 (April 30, 2021): 1,
8–9. https://nihrecord.nih.gov/2021/04/30/pediatrician-who
-uncovered-flint-water-crisis-recounts-experience.

Clark, Amy. "How an Investigative Journalist Helped Prove a
City Was Being Poisoned with Its Own Water." *Columbia
Journalism Review*, November 3, 2015. https://www.cjr.org
/united_states_project/flint_water_lead_curt_guyette_aclu
_michigan.php.

Denchak, Melissa. "Flint Water Crisis: Everything You Need to
Know." Natural Resources Defense Council, November 8, 2018.
https://www.nrdc.org/stories/flint-water-crisis-everything
-you-need-know.

Associated Press. "Doctors Urge Flint to Stop Using Water from
Flint River." *Washington Times*, September 24, 2015. https://
www.washingtontimes.com/news/2015/sep/24/flint-plans
-advisory-about-curbing-exposure-to-lea/.

Longley, Kristin. "Report: Buying in to New Water Pipeline from
Lake Huron Cheaper for Flint Drinking Water than Treating River Water." MLive.com, September 8, 2011. Updated
January 21, 2019. https://www.mlive.com/news/flint/2011/09
/water_treatment.html.

Jackson, Derrick Z. "Environmental Justice? Unjust Coverage of
the Flint Water Crisis." Shorenstein Center on Media, Politics and Public Policy, July 2017. https://shorensteincenter.org

/wp-content/uploads/2017/07/Flint-Water-Crisis-Derrick-Z
-Jackson-1.pdf.

Shafer, Jack. "Newspapers' Embarrassing Lobbying Campaign."
Politico Magazine, June 10, 2019. https://www.politico.com
/magazine/story/2019/06/10/newspapers-embarrassing
-lobbying-campaign-227100/.

Carey, Liz. "One-Fifth of U.S. Newspapers Close in Last 14
Years." *Daily Yonder*, October 22, 2018. https://dailyyonder
.com/one-fifth-u-s-newspapers-close-last-14-years/2018/10/22/.

PEN America. "Losing the News: The Decimation of Local Journalism and the Search for Solutions." PEN America, November
20, 2019. https://pen.org/wp-content/uploads/2019/12/Losing
-the-News-The-Decimation-of-Local-Journalism-and-the
-Search-for-Solutions-Report.pdf.

NIEonline. "Glossary of Newspaper Terms." NIEonline. Accessed
February 6, 2022. https://nieonline.com/coloradonie/downloads
/journalism/GlossaryOfNewspaperTerms.

Saunders, Richard H. *American Faces: A Cultural History of Portraiture
and Identity.* Hanover: University Press of New England, 2016.

Pew Research Center. "Framing the News." Pew Research Center,
July 13, 1998. https://www.pewresearch.org/journalism/1998
/07/13/framing-the-news/.

PBS. "Freedom's Journal." PBS. Accessed February 4, 2022.
http://www.pbs.org/blackpress/news_bios/newbios/nwsppr
/freedom/freedom.html.

Bursztyn, Leonardo, Aakaash Rao, Christopher Roth, and David
Yanagizawa-Drott. "Misinformation During a Pandemic."
Becker Friedman Institute for Economics at University of

Chicago, September 1, 2020. https://bfi.uchicago.edu/wp
-content/uploads/BFI_WP_202044.pdf.

Oxford Reference. "Ritual Model." Accessed February 6, 2022.
https://www.oxfordreference.com/view/10.1093/oi/authority
.20110803100422885.

Stroud, Natalie Jomini. "Selective Exposure Theories." Edited by
Kate Kenski and Kathleen Hall Jamieson. *Oxford Handbook
of Political Communication*, May 2014. Updated January 11,
2018. https://doi.org/10.1093/oxfordhb/9780199793471.013
.009_update_001.

Simkin, John. "Claud Cockburn." *Spartacus Educational* (blog).
September 1997. Updated January 2020. https://spartacus
-educational.com/SPcockburn.htm.

Wallace, Lewis Raven. "Objectivity Is Dead, and I'm Okay with
It." *Lewis Wallace* (blog). *Medium*, January 27, 2017. https://
medium.com/@lewispants/objectivity-is-dead-and-im-okay
-with-it-7fd2b4b5c58f.

Wallace, Lewis Raven. "I Was Fired from My Journalism Job Ten
Days into Trump." *Lewis Wallace* (blog). *Medium*, January 31,
2017. https://medium.com/@lewispants/i-was-fired-from-my
-journalism-job-ten-days-into-trump-c3bc014ce51d.

Wallace, Lewis Raven. *The View from Somewhere: Undoing the
Myth of Journalistic Objectivity.* Chicago: University of Chicago
Press, 2019. https://www.scribd.com/book/428846825/The
-View-from-Somewhere-Undoing-the-Myth-of-Journalistic
-Objectivity.

Lee, Jasmine. "Journalist Discusses the 'Myth' of Objectivity in
the Profession." *Michigan Daily*, January 8, 2020. https://

www.michigandaily.com/news/ann-arbor/objectivity
-journalism-talk/.

O'Toole, Garson. "Finley Peter Dunne." *Quote Investigator* (blog).
February 1, 2019. https://quoteinvestigator.com/tag/finley
-peter-dunne/.

Pulitzer Prizes. "Public Service." Pulitzer Prizes. Updated 2021.
https://www.pulitzer.org/prize-winners-by-category/204.

Wallace, Lewis Raven. "S4 E11: More Truth." Produced by John
Biewen and Chenjerai Kumanyika. *Scene on Radio*, May 27,
2020. http://www.sceneonradio.org/s4-e11-more-truth/.

Spencer, Christian. "Spanking Schoolchildren Is Legal in Many
Parts of US—and Some Kids Get Hit More Often." *The
Hill*, May 19, 2021. https://thehill.com/changing-america
/enrichment/education/554426-spanking-schoolchildren-is
-legal-in-many-parts-of-us.

Sires, Albio, and Nicole Malliotakis. "Prospects for Democracy
in Cuba." By Elizabeth Hoffman. Center for Strategic and
International Studies, August 11, 2021. https://www.csis.org
/analysis/prospects-democracy-cuba.

Gladstone, Brooke, and Josh Neufeld. *The Influencing Machine:
Brooke Gladstone on the Media*. New York: W.W. Norton,
2012.

Kois, Dave. "'On the Media': Comics Edition." *New York Times*,
June 8, 2011. https://www.nytimes.com/2011/06/08/books
/review/on-the-media-comics-edition.html.

Los Angeles Times Editorial Board. "Editorial: 75 Years Later,
Looking Back at the Times' Shameful Response to the Japanese Internment." Opinion, *Los Angeles Times*, February

19, 2017. https://www.latimes.com/opinion/editorials/la-ed
-internment-anniversary-20170219-story.html.

Clark, Tom. "Why Do Editorials Remain Anonymous?" *Guardian*,
January 10, 2011. https://www.theguardian.com/commentisfree
/2011/jan/10/editorial-leading-article-anonymous.

Death Penalty Information Center. "Editorials: Dallas Morning
News Issues Historic Call to End Death Penalty." Editorial,
Death Penalty Information Center. April 16, 2007. https://
deathpenaltyinfo.org/news/editorials-dallas-morning-news
-issues-historic-call-to-end-death-penalty.

Merriam-Webster. "Op-ed." *Merriam-Webster Online Dictionary.*
Accessed February 5, 2022. https://www.merriam-webster
.com/dictionary/op-ed.

Iannucci, Rebecca. "News or Opinion? Online, It's Hard to
Tell." *Poynter*, August 16, 2017. https://www.poynter.org
/ethics-trust/2017/news-or-opinion-online-its-hard-to-tell/.

MPR News. "National Geographic Reckons with Its Past: 'For
Decades, Our Coverage Was Racist.'" MPR News, March 13,
2018. https://www.mprnews.org/story/2018/03/12/national
-geographic-says-coverage-racist-for-decades.

Stovall, Katherine E. "White Mob Violence and the Terror Kill-
ings of Two African-American Veterans of WWI." *Dr. Hilary
N. Green, PhD* (blog), 2016. https://hgreen.people.ua.edu
/uploads/6/3/7/7/63777429/stovall_documentarychapter.pdf.

Lyman, Brian. "'There Will Be Lynchings': How the Advertiser
Failed Victims of Racial Terror." *Montgomery Advertiser*,
April 20, 2018. Updated January 10, 2019. https://www
.montgomeryadvertiser.com/story/news/2018/04/20

/there-lynchings-how-advertiser-failed-victims-racial-terror
-eji-peace-justice-memorial-montgomery/499656002/.

Begos, Kevin. "All Aboard: Newspapers Jumped on Sterilization
Bandwagon." *Winston-Salem Journal*, December 9, 2002.
Updated March 18, 2013. https://journalnow.com/news/local
/all-aboard-newspapers-jumped-on-sterilization-bandwagon
/article_7577c770-8fee-11e2-b8e1-0019bb30f31a.html.

Baleria, Gina. *The Journalism Behind Journalism: Going Beyond
the Basics to Train Effective Journalists in a Shifting Landscape.*
London: Routledge, an imprint of Taylor & Francis Group,
2021. https://books.google.com/books?id=vfcyEAAAQBAJ&
dq=shame+at+what+was+missing:+the+achievements,+
aspirations+and+milestones+of+an+entire+population+
routinely+overlooked,+as+if+Black+people+were+invisible.&
source=gbs_navlinks_s.

New York Times Editorial Board. "Slandering the Unborn."
Opinion, *New York Times*, December 28, 2018. https://
www.nytimes.com/interactive/2018/12/28/opinion/crack
-babies-racism.html.

Deto, Ryan. "Alexis Johnson, Pittsburgh Journalist Banned from
Covering Protests, Lands Job at Vice." *Pittsburgh City Paper*,
October 14, 2020. https://www.pghcitypaper.com/pittsburgh
/alexis-johnson-pittsburgh-journalist-banned-from-covering
-protests-lands-job-at-vice/Content?oid=18177039.

Jones, Nicholas, Rachel Marks, Roberto Ramirez, and Merarys
Ríos-Vargas. "2020 Census Illuminates Racial and Eth-
nic Composition of the Country." United States Census
Bureau, August 12, 2021. https://www.census.gov/library

/stories/2021/08/improved-race-ethnicity-measures-reveal
-united-states-population-much-more-multiracial.html.

Columbia University Libraries Online Exhibitions. "Joseph Pulitzer and the World." Curated by Jennifer B. Lee. Accessed
February 5, 2022. https://exhibitions.library.columbia.edu
/exhibits/show/pulitzer/philanthropy/school-of-journalism.

Wallace, Lewis Raven. "The View from Nowhere." *The View
from Somewhere*, October 15, 2019. Apple Podcasts. https://
podcasts.apple.com/us/podcast/the-view-from-nowhere
/id1481617425?i=1000453580806.

Archives of Women's Political Communication. "Ida B Wells-
Barnett." Archives of Women's Political Communication.
Accessed February 5, 2022. https://awpc.cattcenter.iastate
.edu/directory/ida-b-wells/.

Cools, Amy. "Happy Birthday, Ida B. Wells!" *Ordinary Philosophy* (blog). July 16, 2019. https://ordinaryphilosophy.com/tag
/the-new-york-age/.

Norwood, Arlisha R. "Ida B. Wells-Barnett." National Women's
History Museum, 2017. https://www.womenshistory.org
/education-resources/biographies/ida-b-wells-barnett.

Pulitzer Prizes. "Announcement of the 2020 Pulitzer Prize Winners." Pulitzer Prizes, May 4, 2020. https://www.pulitzer.org
/news/announcement-2020-pulitzer-prize-winners.

Pullella, Philip. "Pope Warns Media over 'Sin' of Spreading Fake
News, Smearing Politicians." Reuters, December 7, 2016.
https://www.reuters.com/article/us-pope-media/pope-warns
-media-over-sin-of-spreading-fake-news-smearing-politicians
-idUSKBN13W1TU.

Taylor, Adam. "Pope Says Journalists Risk 'Becoming Ill from Coprophilia.'" *Business Insider India*, March 15, 2013. https://www.businessinsider.in/Pope-Says-Journalists-Risk -Becoming-Ill-From-Coprophilia/articleshow/21256177 .cms.

Boston Globe. "Spotlight: Clergy Sex Abuse Crisis." Metro, *Boston Globe*, 2002. https://www3.bostonglobe.com/metro /specials/clergy/.

Nanyang Technological University. "NTU Singapore Study Highlights Media's Important Role in Debunking COVID-19 Misinformation." *EurekAlert!*, July 11, 2021. https://www .eurekalert.org/news-releases/859603.

Le Cunff, Anne-Laure. "How to Go on an Information Diet." Ness Labs. Accessed February 3, 2022. https://nesslabs.com /information-diet.

Zhu, Katie. "Slimformation: A Prototype That Helps You Read Smarter, Improve Your 'Information Diet.'" Knight Lab, June 14, 2013. https://knightlab.northwestern.edu/2013/06 /14/slimformation-a-prototype-that-helps-your-read-smarter -improve-your-information-diet/.

Pulitzer Center. "Carol Rosenberg." Pulitzer Center. Accessed February 5, 2022. https://pulitzercenter.org/people/carol -rosenberg.

Solis, Dianne. "Dianne Solis." LinkedIn. Accessed February 6, 2022. https://www.linkedin.com/in/diannesolis/.

Grabe, Maria Elizabeth, and Erik Page Bucy. "Visual Bias." Chap. 5 in *Image Bite Politics: News and the Visual Framing of Elections*. New York: Oxford University Press, 2009;

online: Oxford Scholarship Online, April 2010. https://doi
.org/10.1093/acprof:oso/9780195372076.003.0005.

Snopes. https://www.snopes.com/.

PolitiFact. https://www.politifact.com/.

Google Images. https://images.google.com/.

TinEye Reverse Image Search. https://tineye.com/.

YouTube DataViewer. https://citizenevidence.amnestyusa.org/.

InVID Project. https://www.invid-project.eu/.

Johnson, Clay A. *The Information Diet: A Case for Conscious
Consumption*. Sebastopol, CA: O'Reilly Media, 2012.

Encyclopaedia Britannica. "Areopagitica: Pamphlet by Milton."
Updated March 27, 2020. https://www.britannica.com/topic
/Areopagitica.

Asia for Educators, Columbia University. "Technological Advances
during the Song." The Song Dynasty in China (website).
Accessed February 5, 2022. http://afe.easia.columbia.edu
/songdynasty-module/tech-printing.html.

History.com. "Printing Press." May 7, 2018. Updated October
10, 2019. https://www.history.com/topics/inventions/printing
-press.

Encyclopaedia Britannica. "Publick Occurrences, Both Foreign
and Domestick." Accessed February 5, 2022. https://www
.britannica.com/topic/Publick-Occurrences-Both-Foreign
-and-Domestick.

Clear and Present Danger. "1695: Locke and the End of the
Licensing Act." Clear and Present Danger (website). Accessed
February 6, 2022. http://www.freespeechhistory.com/timeline
/1695-end-of-the-licensing-act/#identifier.

USHistory.org. "The Alien and Sedition Acts." Accessed February 5, 2022. https://www.ushistory.org/us/19e.asp.

Library of Congress. "The Sun (New York [NY]) 1833–1916." Library of Congress. Accessed February 5, 2022. https://www.loc.gov/item/sn83030272/.

Chabon, Michael. "150th Anniversary: 1851–2001; The First Issue: Imagining How a Paper Was Born." *New York Times*, November 14, 2001. https://www.nytimes.com/2001/11/14/news/150th-anniversary-1851-2001-the-first-issue-imagining-how-a-paper-was-born.html.

Schruben, Francis W. "Edwin M. Stanton and Reconstruction." *Tennessee Historical Quarterly* 23, no. 2 (June 1964): 145–168. https://www.jstor.org/stable/42621680.

Risley, Ford. "Birth of the Byline." *Opinionator* (blog). *New York Times*, April 22, 2013. https://opinionator.blogs.nytimes.com/2013/04/22/birth-of-the-byline/.

Detroit Historical Society. "WWJ 950 AM." Encyclopedia of Detroit. Accessed February 5, 2022. https://detroithistorical.org/learn/encyclopedia-of-detroit/wwj-950-am.

Bureau of Justice Assistance. "The Communications Act of 1934." Bureau of Justice Assistance. Accessed February 6, 2022. https://bja.ojp.gov/program/it/privacy-civil-liberties/authorities/statutes/1288.

CBS News. "JFK Assassination: The Fateful Day in Dallas Unfolds." November 22, 2013. https://www.cbsnews.com/news/jfk-assassination-the-fateful-day-in-dallas-unfolds/.

Washington Post. "The Watergate Story: The Post Investigates." Accessed February 6, 2022. https://www.washingtonpost.com

/wp-srv/politics/special/watergate/part1.html.

Lewis, Peter H. "The New York Times Introduces a Web Site." *New York Times*, January 22, 1996. https://www.nytimes .com/1996/01/22/business/the-new-york-times-introduces-a -web-site.html.

Carlson, Nicholas. "How Facebook Was Founded." *Business Insider*, March 5, 2010. https://www.businessinsider.com/how -facebook-was-founded-2010-3.

Brown, Campbell, and Mona Sarantakos. "Introducing Facebook News." Meta, October 15, 2019. https://about.fb.com /news/2019/10/introducing-facebook-news/.

MacArthur, Amanda. "The Real History of Twitter, in Brief." *Lifewire*. Updated November 25, 2020. https://www.lifewire .com/history-of-twitter-3288854.

Owen, Laura Hazard. "Facebook's Pivot to Video Didn't Just Burn Publishers. It Didn't Even Work for Facebook." Nieman Lab, September 15, 2021. https://www.niemanlab.org/2021/09 /well-this-puts-a-nail-in-the-news-video-on-facebook-coffin/.

Braswell, Sean. "Is This German Novel the Deadliest Book in History?" OZY, March 12, 2017. https://www.ozy.com /true-and-stories/is-this-german-novel-the-deadliest-book-in -history/76099/.

Sonneck, G., E. Etzersdorfer, and S. Nagel-Kuess. "Imitative Suicide on the Viennese Subway." *Social Science & Medicine* 38, no. 3 (1994): 453–457. https://ippesbrasil.com.br/wp-content /uploads/2018/07/Sonneck1994.pdf.

Rosenblatt, Kalhan. "Suicide Searches Increased After Release of '13 Reasons Why.'" NBC News, July 31, 2017. https://www

.nbcnews.com/health/health-news/suicide-searches-increased
-after-release-13-reasons-why-n788161.

National Suicide Prevention Lifeline. "The Papageno Effect." National Suicide Prevention Lifeline. Accessed February 5, 2022. https://suicidepreventionlifeline.org/wp-content/uploads /2021/04/Lifeline-Papageno-Effect.pdf.

Washington Post. "Wendi Winters's Last 'Teen of the Week' Interview Was on Gun Violence." YouTube, June 30, 2018. https:// www.youtube.com/watch?v=eg0bOJ2wI2s.

Duncan, Ian, and Nicholas Bogel-Burroughs. "Alleged Annapolis Capital Shooter Jarrod Ramos Had Long-Running Feud with Paper." *Baltimore Sun,* June 29, 2018. https://www.baltimore sun.com/news/crime/bs-md-ramos-search-20180628-story .html.

Hannagan, Charley. "By the Numbers: Taxi Driver Is the Job with the No. 1 Murder Rate." Opinion, Syracuse.com, January 29, 2015. Updated March 22, 2019. https://www.syracuse .com/opinion/2015/01/by_the_numbers_job_with_the _number_1_murder_rate_taxi_drivers.html.

McCarthy, Niall. "The Deadliest Countries for Journalists in 2018 [Infographic]." *Forbes,* December 19, 2018. https://www.forbes.com/sites/niallmccarthy/2018/12/19/the -deadliest-countries-for-journalists-in-2018-infographic/?sh= 4484e0832af5.

Committee to Protect Journalists. https://cpj.org/.

Al Jazeera. "Suicide Bomber Attacks High School in Afghanistan." December 11, 2014. http://america.aljazeera.com/articles /2014/12/11/kabul-school-bombing.html.

International Press Institute. "Zubair Hatami, Afghanistan." International Press Institute, August 31, 2016. https://ipi .media/zubair-hatami-afghanistan/.

Committee to Protect Journalists. "Photojournalist Christoff Griffith Killed at Crime Scene in Barbados." Committee to Protect Journalists, June 26, 2020. https://cpj.org/2020 /06/photojournalist-christoff-griffith-killed-at-crime-scene-in -barbados/.

Harlan, Chico, and Stefano Pitrelli. "Confusion Spreads as Italy Tries to Lock Down 16 Million People." *Washington Post*, March 8, 2020. https://www.washingtonpost.com/world /erkel/erke-coronavirus-lockdown-giuseppe-conte/2020/03 /08/4f72b0da-60fc-11ea-ac50-18701e14e06d_story.html.

Ortenzi, Flaminia, Emiliano Albanese, and Marta Fadda. "A Transdisciplinary Analysis of COVID-19 in Italy: The Most Affected Country in Europe." *International Journal of Environmental Research and Public Health* 17, no. 24 (December 18, 2020). https://doi.org/10.3390/ijerph17249488.

CHAPTER 4

Rudd, Matilda. "Controversial Vegan Blogger Shows Off Her Fit Figure at 40." *Daily Mail*, September 21, 2020. https://www .dailymail.co.uk/femail/article-8754515/Controversial-vegan -blogger-Freelee-Banana-Girl-shows-fit-figure-40th-birthday .html.

Barnhart, Brent. "Everything You Need to Know About Social Media Algorithms." *Sprout Social* (blog). March 26, 2021. https://sproutsocial.com/insights/social-media-algorithms/.

Newton, Casey. "Facebook Rolls Out Expanded Like Button Reactions Around the World." *Verge*, February 24, 2016. https://www.theverge.com/2016/2/24/11094374/facebook -reactions-like-button.

Merrill, Jeremy B., and Will Oremus. "Facebook Prioritized 'Angry' Emoji Reaction Posts in News Feeds." *Washington Post*, October 26, 2021. https://www.washingtonpost.com /technology/2021/10/26/facebook-angry-emoji-algorithm/.

Horwitz, Jeff, and Deepa Seetherama. "Facebook Executives Shut Down Efforts to Make the Site Less Divisive." *Wall Street Journal*, May 28, 2020. https://www.wsj.com/articles /facebook-knows-it-encourages-division-top-executives -nixed-solutions-11590507499.

Sonnemaker, Tyler. "Facebook Reportedly Had Evidence That Its Algorithms Were Dividing People, But Top Executives Killed or Weakened Proposed Solutions." *Insider*. May 27, 2020. https://www.businessinsider.com/facebook-knew-algorithms -divided-users-execs-killed-fixes-report-2020-5.

Munn, Luke. "Angry by Design: Toxic Communication and Technical Architectures." *Humanities and Social Sciences Communications* 7, no. 53 (July 30, 2020). https://doi.org/10.1057 /s41599-020-00550-7.

Streitfeld, David. "'The Internet Is Broken': @ev Is Trying to Salvage It." *New York Times*, May 20, 2017. https://www .nytimes.com/2017/05/20/technology/evan-williams-medium -twitter-internet.html.

Gordon, Billi. "Social Media Is Harmful to Your Brain and Relationships." Reviewed by Ekua Hagan. *Psychology Today*,

October 20, 2017. https://www.psychologytoday.com/us/blog
/obesely-speaking/201710/social-media-is-harmful-your
-brain-and-relationships.

Shaffer, Joyce. "Neuroplasticity and Clinical Practice: Building
Brain Power for Health." Edited by Gian Mauro Manzoni.
Frontiers in Psychology (July 26, 2016). https://doi.org/10.3389
/fpsyg.2016.01118.

Yoon, Kay, and Yaguang Zhu. "Social Media Affordances and
Transactive Memory Systems in Virtual Teams." *Management Communication Quarterly* (July 22, 2021). https://doi
.org/10.1177/08933189211032639.

BBC. "Instagram for Kids Paused after Backlash." September 27,
2021. https://www.bbc.com/news/technology-58707753.

Kamanetz, Anya. "Facebook's Own Data Is Not as Conclusive as
You Think about Teens and Mental Health." NPR, October 6,
2021. https://www.npr.org/2021/10/06/1043138622/facebook
-instagram-teens-mental-health.

BBC. "UK's Youngest Terror Offender, Boy, 16, Sentenced."
February 8, 2021. https://www.bbc.com/news/uk-england
-cornwall-55951628.

Hermansson, Patrik, and David Lawrence. "Hitler Youths: The
Rise of Teenage Far-Right Terrorists." HOPE not hate, September 2020. https://hopenothate.org.uk/wp-content/uploads
/2020/09/HnH_Hitler-Youths-report_2020-09-v2.pdf.

Prothero, Mitch. "13-Year-Old Boy Was Alleged Commander of
Neo-Nazi 'Feuerkrieg Division.'" *Business Insider*, April 15,
2020. https://www.businessinsider.com/13-year-old-alleged
-commander-neo-nazi-feuerkrieg-division-2020-4.

Wagner, Meg. "'Blood and Soil': Protesters Chant Nazi Slogan in Charlottesville." CNN. Updated August 12, 2017. https://www.cnn.com/2017/08/12/us/charlottesville-unite-the-right-rally/index.html.

Alaimo, Kara. "How the Facebook Arabic Page 'We Are All Khaled Said' Helped Promote the Egyptian Revolution." *Social Media + Society* 1, no. 2 (July–December 2015). https://doi.org/10.1177/2056305115604854.

Coldewey, Devin. "Study Finds Reddit's Controversial Ban of Its Most Toxic Subreddits Actually Worked." *TechCrunch*, September 11, 2017. https://techcrunch.com/2017/09/11/study-finds-reddits-controversial-ban-of-its-most-toxic-subreddits-actually-worked/.

Matsakis, Louise. "TikTok Finally Explains How the 'For You' Algorithm Works." *Wired*, June 18, 2020. https://www.wired.com/story/tiktok-finally-explains-for-you-algorithm-works/.

Guynn, Jessica. "Facebook Bans Donald Trump for Two Years over Capitol Riot Posts." *USA Today*, June 4, 2021. Updated June 5, 2021. https://www.usatoday.com/story/tech/2021/06/04/facebook-suspends-trump-two-years-capitol-attack/7545534002/.

Robertson, Adi. "Reddit Bans 'Fat People Hate' and Other Subreddits under New Harassment Rules." *Verge*, June 10, 2015. https://www.theverge.com/2015/6/10/8761763/reddit-harassment-ban-fat-people-hate-subreddit.

Roose, Kevin. "Reddit Limits Noxious Content by Giving Trolls Fewer Places to Gather." *New York Times*, September 25, 2017. https://www.nytimes.com/2017/09/25/business/reddit-limits

-noxious-content-by-giving-trolls-fewer-places-to-gather.html.

Rajendra-Nicolucci, Chand, and Ethan Zuckerman. "An Illustrated Field Guide to Social Media." Knight First Amendment Institute, May 14, 2021. https://knightcolumbia.org/blog /an-illustrated-field-guide-to-social-media.

Times Now Digital. "Here's How to Check Time Spent on Instagram and Set a Reminder to Limit the Usage." Times Now. Updated April 30, 2020. https://www.timesnownews.com /technology-science/article/heres-how-to-check-the-time -spent-on-instagram-and-set-a-reminder-to-limit-the-usage /585271.

CHAPTER 5

Herwick III, Edgar B. "The Slave Who Transformed Cotton Mather from Witch Hunter into Science Innovator." WGBH, July 3, 2016. https://www.wgbh.org/news/2016/07/03/local -news/slave-who-transformed-cotton-mather-witch-hunter -science-innovator.

Niederhuber, Matthew. "The Fight over Inoculation During the 1721 Boston Smallpox Epidemic." *Science in the News* (blog). Harvard University, December 31, 2014. https://sitn.hms .harvard.edu/flash/special-edition-on-infectious-disease/2014 /the-fight-over-inoculation-during-the-1721-boston-smallpox -epidemic/.

Elia, Matthew Joseph. "Ethics in the Afterlife of Slavery: Race, Augustinian Politics, and the Enduring Problem of the Christian Master." PhD diss., Duke University, 2019. https://dukespace.lib.duke.edu/dspace/bitstream/handle

/10161/19806/Elia_duke_0066D_15274.pdf?sequence=1& isAllowed=y.

Wheeler, Rowan. "Onesimus Mather and the Origins of Inoculation in Boston." Paul Revere House. August 22, 2020. https://www.paulreverehouse.org/onesimus-mather-and-the-origins-of-inoculation-in-boston/.

Blakemore, Erin. "How an Enslaved African Man in Boston Helped Save Generations from Smallpox." History.com, February 1, 2019. Updated April 8, 2021. https://www.history.com/news/smallpox-vaccine-onesimus-slave-cotton-mather.

Filsinger, Amy Lynn, and Raymond Dwek. "George Washington and the First Mass Military Inoculation." John W. Kluge Center at the Library of Congress, February 12, 2009. https://www.loc.gov/rr/scitech/GW&smallpoxinoculation.html.

Rosner, Lisa. "Lady Mary Wortley Montagu and Immunization Advocacy." *Books, Health and History* (blog). New York Academy of Medicine Library, March 28, 2017. https://nyamcenterforhistory.org/2017/03/28/lady-mary-wortley-montagu-and-immunization-advocacy/.

Brink, Susan. "What's the Real Story about the Milkmaid and the Smallpox Vaccine?" *Goats and Soda* (blog). NPR, February 1, 2018. https://www.npr.org/sections/goatsandsoda/2018/02/01/582370199/whats-the-real-story-about-the-milkmaid-and-the-smallpox-vaccine.

World Health Organization. "Smallpox." World Health Organization. Accessed February 5, 2022. https://www.who.int/health-topics/smallpox.

Roozenbeek, Jon, and Sander van der Linden. "Don't Just Debunk,

Prebunk: Inoculate Yourself against Digital Misinformation." *Character & Context* (blog). Society for Personality and Social Psychology, February 10, 2021. https://www.spsp.org/news-center/blog/roozenbeek-van-der-linden-resisting-digital-misinformation.

Cook, John. "Inoculation Theory: Using Misinformation to Fight Misinformation." *The Conversation*, May 14, 2017. https://theconversation.com/inoculation-theory-using-misinformation-to-fight-misinformation-77545.

Human Rights Watch. "'Break Their Lineage, Break Their Roots': China's Crimes against Humanity Targeting Uyghurs and Other Turkic Muslims." Human Rights Watch, April 19, 2021. https://www.hrw.org/report/2021/04/19/break-their-lineage-break-their-roots/chinas-crimes-against-humanity-targeting.

Jacobs, Andrew. "At a Factory, the Spark for China's Violence." *New York Times*, July 15, 2009. https://www.nytimes.com/2009/07/16/world/asia/16china.html.

Maizland, Lindsay. "China's Repression of Uyghurs in Xinjiang." Council on Foreign Relations. Updated March 1, 2021. https://www.cfr.org/backgrounder/chinas-repression-uyghurs-xinjiang.

Miller, Cassie. "The Biggest Lie in the White Supremacist Propaganda Playbook: Unraveling the Truth about 'Black-on-White Crime.'" Southern Poverty Law Center, June 14, 2018. https://www.splcenter.org/20180614/biggest-lie-white-supremacist-propaganda-playbook-unraveling-truth-about-%E2%80%98black-white-crime.

Association for Professionals in Infection Control and Epidemiology. "Herd Immunity." Association for Professionals in

Infection Control and Epidemiology. Updated April 6, 2021. https://apic.org/monthly_alerts/herd-immunity/.

Roozenbeek, Jon, and Sander van der Linden. "Fake News Game Confers Psychological Resistance against Online Misinformation." *Palgrave Communications* 5, no. 65 (2019). https://doi.org/10.1057/s41599-019-0279-9.

Lewandowsky, Stephan, Ullrich K. H. Ecker, Colleen M. Seifert, Norbert Schwarz, and John Cook. "Misinformation and Its Correction: Continued Influence and Successful Debiasing." *Psychological Science in the Public Interest* 13, no. 3 (September 17, 2012): 106–131. https://doi.org/10.1177/1529100612451018.

Pennycook, Gordon, Ziv Epstein, Mohsen Mosleh, Antonio A. Arechar, Dean Eckles, and David G. Rand. "Shifting Attention to Accuracy Can Reduce Misinformation Online." *Nature* 592 (2021): 590–595. https://doi.org/10.1038/s41586-021-03344-2.

Postal, Karen Spangenberg, and Kira Armstrong. *Feedback That Sticks: The Art of Effectively Communicating Neuropsychological Assessment Results.* New York: Oxford University Press, 2013.

Gordan, Andrew, Susanne Quadflieg, Jonathan C. W. Brooks, Ullrich K. H. Ecker, and Stephan Lewandowsky. "Keeping Track of 'Alternative Facts': The Neural Correlates of Processing Misinformation Corrections." *NeuroImage* 193 (June 2019): 46–56. https://doi.org/10.1016/j.neuroimage.2019.03.014.

Archie, Lee C. "The Principle of Charity in Philosophy." Philosophy Courses (website). Accessed February 5, 2022. https://philosophy.lander.edu/oriental/charity.html.

Miller, Katherine, and Melanie Rowen. "Looping—Listening to

Understand." Center for Understanding in Conflict. Accessed February 6, 2022. https://understandinginconflict.org/looping/.

Travaglino, Giovanni A., and Chanki Moon. "Compliance and Self-Reporting during the COVID-19 Pandemic: A Cross-Cultural Study of Trust and Self-Conscious Emotions in the United States, Italy, and South Korea." *Frontiers in Psychology* (March 16, 2021). https://doi.org/10.3389/fpsyg.2021.565845.

D'Arcy, Patrick. "How to Listen to People You Disagree With." Emerson Collective, November 2019. https://www.emersoncollective.com/articles/2019/11/how-to-listen-to-people-you-disagree-with/.

Ripley, Amanda. *High Conflict: Why We Get Trapped and How We Get Out.* New York: Simon & Schuster, 2021.

Ripley, Amanda. "The High Cost of High Conflict." By Stefanie Sanford. *The Elective*, May 14, 2021. https://elective.collegeboard.org/high-cost-high-conflict.

Stark, Dave. Review of *High Conflict: Why We Get Trapped and How We Get Out*, by Amanda Ripley. *Words Written Down* (blog). October 2, 2021. http://www.wordswrittendown.com/2021/10/high-conflict-by-amanda-ripley.html.

Norman, Andy, and John Cook. "Infodemic Inoculation: Exercising Thought Intelligence through Whole Brain Thinking with Andy Norman PhD and John Cook PhD." By Lisa Cypers Kamen. *Harvesting Happiness Talk Radio*, June 16, 2021. https://harvestinghappinesstalkradio.com/infodemic-inoculation-exercising-thought-intelligence-through-whole-brain-thinking-with-andy-norman-phd-john-cook-phd/.

National Institute of Mental Health. "Mental Illness." National

Institute of Mental Health. Accessed February 5, 2022. https://www.nimh.nih.gov/health/statistics/mental-illness.

Ogden, Nancy. "How Emotions Can Support Critical Thinking." KQED, March 28, 2016. https://www.kqed.org/education /138183/how-emotions-can-support-critical-thinking.

Food Research & Action Center. "Hunger & Poverty in America." Food Research & Action Center. Accessed February 5, 2022. https://frac.org/hunger-poverty-america.

American Institutes for Research. "National Center on Family Homelessness." American Institutes for Research. Accessed February 5, 2022. https://www.air.org/centers/national-center -family-homelessness.

Reber, Rolf. "What Is Critical Feeling?" *Psychology Today*, April 7, 2016. https://www.psychologytoday.com/us/blog/critical -feeling/201604/what-is-critical-feeling.

Stanford University Center for Teaching and Learning and Mariatte Denman. "The Socratic Method: What It Is and How to Use It in the Classroom." *Speaking of Teaching* 13, no. 1 (Fall 2003). https://tomprof.stanford.edu/posting/810.

Pecorino, Philip A. "Socrates in Prison." In *Introduction to Philosophy*, Chapter 2. Queensborough Community College, CUNY. Accessed February 5, 2022. https://www.qcc.cuny.edu /socialsciences/ppecorino/intro_text/chapter%202%20greeks /Socrates_prison.htm.

INDEX

A

Abbott, Robert S., 136

Adams, John, 151

addiction, 184–185, 219, 225, 302

ad hominem attacks, 57

advertising

    internet and, 145, 211–217

    newspapers and, 108–109,
        112–113, 146–147

affect heuristic, 77–78

agenda setting, 127, 141

algorithms

    about, 209–210, 228

    recommendation, 214,
        229–231, 235

    social media platforms and,
        210–217, 232, 235

Alien and Sedition Acts (1798), 151

Allen, Jennifer, 198

alternative facts, 170–192

alt-right movements, 232–233

American Civil Liberties Union,
    141

Amnesty International, 205

Anderton, William, 105

assimilation bias, 80–81

Associated Press (AP),
    115–116, 152

Austrian Association for Suicide
    Prevention, 164

authenticity of the lying
    demagogue, 32n

availability heuristic, 76

B

backfire effect, 87–89, 93,
    259–260

Bacon, Francis, 14

Bad News Game, 253–255

Baker, Hannah, 164

Banana Girl, 207–209

Beach, Moses Yale, 115, 152

behavior

   changing via brain chemistry,
      72

   news influencing, 166–170

   stories influencing, 70

beliefs

   backfire effect and, 87–89, 93,
      259–260

   BS-proofing your brain,
      248–249, 271, 294–299

   changing minds, 74

   illusion of explanatory depth,
      90–93

   manipulating, 250–251

   pushback effect, 93

   ritual model of communication
      and, 168

   strength of, 100–101

   sunrise problem, 95–101

biases

   about, 75–76, 82–83

   assimilation, 80–81

   backfire effect and, 87–89, 93,
      259–260

   cognitive, 73, 75, 81–82

   confirmation, 14, 79–81

   Dunning-Kruger effect, 81–82,
      275

   heuristic techniques and,
      76–79

   illusion of explanatory depth,
      90–93, 275

   implicit, 75

   journalism and, 103–104

   knowing your, 296

   narrative, 204

   partisan press and, 110–113

   pushback effect and, 93

   status quo, 174

   unconscious, 75, 296

   uncovering, 275

   visual, 203–204

Black America's news publishers,
      134–137

Black Lives Matter movement, 43

Blake, Jacob, 228

Blavity news organization,
      134–135

Blut und Boden, 232

body (inverted pyramid), 119–120

Bondi, Sofia, 194–195

Boston Newsletter, 111

bothsidesism (false balance),
      189–190

bots, 25–26

Boylston, Zabdiel, 242–243

brain

   backfire effect and, 87–89, 93,
      259–260

biased, 75–83

BS-proofing your, 294–299

changing minds and, 74

on collaboration, 89–90

illusion of explanatory depth, 90–93

pessimistic meta-induction and, 84–86

pushback effect and, 93

reward system of, 218

on social media, 217–226

storytelling effect on, 61–73

sunrise problem, 95–101

brainwashing, mass, 250

breaking news, 124–126

Brexit, 42

British Hand, 228

Brown, Michael, 134

Browne, Thomas, 14

C

Capital Gazette, 194–196

Carey, James, 167

Carlson, Tucker, 166–167

Central Park Zoo hoax, 108–109

charity, principle of, 272–274

Cheney, Dick, 169

cherry picking (FLICC), 57–58

Chicago Defender, 136

chronological style of reporting, 118–119

Civil War, 153

clarity, principle of, 273–274

clickbait, 103–110

Clinton, Hillary, 41–42

Cockburn, Claud, 169–170

cognitive bias, 73, 75, 81–82

cognitive immunology, 251

coherence, principle of, 275

collaboration, 89–90

Columbia University, 189, 239

Committee to Protect Journalists, 196–197

commodities versus public goods, 117

common ground, looking for, 276–277

communication, models of, 167–168

Communications Act (1934), 154

community immunity, 252–253

concentration, multitasking and, 222–223

concurrent storage hypothesis, 261

confirmation bias, 14, 79–81

conflict, good, 283–293, 298–299

conflict story frame, 159

Confucius, 257

consensus, sphere of, 175–178

consensus story frame, 159

conspiracy theories (FLICC), 7–9, 58–59

contagious information
about, 1–3, 11–13
fake news, 14–16
going viral, 17–19
how to spread lies, 30–32
information disorder, 45–60
red flags and, 44
social networks and, 11–13,
17–25
Vienna Subway Suicides,
162–165
viral vectors and patient zero,
25–29
words matter, 33–43
continued influence effect, 259
conversations, polarized, 278–280
Conway, Erik M., 56
Cook, John, 54, 57–58, 247
cooperation, principle of, 274
coprophilia, 193
copypasta, 53–54
Cornish, Samuel, 135
coronavirus (COVID-19), 11–13,
17–19, 44, 125–126,
166–167
cortisol, 69
counterarguments, 246–247
Craig, Daniel H. and Helen, 116
Craigslist.org, 145
credence, 100
critical feeling, 256–258

critical thinking
BS-proofing your beliefs,
248–249, 271, 294–299
feelings and, 256–258
principles of, 272–275
viral spread of information
and, 1–3
Crito, 293
Crosky, Robert, 182

D
Dallas Morning News, 180
data points, 20–21, 216
DataViewer tool (YouTube), 205
Day, Benjamin, 152
DeBaun, Morgan, 134–135
debunking
defined, 259
inoculation theory and,
241–255
prebunking versus, 259–261
Vegetable Lambs of Tartary,
5–7
deductive reasoning, 97, 287
deep canvassing, 281
deviance, sphere of, 176
Diamond, Edwin, 15
disagreement
BS-proofing your beliefs, 271,
294–299
good conflict and, 283–285
how-to's of, 261–265

Socratic method and,
286–293, 298–299
ten steps for effective,
265–283
disinformation
Bad News Game, 253–255
defined, 35–36, 45–46
Internet Research Agency and,
40–43
KGB playbook and, 30–32
trolls and, 25–26, 39–43
dopamine, 70, 72–73,
218–219, 224–226
doughnut analogy (Hallin's
spheres), 175–178
Duke University, 181
Dunning, David, 81–82
Dunning-Kruger effect, 81–82,
275

E

editorials, 179–187
Environmental Protection
Agency, 140
ethnic/racial minorities
editorials on, 182–187
Flint Water Crisis, 138–144
manipulating beliefs about,
250–251
in newsrooms, 128–133
eugenics, 85, 182–183
evidence

asking for, 275–276
confirmation bias and, 79–81
illusion of explanatory depth
and, 91
impossible expectations and, 57
inductive reasoning and, 98
logic-based approach and, 60
storytelling and, 73
explainer (process story frame),
160

F

fabricated content, 46, 51–52
Facebook
bad news going viral, 11–13,
17–19, 27–29, 34–35, 42
blocking individuals, 236
brain development and,
223–224
contagious information and,
19–24
launching of, 154
factitious, 16
facts
alternative, 170–192
checking, 198–206
polarized conversations and,
278–280
topic-based approach and, 60
fake experts (FLICC), 54–56
fake news, 14–15. *See also*
information disorder

false balance (bothsidesism),
189–190
false connection, 46, 49
false context, 46, 50–51
false information. *See*
information disorder
Federalist Party, 111, 151
First Amendment, 112, 151
Fischman, Gerald, 195
FLICC strategies
about, 54
cherry picking, 57–58
conspiracy theories, 7–9, 58–60
fake experts, 54–56
impossible expectations, 57
logical fallacies, 56–57
protecting against, 59–60
Flint Water Crisis, 138–144
Floyd, George, 185
Fox, Megan, 50
Fox News, 166–167
frackademics, 55–56
framing news, 157–161
Francis (Pope), 193
Franco, Francisco, 169–170
Freedom of Information Act
(FOIA), 141–142
Freedom's Journal, 135
Front Porch Forum, 225
frugivorous diet, 207–209

G

Galton, Francis, 85
gatekeeping, 127, 141
Gazette of the United States, 111,
151
Ghonim, Wael, 238
ghost papers, 149
Gladstone, Brooke, 177
Gobright, Lawrence, 115–116
Goebbels, Joseph, 232
Goethe, Johann Wolfgang von,
162–163
Goodchild, Peter Lee, 11–13, 44
good conflict, 283–293, 298–299
Goodreads app, 225
Go Viral! (game), 255
"Great Moon Hoax,"
106–107, 152
Griffith, Christoff, 197
groupthink, 299
gudgeion (gudgin), 16
Guyette, Curt, 141–142

H

Hallin, Daniel, 177
Hallin's spheres (doughnut
analogy), 175–178
Hanna-Attisha, Mona, 139–143
Hannity, Sean, 166
Harris, Benjamin, 110–111, 150
Harrison, William Henry, 124
Harvard University, 296
Hatami, Zubair, 196–197

Hearst, William Randolph, 15, 153–154
herd immunity, 252–253
Herschel, John, 105–107
heuristic techniques (heuristics), 76–79
Heyer, Heather, 232
Hiaasen, Rob, 195
High Conflict (Ripley), 283
hippocampus (brain), 68
historical frame, 160
Hitchens, Brian Lee and Erin, 17–19
Hitler, Adolf, 231–232
Hoofnagle, Mark and Chris, 54
Hooker, Joseph, 153
Horn, Steve, 55
humiliation (feeling), 277–278, 285
Hussein, Saddam, 157–159

I

illusion of explanatory depth, 90–93, 275
An Illustrated Field Guide to Social Media, 239
Images.Google.com, 205
Implicit Association Test, 296
implicit (unconscious) bias, 75, 296
impossible expectations (FLICC), 57

imposter content, 46
indoctrination, 250
induction, problem of, 96–97
inductive reasoning, 96–101, 287
The Influencing Machine (Gladstone), 177
information
    contagious. *See* contagious information
    mutating, 3, 12, 28–29
    sources of, 4–5, 202–203
information audits, 200–201
The Information Diet (Johnson), 205–206
information disorder
    about, 45–46
    alternate terms for, 16
    coprophilia and, 193
    copypasta, 53–54
    fabricated content, 46, 51–52
    false connection, 46, 49
    false context, 46, 50–51
    FLICC strategies, 54–60
    imposter content, 46
    inoculation theory and, 246–250
    manipulated content, 46, 51
    misleading content, 46, 49–50
    protection against, 59–60
    red flags for, 44
    satire or parody, 46–49, 107
information warfare, 30–32

influencing behavior, 72, 166–170

inoculation theory (prebunking),
246–251, 253, 259–261

Instagram, 50, 210–211,
223–224, 240

intellectual antibodies,
245–246

Intercept, 234

Internet Research Agency, 40–42

inverted pyramid structure,
119–120

InVID browser extension, 205

J

Jackson, Derrick Z., 143

Jackson, Jonathan, 134–135

Japanese-American internment,
178–179, 181

Jefferson, Thomas, 104–105,
151–152, 192

Jenner, Edward, 244–245

Johnson, Alexis, 185–187

Johnson, Clay, 199, 205–206

Johnson, Samuel, 45

journalists/journalism
activism and, 171–172, 191
under attack, 194–197
bias and, 103–104
fact-checking stories,
204–205
movement journalism,
190–192

myth of objectivity, 170–192

telegraph transforming,
117–118, 152

timeline of major events,
150–154

K

Kaempfer, Engelbert, 5–7

Kansas City Star, 184

Kennedy, John F., 154

KGB, 30–32, 45

Kim Jong-un, 48–49

knowledge deficit model, 279–280

Kruger, Justin, 81–82

L

Lambert, Leon, 157

La Stampa, 193

LA Times, 129, 178–179, 181

lede (inverted pyramid), 119–120

Lee, Henry, 6

legitimate controversy, sphere of,
175–176

legitimate debate, sphere of,
175–176

Lewis, Bryan, 157

lies, spreading, 30–32, 54–60

Lincoln, Abraham, 120–123, 153

listening
shifting disagreements by,
268–272, 275
in Socratic method, 292
trust and, 285

local news
  determining newsworthiness,
    128–132
  Flint Water Crisis and,
    138–144
  framing, 155–157
  ghost papers, 149
  trust and, 149
Locke, Richard Adams, 107
logical fallacies (FLICC), 56–57
logic-based approach against
    FLICC techniques, 59–60
looping (listening technique),
    269–270, 275
Loren, Tammy, 138
Lowy Institute, 235

M

The Magic Flute (opera), 164
magnified minority, 56
malinformation, 36–39, 41, 46
manipulated content, 46, 51
Marketplace (radio program),
    171–172
Martinez, Ramona, 175
Massachusetts Institute of
    Technology, 260
mathematical models, 19–25
Mather, Cotton, 241–243
McGuire, William, 245–252
McKernon, Edward, 14
McNamara, John, 195

media diet, creating, 199–206
memories, outsourcing, 221–222
*Memphis Free Speech and
    Headlight*, 191–192
mental disruptors, 251–252
Mental Immunity (Norman), 298
Merchants of Doubt (Oreskes and
    Conway), 56
Mercier, Hugo, 89
Mexican-American War, 115, 152
miasma, 84
Milton, John, 150
mind parasites, 251
minds, changing, 74
mirror neurons, 67
misinformation, 34–36, 45–46,
    104
misleading content, 46, 49–50
models of communication,
    167–168
Montagu, Mary, 243–244
Montgomery Advertiser, 182
Morse, Samuel, 117
Morse code, 117–119
movement journalism,
    190–192
multitasking, 222–223
mutating information, 3, 12,
    28–29
myth of objectivity, 170–192

N

Nanyang Technological
University, 198
narrative bias, 204
narrative transportation, 67, 70
National Geographic, 182
national news
Flint Water Crisis and,
138–144
framing, 155–157
trust and, 149
National Suicide Prevention
Lifeline, 165
Nazi groups, 228, 232, 235, 250
Nelson, Jeff, 134–135
neuroplasticity, 220
neutrality and objectivity, 174–
175, 186–189
news aggregation, 132
news and newspapers
advertising and, 108–109,
112–113, 146–147
alternative facts and, 170–192
Black America's publishers and,
134–137
breaking, 124–126
contagious. *See* contagious
information
coprophilia and, 193
decline of newspapers,
144–149
fact-checking, 198–206

fake news, 14–16
Flint Water Crisis and, 138–
144
framing, 157–161
how it's made, 155–157
influencing behavior, 166–170
journalism timeline, 150–154
journalists under attack,
194–197
myth of objectivity, 170–192
newsworthiness of, 127–133
nineteenth-century breaking,
113–117
nineteenth-century clickbait,
103–110
partisan press and, 110–113
twentieth-century problems,
117–123
news budget, 155
news deserts, 148–149
news judgement, 127, 132–135
newsworthiness, determining,
127–133
New York Age, 192
New York Herald, 108–109,
120–123
New York Sun, 105–107, 115, 152
New York Times, 47–48, 129,
142, 154, 184–185
New York World, 15, 154
Nextdoor app, 225

Nguyen, Na-Son, 49
Nicolai, Friedrich, 165
Nielsen Total Audience Report, 199
Nixon, Richard, 154
Norman, Andy, 251–252, 298
Norvell, John, 104, 152

O

Obama, Barack, 47–48, 143
objectivity, myth of, 170–192
O'Connor, Anahad, 55
Onesimus (slave), 241–243, 245
Onion, 47–49
op-eds (opinion pages), 180
Operation Iraqi Freedom, 157–161
Oreskes, Naomi, 56
oxytocin, 70–73

P

Papageno Effect, 165
parody/satire, 46–49, 107
partisan press, 110–113, 179
patient zero, 26–29
Pearson, Karl, 85
Penny Press, 107–110, 112, 152
pessimistic meta-induction, 81–83
Phifer, Miles (Relius), 182
photo sources, 205
pigeons, Associated Press and, 116, 152

Pittsburgh Courier, 137
"pivot to video," 154
Plato, 287
Poe's Law, 47–48
polarized conversations, 278–280
Pollan, Michael, 199
Pony Express, 114–115, 117, 152
prebunking (inoculation theory), 246–251, 259–261
Press On organization, 190–191
press passes, 153
press releases, 153
principle of charity, 272–274
principle of clarity, 273–274
principle of coherence, 275
principle of cooperation, 274
principle of rational accommodation, 274–275
problem of induction, 96–97
process story frame (explainer), 160
public goods versus commodities, 117
Publick Occurrences both Forreign and Domestick, 110–111, 114, 150–151
Pulitzer, Joseph, 15, 153–154, 188–189
pushback effect, 93

R

rabbit hole (social media), 214, 226–237

racial/ethnic minorities
  editorials on, 182–187
  Flint Water Crisis, 138–144
  manipulating beliefs about,
    250–251
  in newsrooms, 128–133
radiation, conspiracy theories on,
  7–9
radicalization, 214, 227–229
radio broadcasts, 144, 154
Ratcliffe, Leanne, 207–209
rational accommodation,
  principle of, 274–275
recommendation algorithms, 214,
  229–231, 235
Reddit, 210, 232–233,
  236–237
red flags for false information, 44
representative heuristic, 77
researching news sources, 4–5,
  202–203
Ripley, Amanda, 278,
  283–285
Rittenhouse, Kyle, 228
ritual model of communication,
  168
Rocky Mountain spotted fever,
  61–66
Roosevelt, Franklin, 178
Rosenberg, Carol, 202
Russia Today, 31

Russwurm, John, 135

S

Samuels, Aaron, 134–135
satire/parody, 46–49, 107
Sedition Act (1798), 151
selective exposure, 169
shame (feeling), 277–278, 285
Sherman, William T., 153
smallpox (variola virus), 241–245
Smith, Rebecca, 195
social media
  algorithms and, 207–217, 232,
    235
  another way for, 237–240
  brain on, 217–226
  contagious information and,
    19–25, 49
  into the rabbit hole, 214,
    226–237
social networks
  contagious information and,
    11–13, 17–25
  information disorder and,
    53–54
  viral spread of information
    and, 19–25
Socrates, 286–287, 292–293
Socratic method, 286–293,
  298–299
Solis, Dianne, 202
The Sorrows of Young Werther

(Goethe), 163

Sperber, Dan, 89

sphere of consensus, 175–178

sphere of deviance, 176

sphere of legitimate controversy,
    175–176

sphere of legitimate debate,
    175–176

Stalin, Joseph, 45

Stanton, Edwin, 153

status quo bias, 174

stiflers, 24–25

stockpiling thoughts,
    270–272

stories/storytelling
    Central Park Zoo hoax,
        108–109
    effect on the brain, 61–73
    "Great Moon Hoax,"
        105–107, 152
    harnessing power of,
        280–282
    trust and, 72, 94–95

straight news account, 159

straw man argument, 57

Suicide Prevention Lifeline, 165

sunrise problem, 95–101

superspreaders, 23–25

T

tail (inverted pyramid), 119–120

taradiddle, 16

telegraph, trans-continental,
    117–119, 152

Temple, Will, 182

terrorism, 227–228

13 Reasons Why (show), 164

thoughts, stockpiling, 270–272

Tiger Beat, 47–48

TikTok, 210–212, 233–235

timeline of journalism,
    150–154

TinEye.com, 205

tobacco companies, 55–56

topic-based approach against
    FLICC techniques, 59–60

transactive memory, 220–221

transmission model of
    communication, 167–168

trolls, 25–26, 39–43

Trump, Donald, 14, 32n, 51–52,
    171

trust
    consensus and, 88
    fact-checking news and,
        198–206
    feeling listened to and, 285
    illusion of explanatory depth
        and, 93
    information disorder and,
        53–54
    local/national news, 149
    storytelling and, 72, 94–95

trust (*continued*)

  unconscious bias and, 82

Twitter, 26, 37–39, 50, 154, 212

U

ultracrepidarian, 16

unconscious (implicit) bias, 75, 296

United States Postal Service, 112

useful idiots, 31n

V

vaccines/vaccination, 245–255

variolation, 242–244

variola virus (smallpox), 241–245

VatiLeaks scandal, 193

vectors, 25–26

Vegetable Lambs of Tartary, 5–7

video sources, 205

Vienna Subway Suicides, 162–165

The View from Somewhere
  (Wallace), 172, 189–190

visual bias, 203–204

W

Wallace, Lewis Raven, 170–175,
  186–191

Wall Street Journal, 129

Wardle, Claire, 31

Washington, George, 111, 151, 243

Washington Post, 41, 51–52, 129,
  154, 181

Watergate scandal, 154

Wells, Ida B., 191–192

Wernicke's area (brain), 67–68

Werther Effect, 162–165

Wicker, Tom, 183

Williams, Evan, 215

Wilson, Sharon, 55

*Winston-Salem Journal and
  Sentinel*, 182–184

Winters, Wendi, 194–196

wording, importance of

  about, 33–34

  disinformation, 35, 40–43

  malinformation, 36–39, 46, 50

  misinformation, 34–35

Y

yellow journalism, 15,
  153–154

Yes Men collective, 52

YouTube, 205–206, 210, 232–
  233

Z

Zenger, Peter, 151